DATE DUE

AG 9 '01			

DEMCO 38-296

Facing the Mirror

Facing the Mirror

Older Women and Beauty Shop Culture

Frida Kerner Furman

ROUTLEDGE
New York and London

Published in 1997 by

Routledge
29 West 35th Street
New York, NY 10001

Published in Great Britain in 1997 by

Routledge
11 New Fetter Lane
London EC4P 4EE

Copyright © 1997 by Routledge

Printed in the United States of America
Design: Jack Donner

All photographs, including cover photo, by Caryn Chaden.

Library of Congress Cataloging-in-Publication Data

Furman, Frida Kerner, 1948–
Facing the mirror: older women and beauty shop culture / Frida Kerner Furman.
    p. cm.
Includes bibliographical references and index.
ISBN 0-415-91523-6. — ISBN 0-415-91524-4
1. Aged women—United States—Psychology—Case studies.
2. Aged women—Social networks—United States—Case studies.
3. Jewish women—Social networks—United States—Case studies.
4. Aging—United States—Psychological aspects—Case studies.
5. Beauty, Personal—Psychological aspects—Case studies.
6. Beauty shops—Social aspects—United States—Case studies. I. Title.

HQ1064. U5F84 1997
305.26—DC21   97–12407
CIP

To four generations of beautiful women:

My grandmothers, Ella Karlinsky and Ana Kerner
(may their memory be for a blessing).

My mother, Sara Kerner, and my aunt, Lily Katz.
My sister, Gina Kerner.
My daughter, Daniella Furman.

❧ Contents ❧

❧ Acknowledgments ❧

Many people have helped to make this book possible. Most centrally, the customers and staff of Julie's International Salon allowed me to conceive of this project and bring it to completion. I thank them for their kindness and generosity, for their willingness to share their lives and experiences with me, and for all that they have taught me.

Colleagues and friends have been wonderful in their encouragement and support. I am very appreciative of the members of my women's writing group at DePaul University for their ongoing interest in this work and for their very helpful responses to earlier drafts of the writing. Thank you, then, to Mechthild Hart, Teresia Hinga, Kate Kane, Elizabeth Kelly, and Ann Russo. My special thanks to Mechthild for her encouragement from the very beginning of the project and to Beth for her thoughtful reading of every page of this book, for her excellent editorial and critical skills, and for her generous expressions of friendship. Paul Camenisch and Ann-Janine Morey read the final draft of the book and made valuable suggestions. Riv-Ellen Prell provided me with bibliographic references and organized a very useful conversation about older women with Helen Kivnick and Lucy Rose Fischer during the early stages of field research. Aminah Beverly McCloud and Susan Mezey gave me helpful feedback on the book proposal. Ruth Fuerst and Naomi Steinberg offered enthusiastic and sustaining support during the entire period of this study. Doug Hoekstra, Mari Short, and Jodi Taylor performed the laborious task of transcribing interview audio tapes. Dianne Hanau-Strain generously provided her expertise in her drawing of the salon's interior, as did Caryn Chaden in capturing the salon's life through her photographic work. Charles Suchar introduced me to the technique of photo-elicitation and gave me useful advice about the photographs included in the book. Chana Zelig carefully proofread the final manuscript. My husband, Roy Furman, and my daughter, Daniella Furman, put up with my extended absences from family life during all stages of this work. Roy provided editorial feedback and made numerous trips to the library on my behalf during the months that I stayed at home to write. My grateful thanks to all.

Thanks, also, to the editorial staff at Routledge, and to the anonymous readers designated by the Press, who made many constructive suggestions. I am grateful to the University Research Council and to the Faculty Research and Development Program of the College of Liberal Arts and Sciences at DePaul University for the research leaves and grants that made this study possible.

✨ Facing the Mirror ✨

⅗ Introduction ⅗

What about Julie's International Salon makes me feel that I move into
a different psychological space? Often when I have to go there but feel
some resistance to do so (pressure of other obligations), I remind
myself that it will be a haven from my more driven lifestyle. And in
fact the experience there always confirms that expectation. There is
something safe and comfortable about being there. . . . What is so safe
there? Is it something about the shop culture that reminds me of my
childhood in its more positive moments—time with grandmothers,
aunts? What is so comforting and satisfying about talking about coat
sales? Or exchanging, in a somewhat competitive mood, our latest
physical maladies? There is something very affirming there. It is as if
one feels nurtured without having to do anything in exchange, save
nurture others, which comes naturally and is self-confirming, too.
Why does the concern expressed feel so warming?

—Author's *Field Notes*, October 25, 1991

The very first time I went to Julie's International Salon to get my hair
cut—some eight years ago—I could sense that there was something compelling about it, though I could not quite put my finger on what exactly
was going on there. But it had to do with older women congregated
together in an all-female salon, manifestly for purposes of hair and nail
care, who seemed to be part of a lively and affirming community. For the
next three years I toyed with the idea of doing a study of this beauty
salon. I was held back by respiratory allergies, which I thought would be
incompatible with the aromas of hair care products characteristic of
beauty shops. Finally, in 1991, I could resist the place no longer; I
resolved that I would deal with the air quality as best as I could.

Unlike most scholars who do ethnographic work, I did not set out to
study this setting. It called out to me, as it were. The emotional climate
of women's friendship, support, and camaraderie beckoned to me initially.

Once I actually began the study, I came to realize that women's relationships also conveyed significant moral meanings, as did their views of themselves as women, in general, and as older women, specifically. Other issues readily presented themselves, most centrally the fact that the clientele was largely composed of older women, most of them Jewish, and that they were committed to traditional practices of femininity and beautification. A perusal of the existing literature plus my own knowledge of American culture quickly revealed that little is known about the subjective experience of older women, less about older Jewish women, still less about their self-understanding regarding their physical appearance.

In the course of this study I came to realize the extent to which our society is age segregated. Few of us get to interact in a meaningful way with older people who are unrelated to us; as a consequence, until recently I knew little about old age. May Sarton captures this situation when she writes, "The trouble is that old age is not interesting until one gets there, a foreign country with an unknown language to the young, and even to the middle-aged."[1] This remains the case despite the fact that as a society we are aging very rapidly, constituting a virtual demographic revolution, often referred to as "the graying of America." The number of elderly people is increasing significantly at the same time that the number of children is declining. In 1985, those 65 and over came to exceed those under the age of 18. Those over the age of 85 are the fastest growing age group in the U. S., and they represent a figure 21 times as numerous as in 1900. In 1990 there were 32 million elderly Americans, constituting 13 percent of the population. By 2020, the figure is estimated at 52 million; by 2030, 20 percent of the population will be made up of the elderly. Of those 85 and older, most will be women.[2] These trends relate to dramatic increases in longevity and changes in birth rates—very high for the baby boom, very low at present.

While we have all these figures at our fingertips, as a culture we don't know very much about the subjective, existential, or moral experience of older people. As Thomas Cole puts it,

> Our culture is not much interested in *why* we grow old, or how we *ought* to grow old, or what it *means* to grow old. . . . Focusing narrowly on a reified 'problem of old age,' apart from the actual lives and cultural representations of people growing older, the scientific management of aging [gerontology and geriatrics] denies our universal participation and solidarity in this most human experience.[3]

We know even less about the experience of older women, specifically, as research about them began belatedly in the field of gerontology. Until very recently, older women have been absent from feminist scholarship, perhaps because the energies of younger feminists have been directed to issues that affect their own lives, like reproductive rights and equitable pay.[4] In a 1985 speech to the National Women's Studies Association, Barbara Macdonald took academic feminists to task for their failure to acknowledge older women, charging that younger women see them the way men do, "that is, as women who used to be women but aren't anymore. You do not see us in our present lives, you do not identify with our issues, you exploit us, you patronize us, you stereotype us. Mainly you ignore us."[5] This book is an effort to learn more about certain areas of older women's experience—experience that has been rendered invisible. Simone de Beauvoir wrote that the problem of aging is "carefully passed over in silence: and that is why this silence has to be shattered."[6] My work is an attempt to contribute to the project of shattering the silence around older women's lives.

In the absence of factual knowledge about, and direct exposure to, older women, both mythic and prosaic stereotypes have come along to fill the vacuum: The Wicked Old Witch, the Old Bad Mother, the Little Old Lady "cloud the individuality of every woman past sixty."[7] The dependable grandmother is a more positive stereotype, but it renders the older woman a servant to others. Feminists have done little to contest or reclaim these stereotypes. This may be the case because feminist work has been written, as a rule, from the perspective of younger women: from the daughter's side, not the mother's or grandmother's.

Representations of older Jewish women are even more problematic, for Jewish women must also cope with the stereotype of the Jewish Mother used to characterize them. Generated by Jewish men before the Second World War, the Jewish Mother is the most prominent figure in contemporary Jewish humor today and has attained currency in American society as a whole. She is seen as overprotective, overbearing, self-sacrificial yet demanding attention; she boasts about her children, pushes food upon them, and induces guilt in them.[8]

Women's concerns with physical appearance are often viewed in an ambivalent, if not negative, manner. Our still androcentric culture insists, on the one hand, that women must present attractive appearances if they are to be deemed acceptable and achieve social status. On the other hand, women's preoccupation with appearance is seen as shallow and narcissistic. At a time when many Americans profess commitment to gender equality, women's concerns with physical appearance are likely viewed by many as both anachronistic and embarrassing: anachronistic because women should attend to more important matters, such as the pursuit of interesting careers; embarrassing because women's interest in attractiveness is often seen as competitive, an effort to best other women, when energies ought to be used, instead, to engage in solidarity for the sake of common goals. As a consequence, as Polly Young-Eisendrath puts it, "Because women's concerns for beautiful appearances are so widely conceived as trivial and false, even women are reticent to speak among themselves about appearances."[9] Simply speaking about their looks may ratify the view that appearance is *all* women are concerned about.

Caroline Evans and Minna Thornton argue that "the practices which a culture insists are meaningless or trivial, the places where ideology has succeeded in becoming invisible, are practices in need of investigation."[10] I agree with this insight, and it was this conviction that propelled me to conduct this study of older women and beauty shop culture although I felt hesitant about pursuing my research once I received permission to proceed. Despite my enthusiasm about the beauty salon as a possible site of study, I remember asking a friend, an academic also involved in feminist work, "Do you think it is serious *enough?*" I had evidently internalized mainstream values and was nervous about how such work would be perceived in the academy. My friend was encouraging, and I quickly moved ahead, but my misgivings were not without foundation. I soon discovered that on the face of it, a study of a beauty salon populated by older Jewish women was not taken seriously by everyone; for some, it was a source of amusement. For example, when I answered my home phone one day, a male university colleague's first words were, "Is this Frida Furman's beauty parlor?" I could not read a friend's response after I described the project to him: "That's the thing that needs doing," he said, nodding his head energetically. Was that irony or mild sarcasm in his voice, I asked myself. When I told a colleague in sociology about the study, he assured me, with a laugh, that he knew all about that generation of Jewish women; he was alluding to his mother. Another sociologist seemed intrigued and encouraging, yet he laughed as he described older Jewish women's "blue hair," suggesting that their hairstyles—and by extension, they themselves— were in a "time warp." The director of my university's research council reported on the council's deliberations on my proposal for a leave to pursue field research. Council members needed to be persuaded that the subject and subjects of the study were not trivial.

Nonetheless, in the years since I've been working on this project, there has been a great deal of enthusiasm expressed about it in many quarters. Women's responses have generally been affirming, perhaps because women know, first-hand, about beauty salons and the imperatives regarding beauty experienced by all women in this country. Many have been impressed by the innovative nature of the study. The most enthusiastic reaction to this project has come from academics doing research on women, women with older mothers, older women themselves, and professionals who work with the elderly.

Writing about older, mainly Jewish, women within the context of a beauty salon means entering some unexplored intellectual terrain. There have been gerontological studies of older women, but they usually do not address issues of appearance. Recent writing on feminine beauty tends to focus on younger women. Very little work has been done on older Jewish women altogether. Virtually nothing has been written about beauty salons, as such.[11] On the other hand, gender as a critical analytic category has been at the heart of feminist writing for over twenty years. More recently, an explosion of interest in the body as a site of cultural meaning has been in evidence across many academic disciplines.

In this book I combine some of these interests in new ways. I explore the meaning and experience of the female body for older—mostly Jewish—women in the context of a youth-loving, male-dominated society. Such exploration is not exhaustive: I focus on the body as presented to the world. I investigate the construction and maintenance of the feminine body—and of moral selves—as women recall their lifelong beauty practices, as they discuss, and I observe, their contemporary efforts at the beauty salon (chapter 2). I document and analyze perceptions of, attitudes toward, and experience of the aging body, which slows down, sags, grays, becomes limiting and sometimes painful, acquires wrinkles and added weight (chapter 3). The aging female body comes into deep conflict with cultural representations of feminine beauty, which in U. S. society—and increasingly across the world—today demands youth, slenderness, agility. I discovered in the course of study and writing that such a body is construed and experienced within the context of multiple power relations: male and female, young and old, gentile and Jewish. The body of the older Jewish woman is culturally constructed, I argue, from the perspective of the male gaze, the youthful gaze, the dominant-culture's gaze.[12] Women, like men, are embodied selves, and embodiment has cultural meaning and significance. We cannot understand who women are as socio-moral beings apart from the reality of their embodiment.

The themes of gender and aging cut across the entire book. These are not themes that surface only in women's private thoughts and reflections. At Julie's International Salon, the customers' shared gender and age—among other factors—give rise to a lively community where women unabashedly discuss their aches and pains, their facial lines and double chins (chapter 1). The prohibitions of the public sphere against speaking about these matters are suspended. The beauty salon emerges as a site of support, friendship, and yes, moral action. Women engage in caring work with each other in the course of their weekly visits to Julie's, giving and receiving care in both subtle and obvious ways. Whereas in public, older Jewish women may be perceived as Other, inside the salon they develop a community of selves.

The theme of care surfaces once again in customers' familial relationships. I investigate the expectations women have faced since their youth to care for husbands, children, and parents (chapter 4). I specifically address customers' current obligations to provide care for elderly spouses and their concerns and anticipations regarding who will care for them. As our population ages, caring for the elderly emerges as an urgent issue, one that must question our taken-for-granted assumption that it is women's work. Questions of justice, I suggest, must be raised in the context of caring.

When I told an anthropologist friend of my intention to study a beauty salon, he responded by quoting a line from William Blake's "Auguries of Innocence": "To see a world in a grain of sand." I do not claim in this work to uncover the whole world of older Jewish women's lives. This book addresses their lives outside the beauty salon—their daily activities, intellectual and cultural interests, volunteer commitments, religious and social involvements, and close friendships—only in passing, if at all. It presents their familial relationships, not in the fullness of their being, but from the perspective of caregiving.

The book attempts to meet a feminist goal: to rediscover, revalue, and bring to public view women's experiences that have been obscured, occluded, or devalued because they have been seen as socially insignificant or morally irrelevant. These include experiences in the home and in other aspects of the private sphere, areas of human life that for too long have been neglected or derided in social, philosophical, and religious thought. For purposes of this study, I look at women's lives within the context of the beauty salon, their experience of femininity and of aging, and their work of caring. Instead of seeing these arenas as bereft of socio-moral significance, I believe that they deserve description, analysis, and critique, for they tell us as much about our society as they do about older women themselves. I view study participants as social actors and moral subjects whose experiences reveal a socio-moral order frequently oppressive to women. Women's narratives expose structures of power, inequality, and resistance in the way women perceive their reality, make choices, and live in their worlds. As actors in an inequitable social order, these women often conform to socio-cultural norms—frequently contributing, thereby, to their own subordination—but sometimes defy or use them to their own advantage, as well. Like people everywhere, they live with complexity and paradox. Their perspectives are not always neat and satisfying, and neither are my reflections and conclusions. I sometimes raise questions for which I have no answers, but I let these questions stand to remind us that the complexities and problematics of our collective and individual lives need to be repeatedly confronted and addressed. The book concludes with this awareness, as the problems it raises are massive and therefore not easily resolvable. I offer some suggestions for socio-cultural change, arguing that our best bet, if we are to revalorize women and their experiences in older age, is to resist and contest cultural assumptions and social relations that currently contribute to their devaluation (chapter 5).

This study is broadly interdisciplinary in approach. I engage the fields of sociology, anthropology, gerontology, communication, religion, and feminist studies more generally. I am trained as a social ethicist, however, and the concerns of feminist ethics have guided me most centrally. Feminist ethics recognizes that historically, women's moral identity and moral action often have been ignored or denigrated. Its interests include rectifying this record by, among other ways, investigating spheres of women's moral experience yet unexplored. This field is also involved in identifying, calling to public attention, and critiquing instances of oppression toward women in contemporary society. In the latter case, feminist ethics as a discipline mirrors the more general feminist commitment to justice for women. In addition, a guiding goal for feminist ethics, and for this project, is the well-being of women, as societal arrangements have frequently militated against women's well-being.

In the process of hearing women's voices and observing their worlds, I became aware of the many ways in which our society compromises the well-being of older women. This awareness emerged in an inductive manner as I listened to women's stories and their conversations, as I observed their interactions and other behaviors. In this book I present their experiences via these narratives and observations. I situate and analyze these experiences in larger contexts of cultural meaning and social relations. I then examine the ethical implications of such contexts for women's well-being. Thus, I make ethical judgments, not by distancing myself from the lives of actual people into a realm of abstract principle, but by locating sources of pain, injustice, and virtue in the everyday lives of ordinary women. So, for example, I ask, and attempt to answer, What does it mean when a woman in her seventies insists that she is not older, but middle-aged? What does this tell us about our cultural conceptions of oldness and their impact on women's moral identity? Elsewhere, I investigate why another woman feels shame and disgust about her body, which now has lost its firmness and carries extra pounds; and I question why countless women feel guilty when they can no longer take care of an ailing parent or spouse.

I also identify and celebrate women's moral virtues and moral work within the context of their lived experience—in the relatedness they establish with one another at the beauty salon, in their caregiving to their families, in their resistance to oppressive socio-cultural practices. This study thus operates at both descriptive and normative levels of analysis.[13]

I hold an expansive view of the moral life and the task of doing ethics. The standards of moral value and the many oughts that people live with do not come to them strictly through the evaluative judgments and Thou Shalts/Thou Shalt Nots spoken from home, school, or pulpit. They are also embedded in cultural discourses and visual images that communicate and socialize people into standards of behavior and value, cultural norms, regulations in social relations. These are not only areas for the sociological gristmill, though they are that. All these imperatives communicate moral meanings: what is good or bad, right or wrong, virtuous or evil, responsible or irresponsible, obligatory or optional. They go a long way to constitute moral identity, to shape—or misshape—who we are as moral agents. The ethical task includes the identification and analysis of such meanings and their deconstruction from systems of ideology and power. Since such meanings are to be found in the lives of ordinary people, this approach might be understood as fitting within the ethics of the everyday, as opposed to the more traditional orientation of ethical analysis, which so often has focused on quandary situations resolved via abstract moral reasoning.[14]

In a previous work I argued,[15] following H. Richard Niebuhr, that the ethicist's task is to begin with description, to ask "what is going on" morally in a community, and to discern the community's values, ethos, and identity. "Out of this discourse in the community," Niebuhr thought, "can come an understanding of what ought to be done."[16] I still subscribe to that perspective, but now I believe that the distinction between descriptive and normative tasks is less easily differentiated into two phases. Description frequently implies prescription: Lived experience embeds instances of injustice or moral virtue, patterns of domination and subordination or, conversely, relationships of mutuality. The telling of such experience, by extension, frequently embeds moral judgment, positive or negative. For, after all, both ordinary people and ethicists render such descriptions equipped with some type of moral map. In my case, I entered the field with a set of feminist commitments to justice on behalf of the equality, inclusion, and well-being of women. The next stage of ethical analysis involves the development and clarification of these embedded judgments, their application to larger socio-moral contexts, and the call for needed socio-cultural change.

My commitments to justice arise not only from secular feminist visions, but also from a profoundly religious perspective, that of my own tradition. I see the dignity and uniqueness of every human being at the heart of Jewish teaching, most succinctly articulated in the biblical view of the *imago dei*, the idea that all human beings are made in God's image. Judaism teaches, as a consequence, that all human beings are equally valuable. Prophetic and rabbinic teaching addresses the obligation of all Jews to struggle for the eradication of injustice. In this work I attempt to implement some of these imperatives as I identify and critique sources of older women's pain and disempowerment in unjust social relations, assumptions, and expectations. Older Jewish women, like all other human beings, must be perceived and treated as intrinsically unique and valuable persons. The ultimate goal of my work, then, is liberatory in nature.

Methodology

It was a morning in May at Julie's International Salon. Julie, the shop's owner and my beautician, was cutting my hair when I asked her permission to conduct an ethnographic study of her salon. She happily agreed, suggesting that she herself had more than once thought her customers' stories would make a good read. While Julie may not have known exactly what an ethnographic study entails, she seemed flattered by my interest in her work and her world. She was a fine advocate of this project from the start, enthusiastically introducing me to customers and directing me to potential participants for intensive interviews. Most women I approached about being interviewed readily acceded. Two refused, saying it wasn't their "thing." Everyone at the salon that I spoke with in a more informal manner was interested in the study and happy to discuss my interests. Not a few women told me of their willingness to participate because it might help me with my work. Some women felt flattered that I, a highly educated, professional woman, was interested in them and their lives.

For eighteen months I conducted ethnographic fieldwork at the salon, using participant observation and informal interviewing as research tools. I simply spent a great deal of time there, observing the proceedings as I interacted with women in various ways: one-on-one conversations, group discussions, quiet chats with the staff, the occasional sharing of food. I did not take notes in public during this time because I wanted to establish rapport with people without alienating them in the process. So from time to time I used the shop's restroom to jot furious notes on a small pad. Within a few hours of my visits, I typed out the notes along with my recollections, appending reactions and queries to be pursued further.

A few months of "hanging out" at Julie's and getting acquainted with customers and staff allowed me to identify questions that seemed important in this setting. I then proceeded to conduct intensive interviews in private homes with twenty salon customers,[17] ranging in age from 55 to 86, with a mean age of 73.5 years old. These interviews, which lasted from two to four hours, were tape-recorded and later transcribed. The longer interviews were divided into two sessions. It was not uncommon for women to serve me lunch, tea, or cookies during these visits.

A major goal of these interviews was to explore the relationships among a woman's appearance, her aging, and her self-understanding. Soon after I started participant observation, I discovered that asking women to reflect on their facial wrinkles and other marks of aging was too intrusive and intimidating a request. It got too close to the vulnerabilities women experience as they age. I decided that during intensive interviews I would make use of photo-elicitation as a research tool. In advance of my visit, I asked interview participants to select photographs of themselves from the time of their youth, their middle age, and the current period. During the interviews, I requested that they look at the photographs, tell me something about their lives at the time, and what they thought then, and now, about their appearance as portrayed by the photo and in their recollections. By treating the photograph as a kind of artifact, participants were able to gain some distance from it and to feel less self-conscious. Some women offered me recent photos of themselves taken with a standard camera. In some cases the women did not have such a picture available; I used a Polaroid camera to take their pictures in such instances. Photo-elicitation proved to be a valuable research instrument. Among other things, it facilitated discussion of women's lives that lay beyond issues of appearance. It made it possible for participants to direct the course of the interviews in directions they themselves chose.[18]

Participants in intensive interviews are almost evenly distributed between those who are married and those who are widowed (only one woman was divorced in her youth and remains unmarried). Sixteen of the twenty currently reside in the metropolitan area of their birth. Only one is foreign-born. Many have children and grandchildren living in the area; others do not. Nine women completed high school, three are college graduates, and two others earned master's degrees. One received a midwifery diploma following high school, while five never finished high school, as economic necessity demanded they get jobs to help their families. All would consider themselves to be middle-class, though they represent a wide economic range, as evidenced by their homes, which reveal modest to affluent means. Fifteen out of the twenty own their residences, whether house or condominium; the others rent. During the course of this study, one woman, a widow, was moved into a residential facility by her family. Eighteen of these twenty participants are Jewish, roughly representing a similar ratio of Jewish to non-Jewish customers at the shop. Needless to say, the names of the salon and of everyone associated with it have been changed to safeguard confidentiality.

As a consequence of the particulars just listed, the women of this study represent a specific social location in American society: They are white, middle-class, and mostly Jewish. They are also older and American. I have every indication that they are also heterosexual.[19] Despite the diversity found among American women, these women share with other women certain characteristics and experiences related, especially, to their gender and age. Jewish middle-class women may also represent a highly success-ful adaptation to American middle-class values,[20] which may speak for the experience of other women, as well. While my findings and interpreta-tions may not be generalizable to all American women, I believe they sug-gest some shared experiences, especially when seen against a backdrop of dominant cultural meanings regarding the body, physical appearance, aging, and old age in the United States today.

As a Jew, I shared most study participants' ethnicity, which made for easy entry into the field site and for generally comfortable rapport. Shared gender and class status undoubtedly contributed as well.[21] I am certain that my being a woman was a critical asset in data-gathering about physical appearance, the beauty shop, and aging. Unlike me, though, virtually all the women were born and raised in the United States; most are second- or third-generation Jews, whose parents or grandparents were immigrants from Eastern Europe. I came to this country from Chile at age thirteen. Some aspects of Jewish American culture frequently manifested in women's relationships, discourses, and behaviors at the beauty salon were conse-quently not necessarily self-evident to me. This provided me with a certain measure of distance, thereby preventing me from "going native." On the other hand, areas of shared experience gave me access to subtle and some-times subjective meanings that might be lost on the complete outsider.[22]

Other factors separated me from study participants, the major one being age. At age forty-eight, I am one generation younger than most of the women in the study; I am two generations younger than those in their mid-eighties. Generation and educational level undoubtedly colored other differences between us, most notably my strong feminist perspec-tive and the absence of explicitly feminist awareness and analysis on the part of most study participants. While I honor women's views and work toward making these visible, I sometimes disagree with them.

Procedurally, I took a phenomenological perspective in initially grasp-ing and reporting women's experience from their own point of view.[23] It was especially important for me to place their voices at the center of the text. In this book I try whenever possible to allow a woman's own words to express her individuality, hence I refrain from editing repetitions in a woman's speech, for example, because I want to retain her inflection and her usual manner of self-expression. My analysis and critique arise induc-tively from women's narratives. I do not absent myself from the text, however; I report my engagement with women's discourses, and I frequently let the reader in on my responses, puzzlements, and worries. In short, I take a position against the erasure of myself from the text.

The text that emerges is ultimately of my own making. More than a decade of reevaluation and critique of ethnographic method and writing has demystified the notion that ethnographic work achieves an objective rendition of observed reality.[24] After all, while I let women speak for themselves about a variety of topics in the text, it was I who structured the sequence of topics, selected quotable speech, and often pulled out of the interview context a woman's particular viewpoint. The ensuing text, therefore, is a product of my mind and goals. In the end, it represents my interpretation of other people's reality.[25] I have to trust that the epistemological dilemmas raised by this method nonetheless allow the reader access to older women's experience.

The ethnographic process was demanding, exciting, and politicizing. This is an extraordinarily labor-intensive approach. In my experience, the richness of the process itself via its intense engagement with other people is compensation enough for the long hours involved in the field; the sorting, organizing, and analyzing of data; and, eventually, the writing. I feel personally transformed by how I now notice and relate to older people. I have become extremely sensitive to the ways in which older women are culturally represented and talked about. I support Evelyn Rosenthal's clarion call to feminists to enter into an analysis of ageism parallel to that leveled against sexism in order to uncover "similar mechanisms at work constructing the nature of old age. . . . By investigating the lives of old women, we can challenge stereotypes, critique old age as a social construction, and discover that much of what we women fear about our own aging is not natural to old age."[26]

By temperament and conviction, I choose to study living people whom I can see, hear, and interact with. In this regard I differ from most social ethicists, who until recently almost universally relied on the written word as a source of their work. I have wanted here to investigate directly the social dynamics and cultural values and judgments that shape older women's lives. What better way to do so than to study women in their flesh and blood—in person, in their bodies. Ethnography is a congenial approach to me as a feminist, as it offers me a possible route "to get closer to women's realities" since it "makes women's lives *visible*, just as interviewing is an important feminist method if it makes women's voices *audible*."[27]

The ethnographic process also raises a set of serious moral issues, issues that perhaps are ultimately unresolvable. Working with people in an ethnographic setting potentially leads to power inequalities and exploitative relations. The method of participant observation in fieldwork, for example, is not ethically neutral. On the one hand, it may produce an objectification of study "subjects" or "informants" if the researcher emphasizes observation over participation, thereby converting participants into objects of the ethnographic gaze. The ethnographer is then the authority who can define and characterize her subjects in whatever way she sees fit, under the protection of scientific "objectivity." On the other hand, the ethnographer who becomes a full participant may enjoy closeness with study participants while the study lasts but then may walk away from people, as well as from the setting. She enters a "culture of indebtedness"[28] but may not readily know how to reciprocate. Either situation gives rise to the question of ethnographic representation: how one characterizes those one studies.

Following interviews in private homes, more than one woman asked me to come back and visit. A few called me at home weeks and sometimes months later. One calls me annually, "just to say 'hello.'" What long-term responsibilities, if any, does the ethnographer have toward participants? Are these any different when participants include people who are potentially dependent, e.g., children or the elderly? Does this situation set up an experience of abandonment? In what ways is the ethnographer accountable to study participants? I asked myself these additional questions during the period of field research and thereafter, prompted at times by participants' needs.

I don't have satisfactory or definitive answers to these questions. During the data-gathering facet of this project, I tried to engage in reciprocal relationships with Julie's women, inasmuch as I entered into mutual exchanges, attempted to reveal my vulnerabilities, and moved beyond simply eavesdropping on theirs. I had to earn their trust. Often this happened once I expressed interest in them, shared my own experiences, offered my emotional support for their situation, and became present to them.

In representing the women of this study, I made an effort to enhance their subjectivity by allowing them to speak for themselves as much as possible. I tried to provide an empathetic picture of who these women are. I include myself in the text, revealing sometimes my exchanges and disagreements with them. I refer to them as "participants," not subjects, in an attempt to contest objectification and the asymmetry of the researcher/subject tradition.[29]

I have tried to be accountable by writing a book that, I hope, is accessible to everyone at Julie's International Salon, one that avoids technical jargon and "academese." I have also requested from my publisher that the font size be large enough for older people to read without difficulty. While I do not resolve the ethical issues at hand, I have struggled with them, as have others, including an increasing number of feminist ethnographers. The issues are broad and contested, but they need to be addressed nonetheless.[30]

Cast of Characters

Study participants weave in and out of the text throughout this book. In an effort to provide a coherent image of each individual at the beginning of this study, and for the reader's future reference, I draw a thumbnail sketch of each woman at the time of the interviewing process. In addition to the twenty participants in intensive interviews, I include salon staff members and a few customers whose voices are heard repeatedly in these pages. Names are listed alphabetically under each category.

Participants in Intensive Interviews

Alice, seventy-two, is a practical, straightforward, emotionally reserved woman with short brown hair. Widowed for the last eleven years, she was married for thirty-six years and has three daughters.

Anna, sixty-eight, is a solidly built, practical, generous woman with a keen sense of responsibility, a warm smile, and very short salt-and-pepper hair. Married for forty-three years, she has been widowed for the past six. She is the mother of a son and a daughter, Jenny, forty-two, who routinely accompanies her mother to the salon.

Beatrice, eighty-two, is a petite, bespectacled, silver-haired woman who wears a mantle of vulnerability. She is an intense person, with firm opinions and a sure sense of self. Married for fifty-five years to her ninety-year-old husband, she has no children.

Beth, fifty-nine, is a handsome, expressive, friendly woman with beautiful, natural silver hair. She returned to college after her children were grown and is now enjoying a professional position. Married for forty years, she has four children.

Clara, eighty-five, is a thoughtful, reflective, articulate woman with light-colored hair, a beautiful face, and a sunny smile. Widowed after fifty-three years of marriage, she is the mother of two children.

Dori, sixty-four, is a blue-eyed, light-haired, attractive woman—friendly, outgoing, and high-spirited. As a result of a car accident thirty years ago, she is a paraplegic and uses a wheelchair. Married for forty years, she has three children.

Edie, fifty-five, is a jovial, outgoing, optimistic woman, short in stature, with glasses and brown hair. Five years ago she suffered a massive stroke; through sheer hard work and perseverance she has regained most of her speech and mobility. Divorced following a brief marriage in her twenties, she has one daughter.

Evelyn, seventy-seven, is a small, intense, intelligent woman with light brown hair. The mother of two children, she has been widowed for some five years following a forty-five-year marriage. The loss of her husband has left her in a continuing state of depression she seems unable to shake.

Harriet, seventy-two, is a short, witty, quick-minded and quick-tongued woman with auburn hair and sharply delineated eyebrows. Married for forty-four years, she has been widowed for the past eleven. She has three children.

Leah, eighty, is a gentle, kindly, heavy-set woman with eyeglasses, golden-blond hair, and the habit of earnestly looking right into her interlocutor's eyes. Recently widowed for the second time, she is the mother of a son and a step-son.

Lucy, sixty-two, is an amply built, intelligent, opinionated woman with blue eyes, blond hair, and a handsome face. Married for forty-two years, she has two daughters.

Marny, sixty-four, is an intelligent, articulate, statuesque woman with brown hair and a stylish, sophisticated demeanor. Currently the owner of her own store, she has been married for forty-four years. She is the mother of three children.

Martha, sixty-seven, is a thoughtful, articulate, highly accomplished, brown-haired woman, now retired after a successful career in public service. Widowed twice in her youth, she is now married, with no children of her own.

Merle, eighty-six, is an intelligent, thoughful woman who gives careful consideration to her words before she speaks, a tendency nurtured perhaps during her long career as a school teacher. Bespectacled, blue-eyed, with beautiful silver hair, she carries herself with a kind of patrician grace. Married for sixty-two years, she has a daughter.

Reva, seventy-five, is a tall, serious, reflective woman with ash-blond hair and a tailored look. Married for forty-five years, she has been widowed for nine. She has two daughters.

Sadie, seventy-nine, is a thoughtful, emotionally intense yet publicly reserved woman who wears glasses and blond hair in a kind of pageboy style. Married for thirty-five years, she was widowed eight years ago. She is the mother of three children.

Sara, seventy-eight, is an intense, talkative, self-assured woman with a slight build and salt-and-pepper hair. She has been married for fifty-six years and has no children.

Shelley, eighty-two, is a small, thoughtful woman with a reflective temperament, an intelligent face, and short brown hair. Married for fifty-eight years, she is the mother of two sons.

Sylvia, seventy-seven, is an intense, inquisitive, expressive woman, small in stature, with platinum-blond hair. Born in Poland and a survivor of the Second World War, she has been married for fifty-three years; her husband now suffers from Alzheimer's. She has two children.

Teri, eighty-six, is a friendly, warm, life-affirming woman with a sunny disposition and light, ash-blond hair worn in curls atop her head. She was married for thirty years and has been widowed for the last twenty-four. She is the mother of one daughter.

Other Active Participants

Blanche, in her seventies, is a short, serious, intense, talkative woman with auburn hair. She is married and has children.

Carmela, in her seventies, is a short, plump, friendly and interactive woman with a round face and golden-blond hair. She is married and has children.

Pam, mid-sixties, is an attractive, friendly, chatty woman with blond hair. She is widowed and has no children.

Shaina, in her seventies, is an imposing, self-mocking, handsome woman with an ascerbic wit and silver hair. She is married and has children.

Salon Staff

Helen, in her forties, is principally responsible for hairwashing. She is a short, brown-haired, sweet, gentle woman, with a kind word for everyone. Greek by birth, she is married and has no children.

Julie, in her late thirties, is the shop owner. She is a kind, accepting, diplomatic woman with black hair and an attractive face. Born in Korea, she is married and has three children.

Karen, in her forties, is a part-time beautician, working at Julie's only on Saturdays. She is a quiet, reserved, good-looking woman with golden-blond hair. The only American-born staff member, she is divorced and has no children.

Svetlana, in her fifties, is the manicurist. She is a short woman with a round face, brown hair, friendly eyes, and an earnest yet reserved disposition. Born in the former Soviet Union, she is married and has two daughters.

Verena, in her late fifties, is a beautician. She is a blond, handsome, amiable woman who often speaks her mind. Born in Germany, she is married and has three children.

Victoria, in her thirties, is a beautician. She is a thin, lovely, friendly woman with reddish brown hair and a ready smile. Born in Greece, she is married and has three children.

CHAPTER ONE

Women's Territory

Community and the Ethic of Care at Julie's International Salon

❧

She has women friends here who will neither let her starve nor weep.
            —E. M. Broner, *A Weave of Women*

Julie's International Salon—Julie's, for short—is located in a residential neighborhood of a large midwestern city. More precisely, it is to be found in a nondescript mini shopping strip at the intersection of two busy streets. A large picture window sports the shop's name, along with hair-design posters, which are tastefully displayed and infrequently changed. Not uncommonly, hand-written signs, posted on the window or the glass door, note changes in shop hours; they decidedly convey an air of informality to the place. Moving indoors, the customer first steps into a rectangular reception area. To the left of the entrance is the shop's desk; it serves as a cashier's station and is not regularly staffed. It is usually Helen, who is in charge of hair washing and general shop upkeep, who transacts payments behind the desk. On a wooden surface over the desk, a pen is attached to a chain for the convenience of customers writing checks. Salon pocket calendars often rest sloppily on this surface for the taking. Several chairs are arranged haphazardly near a television set. Two walls are lined with wood-grained, glass-faced cabinets that display various kinds of merchandise for sale, including custom jewelry and women's clothing. Some of this merchandise has remained in place for years and looks rather shabby for wear. A small room to the right of the entrance functions as a coatroom.

Customers arrive at Julie's in various ways. Many drive their own cars, which they park in the shopping strip's parking lot, within view of the beauty shop. Some are dropped off by husbands, or more rarely, by children or friends. A few walk from their homes in the vicinity of the salon. Still others take cabs. On occasion a woman on a wheelchair or a walker is brought in by a companion, or a very elderly, frail woman is helped to negotiate her way into the heart of the shop.

The "inside" area is partly painted and partly wall-papered in soft colors—pink and gray. This area is longitudinally divided by a long wooden cabinet used to support three large, two-sided mirrors and store beauty supplies and equipment. Three cosmetology chairs are located on either side of the cabinet. There are spaces between the mirrors that allow beauticians and customers to see and talk to each other across the division separating the stations. Three hair washing stations, consisting of a chair and a wash basin each, are situated against one wall. Usually only one of these stations is used for its designed purpose. There is also a small bench against the wall behind Julie's station, which one first encounters after entering the shop. A similar bench resides behind Victoria's station, immediately opposite Julie's on the other side of the room divide. These benches and chairs provide opportunities for socializing while customers await their turns.

The back part of the shop, beyond the main "inside" room, consists of a large area lined on opposite sides by old-fashioned hair driers—fourteen in all—the type used to dry hair set in rollers by placing a kind of helmet over the head and adjusting the heat to personal comfort. It is in this area that Svetlana, the manicurist, works, using a portable cart that holds her supplies and provides a working surface. A small kitchen and a bathroom are connected by a small corridor, in which is located a coffee station: coffee pot, cups, and virtually always sweets to eat.

The interior's accent is on functionality, not glamour. In fact, the place is characterized by homeliness and an unkempt flavor: It is not unusual to see hair curlers or towels on the floor, for the TV to be blaring even when no one is watching, and for people to be yelling from one part of the shop to the other. These very characteristics may in fact facilitate the communal nature of social interaction there, as the sociologist Ray Oldenburg argues in *The Great Good Place*, where he studies coffee shops, taverns, and cafés—neighborhood places where people used to hang out, away from both home and work. According to Oldenburg, these features discourage pretension among those who gather there, thereby encouraging social leveling[1] and hence an atmosphere conducive to friendliness and social exchange.

Adding to the shop's informality is the occasional presence of staff members' children "hanging around" during school holidays. Julie's three children typically occupy the reception area during these times. Victoria's oldest son watches television when he comes in with his mother on Saturdays. Customers delight in and fuss over the children, who are never perceived as a nuisance in this context, even when they run around the shop or raise their voices in gleeful play or discord. Informality is also reflected in the self-presentation

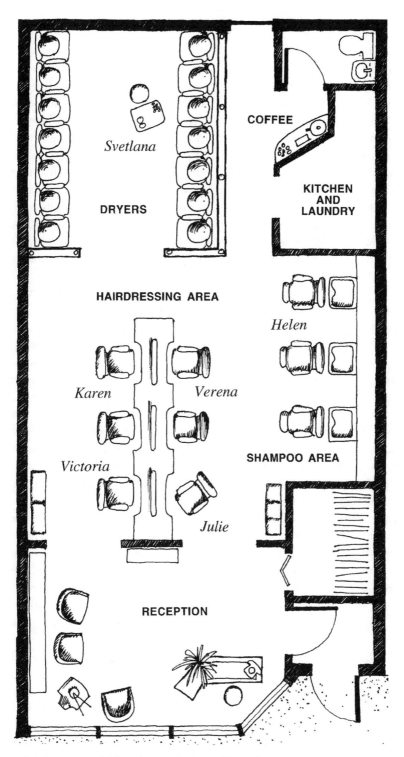

COFFEE

KITCHEN
AND
LAUNDRY

Svetlana

DRYERS

HAIRDRESSING AREA

Helen

Karen

Verena

Victoria

SHAMPOO AREA

Julie

RECEPTION

Julie's International Salon. *Drawing by Dianne Hanau-Strain.*

of customers when they come to the shop. Many are very casually dressed and wear no makeup at all.

In the past, the neighborhood was characterized by a heavily Jewish population. While the neighborhood is more mixed than it was some twenty years ago, the older population is still predominantly Jewish (there is currently an influx of young Orthodox families into the area). The salon's clientele is mostly drawn from the neighborhood. It is largely female, American-born, middle-class, older, and Jewish. Not all Jewish customers are of the same stripe, however. They range from those involved in some branch of religious Judaism, to those active in the local Jewish Community Center, to women who have no formal connection to any Jewish institution yet have strong Jewish identities. For most customers that identity appears to be shaped by ethnic rather than religious meanings, in keeping with similar patterns generally observed among second-generation Jews.

In a real sense the shop follows the Jewish calendar, as major Jewish holidays are marked by appropriate decorations throughout the year. The shop closes on Yom Kippur and displays a lit electric menorah on the window during Hanukkah. Women freely offer each other holiday greetings. Speech is frequently sprinkled with Yiddishisms when Jewish customers speak together. Discussion of holiday foods and family dinners is frequent. Food brought into the shop for sharing often is "Jewish style."

The salon staff is non-Jewish (save for the manicurist) and foreign-born: Korean, German, Russian, Greek. It is also exclusively female. As a consequence, the shop constitutes an all-female space wherein it is rare to see men at all. Occasionally men come in, usually to pick up their wives, in which case they wait in the reception area, behind an invisible border that separates it from the "inside" of the salon, where the "action" is. On rare occasions men do enter this "inner sanctum." I am told that a few men are customers, although I have never seen one in that role in all the years of my visits as customer or researcher. Some men occasionally come into this space to chat briefly with a spouse or parent, in which case they are most commonly ignored, that is, rendered invisible. In short, this is principally "women's territory."[2] In this regard Julie's is an old-fashioned shop since unisex hair salons, which serve women and men and are typically staffed by both sexes, are now the norm. Julie's also continues to offer certain services largely unavailable in today's typical salon, namely, hair setting. It is common to see here, but not elsewhere, women getting their hair set in rollers and then sitting under hair driers before being "combed out."

To the untrained eye, customers might look alike, reflecting the tendency to homogenize the Other—in this case, older Jewish women. But if you spend any time at Julie's you notice that, like anyone else, each woman has a unique personality and presents a distinct public persona. What they share is an unprepossessing yet unmistakable presence that seems to announce, "Here I am."

The Salon as Community

By now it should be clear that in no way is this an upscale salon. According to Marny, a long-term customer, this is a "good, old-fashioned beauty shop. I don't know if there are many left. There are a million of the 'la-la-la' salons downtown and in the suburbs; and they put up high prices and high names. . . . What's different about Julie's is there is no pretense. . . . What you see is what you get." Lucy, an affluent customer who commutes a fair distance to Julie's, suggests that the run-down nature of the place is "comfortable for the haves and it's comfortable for the have-nots. And there's plenty of haves there. . . . It's a real melting pot."

Whereas for Lucy the attraction of Julie's is its socio-economic variety, for Edie the pull is its cultural diversity, the fact that the staff is multinational: "Julie's is an *international* beauty shop. Did you know? . . . It's beautiful. And we all get together. We all like each other. . . . We get along beautiful. You go to a different beauty shop, you have to sit there and nobody is talking to nobody."

A similar note is struck by Anna, who, as we will see, is a Thursday customer who takes charge of bringing food to the beauty shop for everyone's consumption. She tells me, "We have a very international organization: Julie being Korean; Verena being German; Helen is Greek; Svetlana is Russian; the other girl, Victoria, is Greek; Karen is an American; and I'm Jewish.[3] All of this melds together. We have no problem with it. So it's very international. To watch Julie eat Jewish food is hysterical. She loves it!"

The fact that the staff is foreign-born—save for one beautician, Karen, who only works on Saturdays—contributes to rather than detracts from the communal ethos at the beauty shop. This is because these women—all substantially younger than their clientele—share some fundamental values with their customers. These include a central commitment to family, conservative cultural values, and an appreciation for the value and experience of old age. By American standards, these workers reveal values of an older generation— hence the fine fit with their customers.

In an effort to articulate the meaning of community for modern people, Martin Buber wrote,

> Community . . . declares itself primarily in the common and active management of what it has in common, and without this it cannot exist. . . . The real essence of community is to be found in the fact—manifest or otherwise—that it has a centre. The real beginning of a community is when its members have a common relation to the centre overriding all other relations.[4]

Buber refers here to what might be called an *intentional* community—people purposefully drawn together by a core set of concerns. Here I argue that community at Julie's is of an *unintentional* sort: Without planning or design, Julie's emerges as a group of individuals—a different group depending on which day of the week their appointments fall—who enter into ongoing relations with one another around a shared set of concerns. Narrative theologians suggest that community is constituted by those people who share stories, stories with a mythic and symbolic depth emerging from the past that speak to people's contemporary experiences.[5] I believe a variation of this sort of storytelling takes place at Julie's that forges this beauty salon into a community.

Community becomes possible among customers for a variety of reasons, including the casual style of the physical environment already described, but also because of shared structural commonalities, including age, gender, ethnicity, and in many cases, marital status, since virtually all customers are either married or widowed. The stories women tell, though seldom of a religious or mythic nature, draw them into shared universes of meaning. The stories, as we will see in this and other chapters, relate to the experience of being female in a society that demands the display of a feminine appearance; the reality of aging and physical decline; the history of many customers as second- or third-generation American Jews; their background as mothers and homemakers, caregivers par excellence. Storytelling is complemented by action, so the salon becomes a site for the performance of caring deeds, as well.

Despite the values shared by the staff and clientele and the latter's appreciation of diversity, there are some built-in tensions between customers and staff tied to their respective roles. A customer, after all, is an employer of sorts, a beautician or manicurist an employee. These power inequalities surface on occasion. During "slow" days, for example, when bad weather keeps customers away, Svetlana shows me her appointment book, anxious about the number of customers she can count on for the day. In this way she reveals her economic dependence on her regular clientele. Julie often shares her frustrations with me about difficult customers: those who routinely arrive late, those who rush her, those who make unreasonable demands, those who dislike one another and use her as an intermediary. Verena is more spontaneous about expressing her aggravations directly and sometimes wrangles with some customers. But I also observe that she seems to get along very well with many of her customers. "I like more than I dislike," she says, adding that she simply ignores difficult customers, stays quiet, and does her job. Julie confides that despite the stress that some people and situations engender, when she's away from the shop for a day she misses it. She appreciates the close ties she has with many customers, recognizing their unusual nature in a work setting. If friendship and community emerge from relationships among equals, then the communal life at Julie's is centrally a phenomenon experienced by the shop's clientele. What is significant at Julie's is that despite the power inequalities between customers and staff, as we will see, staff members frequently partake in communal life and find areas of reciprocal sharing with many customers.

In chapter 2, I will discuss at some length what motivates customers to frequent beauty salons. Here I turn to a more specific question, namely, why they choose to patronize Julie's International Salon, in particular. We should keep in mind that most customers have standing weekly appointments; most also have a long-standing relationship with this particular beauty shop, in some cases antedating by many years its 1982 purchase by Julie.

A few customers cite convenience as the key reason for going to Julie's. These are women who live in the immediate neighborhood and walk to the salon or get there via a short car ride. This is not a sufficient reason, however, as there are other shops in the general area that could command their patronage. For these and other women, the competence and efficiency of their beautician is a real draw. In the case of two beauticians, Verena and Victoria, many customers followed them from other shops years ago. Women laud not only the work of their beauticians, but also the fact that these are nice people, people they have grown fond of, people who care about them. Edie celebrates the fact that "Victoria and I get along so beautiful." Referring to Verena, a woman tells me, "She's good. She listens to you, she sympathizes, she talks, she laughs at you, she makes fun at you." In short, she is attentive. Customers frequently cite their affection for Helen, the "shampoo girl," who always has a kind word for everyone. As Teri sees it, "Helen greets you like you're a long-lost relative."

Julie, the owner of the shop, is the object of greatest admiration because she is seen, not only as a capable beautician, but as the tone-setter for the salon. And it is the shop environment that seems central to customers' enjoyment of the place and their desire to continue their association with it. People characteristically mention Julie's warm personality and calm demeanor. She is seen as "a kind, delightful woman"; a "sweet girl—she's got the patience of a saint"; a "hard-working, nice girl"; a "good person"; "friendly, pleasant"; "very accommodating." One woman tells me that Julie is "very nice. I feel she has a Jewish heart," that is, Julie is able to bridge their ethnic differences. Julie is also seen as a capable manager since there is no tension evident among the staff, a situation commonly reported about other beauty salons. Many women also value Julie's insofar as there is seldom any bickering among customers as is usual elsewhere: "Nobody gets on anybody else's nerves," says Anna. "Nobody is hollering, 'Me first,' which is horrible." Perhaps Martha best captures shared perceptions when she declares that Julie "creates a very warm, accepting atmosphere, and people who are there respond in kind."

Anna says that Julie's is "like family . . . like a second family to many women," a sentiment echoed by other customers and staff, as well. Reva calls it "family-style," while Martha suggests that "It's a friendly, homelike atmosphere. You become part of the family." Some customers, though not the majority, are in fact integrated into Julie's family, at least in symbolic terms. Martha recounts occasions she and her husband were invited to celebrate Julie's family events, including a baby shower, a birthday party, an open house, a wedding: "My husband and I got to know her whole family." Apparently a few other salon customers were also guests at some of these happenings. Another case in point is a customer named Pam. When Pam arrives for her usual Thursday appointment one December morning, she is thrilled to see Ceci, Julie's youngest daughter. She takes Ceci into her arms, kisses her on the lips, and asks Julie why "Grandma Pam" wasn't told Ceci would be there. The child and the older woman spend some intimate time together. On another occasion, as Pam leaves the shop, she tells Julie, "Tell my little girl I love her."

Images of home also are repeatedly used to capture the essence of this beauty shop, as when Alice declares, "It's like a home meeting grounds on Thursday," the day of her standing appointment. There is something informal and unselfconscious in the behavior of many women that does suggest home. When the shop phone rings, customers frequently answer it, sometimes providing information, sometimes getting involved in conversations of their own, such as trying to discover if the two parties have met. At times the phone call is for a customer, not only, say, from a husband wanting to know the desired pick-up time, but also from other customers who know where to find each other. There is a high level of trust operative in this setting, judging by the intimate nature of some of the conversations. In addition, women frequently leave their purses unattended for long periods of time while they are getting various kinds of service. In her no-nonsense style, Anna comes in one day with a package of Band-Aids wrapped in foil, saying in a bantering style to Julie, but really addressing herself to the entire shop, "What kind of shop is this?" She explains that another customer phoned her after Helen cut her finger, telling her to bring some Band-Aids. A bit later that customer calls Anna to confirm that in fact she has brought the needed first aid. On another occasion I see Anna emptying out a trash can.

To the degree that families ideally are places where one receives support, love, and acceptance, Julie's does in fact resemble a family setting. We should keep in mind, however, that in using the metaphor of family to characterize the salon, women are undoubtedly banking on culturally romanticized images of the family. One way in which this family ethos is manifested is through the ongoing experience of "being," as opposed to "doing," of most customers. While the staff is in fact "doing," engaged in purposive and functional work, the customers, sitting together talking, waiting their turn, or chatting with their beauticians, are unconditionally accepted as they are, with no need to demonstrate their worth through concrete accomplishments. In some ways the experience feels like that of women spending time together at family gatherings with other women: talking about their lives and memories, enjoying the company, in no rush to get anywhere in particular. A different sense of time seems to prevail, suggesting that the building and maintenance of community cannot be rushed.

When characterizing Julie's distinctiveness, customers refer to the warmth, camaraderie, and friendliness they find there. Clara observes that "it's different because you will find that most of the women that go there seem to know one another. They're very friendly. It's almost like an organization, a club, you know? It feels that way. . . . It's very informal. And I'm a very informal person. I really am very informal. And I like that feeling. It's like walking into a friendly room." Clara believes that some customers who have made friends at Julie's "have looked for friendships." Others, like herself, "are busy in their own world. They have their own friends, they have their own families. And this is just an hour or two of talking and laughing and companionship, and that's it." Nonetheless she is adamant that this shop is unique, "one of its kind. People feel happy there. You can see when they walk in; they're just happy to be there."

Many women experience Julie's International Salon as a site of friendship among customers, even if they themselves do not partake of it intensely, as in Clara's case. On a Friday morning, I am talking to Beth in the back area of the shop. She keeps her eye on Julie to make sure she does not miss her turn. I ask her why she comes to Julie's, specifically. "'Cause I like the way [Julie] does my hair. And I've met some nice girls here. And we call ourselves our 'beauty shop friends.' They know about my family; I know about their family. And we chit-chat. And how are my children? they ask me. How are my grand-children? How is the sick husband? So, it's been very pleasant." Acknowledging that she does not see these friends outside the shop, she nonetheless explains, "But if the beauty shop friends are sick, I call them, you know. 'Where are you?' And they've called me to congratulate me [on the birth of a grandchild]. And so it's a nice relationship that I have with the people that I've met here." Beth is a married, busy professional with an active social life and a close relationship with her four grown children and several grandchildren.

Dori, a married mother of three adult children and physically challenged due to a serious car accident many years ago, views her Saturday visits to Julie's as "my one social outing for the week." Her perception of her relationships there is surprisingly similar to Beth's, despite the great differences in their life situations. "I call the beauty parlor a social club. I've been going for so many years, and we're dealing with friends; we're good friends. I tell them about my family, and they tell me about their families. And we're more than just casual acquaintances." She asks me if I am familiar with Anna's renowned baking. Dori ordered a cake from Anna that she shared with her "social club" the previous Saturday because "I consider them my friends, and I wanted them to help celebrate my [wedding] anniversary." It is Anna who tells me that although she could do her own hair if she wanted to, she goes to see Verena at Julie's because "It's my one day out. It's a lift. It's being with the good people there. Nobody wants to miss it. When we miss a day, we're all very unhappy." For Anna it is her "one day out," not because she is house bound, but because she has other demands on her. A visit to Julie's offers a needed respite from a fast-paced life.

When I phone Leah to schedule an interview for a Friday, she quickly responds, "Never on Friday. That's my therapy day at the beauty shop. . . . You go in and you talk to this one and that one and listen to their problems. And you say, 'Oh, my problems aren't that bad.' And you look forward to seeing the same people, week in and week out. And if you don't see them, you wonder if everything is all right." Leah is among the many women who phone other customers when they don't show up at their accustomed time. Beauticians commonly do the same.

Teri tells me, in no uncertain terms, "There's something about that shop that you're never gonna find anywhere. The closeness, you know." She illustrates the attention she receives from the moment she enters Julie's. "First of all, they bawl the heck out of me, if I come in . . . a little after 11:00 [her appointment time], 'You're late!'" If she arrives a few minutes early, Verena, Teri's beautician, teases her by saying, "What are you doing here so early?" "So I look at Julie and I says, 'You know what? One of these days I'm gonna find me a beauty shop where I get a little respect! [laughs]. Well, then I start talking and never shut up. . . . I've never experienced anything like I'm going through now, going to this shop." She describes the friendliness and warmth of all staff members. She has already told me how talented Verena is at doing her hair. Now she adds, "She is more than a beautician. I would say she's a friend."

At another point in our interview, Teri, who is eighty-six, and I are discussing her life as a long-time widow. She tells me about her occasional loneliness in the context of a rather active life. "I live for this Thursday [her appointment day], would you believe? Because I'm gonna see all these gals. It's not a chore going to the beauty shop; it's a day out. That's the way I feel. These gals are just, just wonderful. . . ." She refers here to both staff and customers. I ask her how long she spends at the salon. She arrives at 11:00 A.M. Then she waits for Anna to take her home, somewhere between 2:00 and 3:00 P.M. "The whole day. But I don't feel like it's wasted because I enjoy it. I enjoy every minute of it. You talk with this one and that one. . . ."

Beth, Dori, and Teri characterize their relationships at Julie's as friendships; Anna and Leah do not label them as such, but they suggest as much. If we are to appreciate the significance of these relationships, it seems to me that we need to develop a more expansive view of friendship than the one that is culturally dominant. Historically the West has been, and continues to be, strongly influenced by classical Greek views of friendship, most notably Aristotle's.[6] Aristotle saw friendship as a central relationship in social life. He placed various forms of friendship into a hierarchy, moving up from acquaintances, to companions, to intimates. In this view acquaintances are plentiful, companions fewer, and intimates few and far between in a person's life. In other words, for Aristotle the quality of friendships and their quantity are inversely related: The more friends you have, the lesser the quality of the friendships; the fewer, the higher.

Some of Julie's customers have active friendship networks outside the salon; some have lost most of their friends to moves or to death. In general, women do not socialize with each other outside the salon; their relationships are contained within it. But it may not be productive to make the judgment that customers and staff at Julie's International Salon are acquaintances as opposed to friends because many have more long-standing friendships with others outside the shop that engage a larger domain of their lives. To differentiate between acquaintance and friend by placing them along an Aristotelian hierarchical scale, while useful in making certain distinctions, may well belittle the significance of the relationships that do exist. Judging by what I see at the beauty salon, the theologian Mary Hunt's perspective on women's friendships is accurate and her proposal promising:

> Women friends, lots of them, are necessary for women's survival in an often unfriendly environment. . . . [M]y proposed model is not hierarchical, nor does it differentiate by gradation or degree the importance of various friendships. . . . It reflects women's experience of variety and diversification in friendships.[7]

Beauty-shop friendships, then, may be seen as neither better nor worse than other friendships. They are different from other friendships, perhaps, because they are limited to a particular space and time, but the significance of such relationships is not thereby diminished; rather, it is particularized.

The importance of friendship in women's lives has a long history. The biblical book of Ruth tells the story of a deep and abiding friendship between Naomi and Ruth. Records of women's friendships reach us from the medieval cloisters and religious communities of Christian Europe.[8] Recent scholarship has unearthed powerful and passionate friendships among women in eighteenth- and nineteenth-century America, friendships that were culturally accepted and encouraged.[9]

Recent feminist work has attempted to understand contemporary women's friendships from a theoretical perspective. This work frequently takes a gender-based approach, suggesting that women's friendships are distinctive because they involve women's distinctive psychology. In the classic book, *Toward a New Psychology of Women*, the psychiatrist Jean Baker Miller argues that "women stay with, build on, and develop in a context of attachment and affiliation with others. Indeed, women's sense of self becomes very much organized around being able to make and then to maintain affiliations and relationships."[10] While the desire for affiliation is a human need, in American society, autonomy and independence are touted as traits of the healthy male. Women's efforts in these directions have been discouraged until recently, for the appropriate mark of femininity is seen as connection, not separation; service to others, not competition. These distinctive forms of personality development are not thought to be "natural," that is, biological, in nature. Rather, they are mediated by existing societal arrangements and cultural values.[11] Women's commitment to emotional connection is associated with several important dimensions of their friendships. Empathy is seen as central by some authors, while others emphasize attention, reassurance, or comfort.[12]

The significance of friendship in older age has been recognized empirically only recently. Women's life-long tendency to have significant friendships is often intensified in old age.[13] Because old age is a time when people frequently experience multiple losses, researchers are now beginning to see friendship as one way to come to terms with them. As Dorothy Jerrome puts it, "Friends play a vital role in the process of socialization to old age. They impart instrumental knowledge, provide an opportunity for role rehearsal, and set controls on behaviour. . . . Friends provide protective isolation in managing confrontations with the wider society. . . . There are certain periods of life when friends are particularly important, and old age is one of them."[14]

Friends are important sources of support while mourning the loss of a spouse, especially for women. At that time the older person needs to talk about loneliness with a peer who understands her pain: "Since female gender identity may be partially defined in relations to others, such events can lead to a loss of a sense of self and depression. . . . Friendship can serve as a critical source of help in coming to terms with these changes. . . . Understanding and equal give and take among peers may be more possible than with children."[15] Friends sometimes are more important than family relations to morale and well-being.[16] They provide companionship and the capacity for enjoyment, for having a good time.

As I observe the relationships at Julie's, I see women as friends, engaged in relationships with one another that involve attention, support, and mutual responsibility—in short, caring. These are significant relationships, relationships that clearly provide meaning and value for many women, and hence need to be acknowledged and celebrated for the emotional and moral work that they embody. That they happen within private space, or, more specifically, the culturally trivialized context of a beauty salon, is irrelevant from an ethical point of view. It is time to begin breaking down the socially constructed division of private versus public space when analyzing moral disposition and moral action. In doing so perhaps we can start recognizing the social nature and social value of women's caring work.[17] What we see at Julie's is neither the classical confrontation with major moral quandaries nor the heroic deed on behalf of ideal principles characteristic of the Western ethical narrative. Rather, we find there women as moral actors, engaged in an ethics of the everyday, designed to sustain women's spirits in the midst of their usual, quotidian existence. Pared down to essentials, it involves two basic components: being present to one another, on the one hand, and responding to need—which might entail comforting, celebration, or companionship—on the other.

Modes of Caring

Gerontologists, working out of a social science perspective, are especially interested in how a rapidly changing society like ours provides support to the elderly. To that end, they have investigated social networks that include the older person's kin, friends, and neighbors.[18] They generally explore social support in functional terms, that is, what it entails and how it functions. I am interested, as well, in the moral dimensions of support, what feminist scholars might call care or caring.[19]

Interest in care as a moral value emerged with some urgency following the 1982 publication of Carol Gilligan's book, *In a Different Voice*. Interested in developing a model of women's moral development, Gilligan concluded that women tend to discern their moral responsibilities within the concrete realities of their relationships.[20] Theirs is an ethic of care based on human connection. A woman might care for her elderly mother, for example, not because she experiences this as a moral duty, but because she loves her mother. By contrast, Gilligan reasoned, men are more likely to use abstract moral principles—such as human rights and justice—in determining the appropriate course of moral action. Gilligan's argument has given rise to a great deal of debate, and there is no broad consensus regarding her conclusions. A major point of disagreement among feminists is whether women are caring due to their psychological development, i.e., their personality, or whether women care as a result of their subordinate status in society.[21]

Academic debates aside, in recent years much thought has been given to the meaning of care and to the possibility of a viable ethic of care, which would place caring at its center. For our purposes, in identifying what care or caring involves, I begin with Gilligan's own words: "The ideal of care is . . . an activity of relationship, of seeing and responding to need, taking care of the world by sustaining the web of connection so that no one is left alone."[22] Social ethicist Barbara Andolsen expands this definition when she writes,

"Care names an ongoing pattern of actions that are designed to create and sustain positive relationships among human beings. The one who acts from a stance of care responds to the one-cared-for in a fashion that minimizes harm, comforts and, to the extent possible, increases opportunities for growth and joy."[23] That caring is an essential aspect of our lives as human beings is empirically verifiable: We all need care in order to thrive. But the Western ethical tradition typically has not acknowledged it as a practice worthy of moral value. Many observers assume this is the case because caring mostly has been the work of women and other disempowered persons.

Julie's International Salon is a business establishment whose central purpose is to provide certain services—hair and nail care—for the sake of profit. However, I believe that it frequently functions as an unintentional community for its participants through its friendly relations of caring. As such, it provides many women with a sense of belonging and affirmation, often in contrast to the impersonal nature of the public square, which renders older people—especially older women—invisible and hence irrelevant. Care often is expressed using distinctively female modes of communication, humor, and bonding. In short, I believe that this setting presents important features of what feminist scholars call "women's culture."[24] I have already discussed some ways in which people at Julie's extend care to each other. In what follows I more explicitly explore mechanisms that forge this beauty salon into a vibrant community.

Illness-Talk

It should not come as a surprise to hear talk about ill health at Julie's. However, I am not prepared for the centrality of such a topic in the exchanges between customers and beauticians, and customers among themselves, because speaking about our ailments is not typically acceptable except with close family members. Older people are frequently caricatured about their alleged preoccupations with their ailments; consequently many are forced into silence about these matters for fear of social disapproval. These cultural tendencies reveal a profound denial of physical decline and death in our society (themes we will return to in chapter 3).

By contrast, at Julie's one of the first things the beautician asks a customer, or that customers ask each other, is "How are you feeling?" and, if applicable, "Are you feeling any better?" or "How is your husband?" Women do not hesitate to respond with a health bulletin. What is significant, however, is that health or illness talk is reciprocal. No one has the exclusive right to speak, and no one seems to take advantage of a captive audience. Conversations about illness frequently involve advice-giving on the part of the listener, as when Shaina, recovering from an especially difficult bout of Crohn's disease, suggests it would be some time before she can clean her house the way she likes it. Verena responds that Shaina should not worry or hurry about this because, after all, "No one is going anywhere," by which she means, "You have no reason to pressure yourself."

Customers exhibit a capacity for laughing at themselves, at their aches and pains, and at their intense engagement in such matters. For example, Blanche and Carmela, along with Claire, find themselves discussing various surgeries that they've had, stimulated by the fact that Blanche recently had cataract surgery. They first compare notes on that type of surgery; Blanche then talks about the hysterectomy she had years back, and so forth. Rather spontaneously, Blanche breaks into this discussion by saying, "Look at us, talking about cataracts, hysterectomies, hospitals!" They all laugh in this moment of self-recognition and amusement at themselves.

At times, illness-talk becomes competitive between customers, such as the time when Sara comes into the shop and I ask her whether she has recovered from a protracted illness. She playfully says, "I no longer answer that!" only to list the various maladies that she'd been afflicted with: upper respiratory infection, sinus, bronchial infections, and so on. No sooner does she get this out than Shelley pipes in with *her* litany of upper respiratory ailments. At times the two women interrupt each other in this discussion. What is distinctive for me about this exchange is not the comparison of ailments as such, but the joy and zest of the exchange itself. It represents an example of what linguist Deborah Tannen[25] calls troubles-talk or lament-talk and applies, as well, to much of what I have said so far about illness-talk: Women talk to one another in search of connection and intimacy, to forge friendships and establish rapport.

Frequently it is the exchange of problems that cements this bond between women, and at Julie's, health issues constitute a primary conduit to intimacy and mutual support. For Sara and Shelley the joy comes not from having been ill but from the ability to share the symptoms with such abandon, completely free of the fear of judgment, secure that their conversation partners offer acceptance and recognition of the suffering endured. These exchanges support the observations of psychotherapist Rachel Josefowitz Siegel in her work with a support group for older women: "Our need to talk of death, dying, and loss of function seemed intensified by our awareness that these topics were shunned in other settings."[26]

A more indirect form of lament-talk is generated by Julie after she learns of Mary's stomach cancer and its devastating prognosis. As soon as Mary is out of earshot, under the drier, Julie quietly proceeds to tell one and all about the terrible news, which Mary, unusual in her privacy, has only shared with Julie, her beautician. Julie's spreading of the news serves at least two purposes. One is to relieve herself of the burden of the news; another is to bind others into a community of lament, those bonded together quietly but painfully as "knowers" of a tragedy imminent in their midst.

In their friendly relations, people at Julie's are aware and accepting of one another's needs. A woman *acts* on this awareness by expressing concern and eliciting her interlocutor's articulation of her experience and worries. Julie believes that "women feel better if they can discharge all that they are feeling, let it all out. They don't get depressed that way." In facilitating this therapeutic behavior, Julie and others engage in caring action.

Some women probably lack sources of support elsewhere. Carmela, for example, is telling me about her worries that she might have a serious medical problem. She says how much she enjoys talking with me because "it's good for me," adding that she cannot talk to her husband about such worries. I ask who she talks to about things that concern her. "Myself," she responds. "I talk to myself in the mirror." Her daughter is like her husband, so "there's no one to talk to." In like manner, Beatrice feels she cannot talk to her husband about the awful time she is going through, which she is discussing at the shop: "He knows my anxieties and fears." "Is he able to help you?" I ask her. "No. Not one bit. Not one bit. He just doesn't understand. He can't." Paula Caplan may be referring to the experience of such women at Julie's when she writes, "There is some historical evidence that, until recent years, most women did not expect real sharing of feelings and supportiveness from husbands; for this, they turned to their women friends and relatives, and they believed this was natural."[27]

Discursive Detail

At Julie's, much of the women's talk includes a generous amount of detail, whether the conversation involves illness, travel plans, reports of vacations, narratives of childbirth, or the making of chicken soup, down to the last ingredient. I am initially perplexed by the number of particulars used to communicate women's experiences. I have to confess that at times I feel distracted by the seemingly incessant recitation of details.

Tannen suggests that women in general use more detail than do men in their conversations. "The exchange of relatively insignificant details about daily life sends a metamessage of rapport and caring," she writes. "The noticing of details shows caring and creates involvement. . . . Because women are concerned first and foremost with establishing intimacy, they value the telling of details."[28] I think Tannen is helpful here. However, when applied to Julie's, I believe her explanation needs further specificity.

First, the women at Julie's have time to devote to leisurely conversation, a luxury not afforded to those of us wearing several hats and always short of time. Second, my observation at Julie's beauty shop is that conversations typically concern private as opposed to public life; it is rare to hear discussions of public events or the expression of political concerns. This is not to say that these discussions are entirely absent or that women are uninterested in them. Rather, the beauty shop offers a special location where personal life can be highlighted. What we have, then, is the exchange of lived experience, which for most of these women relates to the actual condition of their lives—their joys, sorrows, chores, responsibilities. Detail, I believe, serves not only to communicate personal experience but to encourage listeners vicariously to partake in it.

When Carmela tells about a cardiac episode that lands her in the hospital for some days, she spells out the exact chronology of events: what she was eating when she felt faint, what she said, what her husband replied, and so forth. Likewise, in the course of a couple of hours, Verena repeatedly reports in great detail on her vacation to a resort with her sister, a vacation involving lots of time at the beach. Both narratives allow the speaker to re-live her experience each time she tells it; the detail furnishes the nitty-gritty of the experience to the listeners, in this way inviting the vicarious participation of the listeners in that very experience. The sharing of conversation around the details allows for active involvement in the here and now, as when Verena notes that while at the beach, her legs became itchy after she put on suntan lotion. Everyone within hearing range, including me, jumps in to offer an explanation as to why Verena's legs became itchy. In short, we partake directly in her experience because she takes us with her as she recollects it in such palpable detail. The result is that such patterns of sharing cement and fortify social connections. They also involve mutuality and inclusion: Everyone is given a hearing when it's her turn to tell her story; everyone is implicitly invited to participate in the collective response when someone else is telling hers. I have never seen a woman excluded from social discourse at this beauty salon.

A word should be said about the popular characterization of women's discursive exchanges as gossip. This characterization usually views in a negative light women's tendency to talk about others because it assumes that the intent is negative; hence the notion that women are "catty" in their treat-ment and/or evaluation of other women. At Julie's there is a considerable amount of discussion of absent women, especially women who are customers of the shop. Very rarely is the discussion negative, however. Only once have I heard what might be considered negative gossip. (I am told that two women sometimes engage in bad-mouthing others who are not salon customers; but these women are neighbors and have a relationship independent of the shop.) Typically conversations about absent others revolve around such things as a woman who did not show up today because she is ill or a woman whose husband passed away recently and she's having a hard time. If evaluative comments are made about these absent women, generally they are positive in nature, expressing fondness for them and concern about their situations.

In her study of gossip as a form of communication, Sally Yerkovich argues that gossip is at heart a sociable process and consequently "the content of the talk is not as important as the interaction which the talking supports.... While describing an absent party, the substance of the moral characterization serves also to reinforce the existing social bond of the gossipers."[29] In other words, talking about other women in the manner that it is done at Julie's serves to strengthen the connections among the conversation partners: By making present to the others the women who are not physically there at the moment, this form of talk creates an opportunity for the expression of care and support.

When I start fieldwork for this study, a woman friend, an academic, suggests that I will probably find the conversation to be boring, restricted to topics that are narrow in scope. She is mistaken. I come to see that in these women's verbal exchanges about food, illness, family, and everyday experience, they are attending to important areas in their lives. By sharing recipes or shopping tips, or discussing their grandchildren's weddings or their husbands' infirmities, they are deepening their skills and insights regarding those things for which women of their generation are held responsible. Until what women do in so-called private space—the domestic sphere—is appreciated for its contributions to everyone's lives, women's discourse about these matters will continue to be trivialized, devalued, and dismissed as an area unworthy of investigation.

Concern and Affection

In their expression of care, it is not uncommon for customers to compliment one another on their clothes or their looks, often in generous and affectionate terms. For example, when Teri comes into the shop after a week's absence due to illness, Beatrice expresses delight in seeing her. She asks Teri how she is feeling, gently grabbing Teri by the loose folds of her neck; turning to me, she asks rhetorically, "Isn't she pretty?" adding, "And sweet, too." Then there is the time when Carmela greets Blanche with a cheerful "Hello, sweetie." When Julie is working on Carmela's hair, Carmela talks of her imminent departure for Phoenix, where she goes for six months each year. With a deep sigh, Blanche says, "I'm so sorry," clearly referring to the prospect of Carmela's absence from the shop. Turning to me, but within Carmela's earshot, Julie says, "I will miss her."

On another occasion, Julie tells me that she recently had her braces tightened and is now feeling uncomfortable. A bit later, Anna comes by. Noticing Julie's discomfort around the mouth, she asks her if she has retainers on. "Not yet," Julie replies. Anna then recounts that when Julie first put on the braces, she covered her mouth in embarrassment. Anna yelled at her, telling her to uncover her mouth and to show that beautiful smile. Now Anna says to Julie, "We are so proud of you for doing that," that is, for getting braces as an adult.

There is no uncertainty in these verbal expressions: They directly communicate the significance a woman plays in the others' lives. In this setting women tell one another they are valued. To my mind this represents more than a psychologically therapeutic gesture. It stands for deep affirmation of another human being, hence carrying moral as well as religious significance.

Nonverbal ways of offering support are also operative at the salon. On Saturday mornings Julie comes into work a bit early in order to pick up a group of customers at a nearby high-rise apartment complex. Another customer takes them home. When I hear about these arrangements, two people simultaneously announce, "Julie is our driver!" Anna routinely drives Teri home. A woman tells me that when she was sick in the hospital, Julie and her husband went to see her. On occasion beauticians go to customers' homes, or vice-versa, to do or to touch up a woman's hair if a special occasion calls for it and the shop is closed.

The supportive environment of the shop is revealed in moving stories about two long-term customers who used the salon as a base following the death of their spouses. Pam, who lives nearby, would show up at the shop a good deal, until she stopped, being made self-conscious by customers' surprise on seeing her there all the time. The other customer, now deceased, used the shop as a "second home" for some three years after becoming a widow. Clearly for these and other women, Julie's provides a therapeutic context that helps to relieve depression and contributes to self-esteem by providing an environment rich in companionship and support.

There is a great deal of affection and physical contact expressed in this setting, as well. The ethnic background of women at the salon may explain these phenomena. They readily reflect my own experience of the warmth and affection frequently evident in Jewish communal and familial settings. It is usual to see customers kiss or hug the shop staff. Slaps on the rear-end are not uncommon, frequently delivered by customers onto staff members; I also see this gesture of familial affection made by a beautician toward a customer, and even between customers. Touching goes on all the time, by staff as they work on women—during hair washing, cutting, setting, and so forth, but also during pedicures, which include leg massage. But there is also a great deal of hugging and touching between customers, as when one woman touches another's arm very tenderly, offering comfort and empathy on the loss of the second woman's mother. Another time I notice a very loving exchange between Sylvia, whose husband suffers from Alzheimer's, and Paula, who has a boyfriend in a nursing home, also with Alzheimer's. The two stand quietly together, bringing each other up to date. Sylvia, a Holocaust survivor and hence one of the few European-born customers of the shop, looks directly into the eyes of Paula, a non-Jew, as she gently caresses her arm, plaintively exclaiming, "Oy vey! All I can say is, Oy vey!"

I am reminded in this regard of an insight from May Sarton's novel, *As We Are Now*. The protagonist, Caro Spenser, is a woman in her seventies who writes in her diary, "I cannot imagine what it would be like to feel a tender caress—my skin is parched like the desert for lack of touch."[30] When I first approach Julie about doing this study, she provides me with the following observation: "Beauticians are like psychiatrists," she says, "in that customers talk to you about their most personal problems." "Why do you think that is?" I ask her. "Because you touch their hair," she replies.

At Julie's, women's caring for others is embodied work. In this regard it represents the meaning of care in its fullest sense. For we might feel disposed toward empathy or compassion toward, or support of, another. Until we enact such inclinations, however, we have not *acted* morally. As social ethicist Beverly Harrison notes, "Feelings deserve our respect for what they are. . . . Moral quality is a property of acts, not feelings, and our feelings arise in action. The moral question is not 'what do I feel?' but rather 'what do I do with what I feel?'"[31] While dispositions and emotions are an important part of caring, then, caring must also be seen as a *practice*.[32] Women at Julie's enact care through action: kind words; touch and physical expressions of affection; attentiveness and response to others' presence and needs. Perhaps Clara is not at her most articulate when she muses as follows, but she gets her point across: "I think that attention—perhaps attention—is the most, what can I say, good emotional fruit that older people experience."

Humor

Humor is an important dynamic at Julie's, used to communicate affection and support, to deal with conflict, and as a vehicle for plain fun. Humor often takes the form of bantering, as women—customers and staff alike—playfully ridicule one another without the slightest evidence of hurt feelings or self-consciousness as a result. While this kind of humor is foreign to my own upbringing as a Jew in Latin America, I observe it among other Jewish American women of that generation; for example, in the way my mother-in-law interacts with her women friends.

It is the day before Halloween. Blanche is sitting at a beautician's station; her hair is covered by a white plastic bag, some streaks of dark dye peeking out from the bag onto her forehead, her eyebrows thick with hair coloring as well. A customer spiritedly yells at Blanche as she heads for the back of the shop, "Go like that tomorrow. You'll scare someone."

Julie is continually teased by customers and staff about her tendency to be scissors-happy. Pam routinely makes fun of Shaina's loquaciousness. One time, for instance, Pam approaches Shaina, who is sitting under a drier. To one and all, but most of all for Shaina's benefit, Pam declares, "It's quiet today because Shaina is keeping her mouth shut!" At that very instant Shaina gets up and struts around the room, saying in an ironic tone, "I'm just an old bag." A few months later, as Shaina leaves the shop, she calls out to Pam, "Good-bye, noisy!"

Women's behavior toward one another, at Julie's and elsewhere, is characterized by an attempt to establish connection and develop closeness. Conflict is especially difficult for women because it threatens to disrupt connection and break the bonds of friendship. I am not surprised to find that conflict and tension are not openly handled at Julie's. Especially interesting is the use of humor to cope with conflictual situations. Harriet has been patiently waiting to be "combed out"; she seems to think she's next. Julie attends to another customer first. Harriet expresses her frustration in a joking, mocking, theatrical fashion by playfully "beating" Julie on the arm while, pretending to cry, she says that it was her turn. Julie humors her by smiling sweetly, then goes about her business. At one point Verena diffuses potential tension between customers by humorously barking out, "I'm the policeman. I'm handling traffic!"

A good deal of humor revolves around issues of appearance and aging and is frequently directed toward the self. Evelyn expresses admiration for Anna's talent in cooking, crocheting, and cross-stitching. "All nervous energy," she declares, "but then Anna is only sixty-six. I am one hundred and six! I feel like Methuselah!" On another occasion, when Julie is combing her hair, Shaina pulls at her own neck, loudly exclaiming for all to hear, "Turkey neck!" Then to Julie she says, "There is something wrong with this mirror—at home there is no double chin!" Everyone around shares in the fun, with one woman suggesting the construction of a contraption that would link a wire from ear to ear, hence making it possible to hide the neck. In like manner, witticisms about pregnancy abound when women look at themselves in the mirror and suggest that they look rather far along in pregnancy. The sociologist Arlie Russel Hochschild observed a similar pattern in her study of a residential community of older women: "There were many jokes concerning pretended pregnancy."[33]

Women's humor has frequently been interpreted as being self-deprecatory, revealing women's negative self-esteem. Scholars are now revising this interpretation, however, in some cases beginning with Freud's assertion that "humor is not resigned but rebellious": It allows people to assert themselves against the unkindness of their real circumstances.[34] In this manner, Mary Crawford argues that the apparent self-depreciation in women's humor may in fact reveal an intentional desire on women's part "to increase group intimacy through self-disclosure and a goal of satirizing the negative and contradictory role messages directed at women."[35] The social unacceptability of women's aging, the loss of youthful bodies and feminine attractiveness may in fact be contested by some women at Julie's through this kind of humor. Laughing together at double-chins or enlarged bellies serves to bond women around the inevitability of aging. It does not reveal a resigned attitude, however; rather, it pokes fun at our society's unrealistic expectations that women remain forever the icons of youthful beauty and sexuality.

Food

Another ongoing feature of community life at Julie's International Salon is the constant presence of food, in its physical reality or as part of the conversational fare. It is very common for women to discuss their cooking plans, especially around holiday time. Frequently I hear discussions of food shopping needs and information exchange about food sales or recipes. On one occasion Verena is looking through a stack of food coupons that a customer has brought her. On another, Svetlana tells me of a successful expedition to the local supermarket, where she purchased a huge salmon she plans to share with her *machuten* (Yiddish for father-in-law).

An extension of this interest in food is to be found in the cookies, fruit, and cakes always available for consumption at the shop; these are brought in by a large number of customers on a routine basis. Such nurturing offerings are quickly opened and displayed for the taking, near Julie's work station or by the coffee pot near the rear of the salon. Beauticians frequently offer such goodies to the customers, who almost always indulge. The familial ethos of the shop makes it possible for a customer to exclaim, soon after her arrival, "Is there something to eat in the refrigerator? I'm hungry." With that comment, off she goes toward the kitchen in search of a tasty bite.

Even more intriguing is the consumption of full meals at Julie's. Some women bring sack lunches with them, which they consume while they sit under driers, often sharing morsels with their neighbors. Frequently a staff member telephones a food order for a customer to the Thai restaurant next door. Customers will eat their lunch while under the drier or at a work table at the very rear of the shop. It is thus not unusual for the pungent fragrances of egg rolls and stir fries to mix with the less appealing smells of permanent fluid, hair spray, and hair dyes.

Thursday is an unusual day at Julie's. Beginning in late morning, the "Thursday clique" or "Thursday club" begins to congregate, a group of about ten women who have known each other for years as customers of the shop. Anna, a high-energy woman in her sixties, brings home-cooked lunch for the whole salon every few weeks. When she is not cooking herself, she telephones from home and takes fast food orders, which she picks up at Wendy's on her way to the beauty shop. A number of customers continue to be impressed by this feature of beauty salon life. Martha, for example, recalls telling friends about her experience at Julie's: "Oh, I would tell people, else-where, you know, that I just had my lunch at the beauty shop. And I'd tell them about what we're having [to eat]. Well, nobody would believe me. Where else could you go where this takes place?"

One Thursday Anna arrives with a home-cooked feast in tow. Soon enough, people find out she unexpectedly had her hair done the previous day because of a special social engagement. Some of the women express amaze-ment and admiration about Anna's generosity in especially coming to bring lunch. Thus Shaina tells her, "You are nice," while Reva proclaims, "You are something!" Anna simply replies, "I wouldn't miss it," as she begins to serve her delicious repast. As I suggested earlier, in general these women do not socialize outside the shop, save for those who have had pre-existing relation-ships. However, members of the "Thursday clique" plus the shop staff take Anna out to a nice restaurant once or twice a year as a gesture of reciprocity.

The meaning of food in social life is of course far more complex than simply meeting biological survival needs. Bringing food to the salon and eating meals together are not activities related to hunger per se but to social relationships. As Lee Klosinski writes, "Eating together is a social event which involves people in matrices of reciprocity and mutuality."[36] It is diffi-cult to identify precisely what motivates women, including Anna, routinely to bring food into the shop. On a most basic level, women feed their families.[37] If Julie's is like family for many, then feeding its participants may seem like a natural extension of women's usual work. At another level these offerings are concrete expressions of a nurturing impulse. Such expressions of affection and care are rather common in the Jewish culture in which most of these women grew up. The food may also signal reciprocity for the care and sup-port these women receive from customers and staff alike.

Food and commensality frequently serve to demarcate boundaries between one group and another. At Julie's, the Thursday customers see themselves as being a special group—distinct from others at the shop—in part because their full-fledged commensality behaviorally sets them apart. But food creates bonds between people as well. We don't typically share meals with strangers. Indeed, the Thursday clique is an identifiable group at Julie's, the women feeling especially connected to one another and cognizant of their more intense level of interaction. For, as Jerrome suggests, "Commensality—a ritual expression of solidarity through eating and drinking together—is important in the expression and consolidation of women's friendships."[38] In short, members of the "Thursday clique" sacramentalize their friendship in those moments when, as it were, they "break bread" together.[39]

Coda

As we have seen, many customers attribute the caring ethos of the salon to Julie, the owner. We have also seen that the communal nature of this shop results from an ongoing and diverse set of social exchanges among many women, exchanges I have characterized as caring expressions of friendship. While Julie may set the tone for such a climate, it is the women themselves—staff and customers together—who construct and maintain this unintentional community. A particular style of communication and friendship prevails there, not the least because as part of the rituals of beautification, women literally as well as emotionally "let their hair down." As a number of customers put it, at Julie's "people can let it all hang out."

This is not, however, always an uncomplicated process. Power dynamics, as earlier suggested, sometimes make for tense situations rather than occasions for caring. A customer I see only a couple of times wonders whether she needs to get her hair colored before Verena goes away on vacation. They agree that she will have it done during Verena's absence. The woman is anxious about Verena leaving the color formula at the shop for another beautician to use. Verena seems weary and a bit out of patience, but she nods her head emphatically, indicating that she will do so. Then looking at herself in the mirror, the customer requests that Verena prepare a different formula for her hair color, because, as she puts it, "This hair color looks dirty, to my eyes." Verena immediately retorts, "Wash your eyes out!" The customer replies, "Wash your mouth out!" as she jestingly slaps her on the cheek. Both of them break into peals of laughter, and the customer goes on to get her hair washed, asking Verena, "Have you ordered for me yet?" "No, darling," replies Verena, "I did not have a chance. But don't worry, you'll have it when I come back." This she says looking away from the woman, eyes rolling with impatience and weariness.

Despite the friendly and happy mood typical at Julie's, there are moments of stress not always cushioned by humor. These are few and far between and involve customer-staff relations. Although in my judgment the latter are generally relations characterized by caring, at an important level they remain unequal relations: Staff members are economically dependent on their clients and hence must show themselves in their occupational persona as well as in their role as customers' friends. On rare occasions I have heard Verena call out in frustration, "This business drives me crazy. I'm going to get out one of these days!" In a more dispassionate moment she confides that "dealing with the public" is the most difficult aspect of her work, that is, responding to the sometimes unreasonable demands or complaints of some of her customers. Beauticians are expected to display a cheerful disposition and be available—emotionally and otherwise—to their clients. This is reminiscent of

Hochschild's claim that certain kinds of work—especially those held by women in social service jobs—require "emotional labor," wherein "the emotional style of offering the service is part of the service itself."[40] Julie and Verena recollect their early days as beauticians when they would go home every day and cry buckets because of the tensions they experienced with some customers.

Under usual circumstances, Julie recognizes that customers need to feel that her full attention is focused on them: "When I am with a client, no one else is here." Working on a woman's hair and making eye contact through the mirror, she usually appears to be willingly and happily engaged in friendly communication. I ask Julie what she does when she is in a bad mood and does not feel like relating. "I just listen. I let the woman talk. Sometimes [beauticians] may not even hear what the woman says, but we simply repeat, 'Mmm hmm.'" This response is meant to encourage the customer to talk. While it may be perceived as therapeutic, it may also serve to mask Julie's withdrawal from engagement, at times a necessary form of self-protection. Yet I also hear many conversations in which beauticians confide in their clients about what is troubling them. Sometimes the trouble involves conflictual relations with another customer, sometimes family dilemmas. Their emotional expressions are therefore not restricted to "emotional labor." They also represent genuine feeling and a search for the satisfaction of their own needs. A great deal of reciprocity is therefore operative in the relationships with many customers. "It hurts the beautician when a client dies," Julie tells me with a great big sigh after recounting the death of a woman some years back. Her emotional attachment is evident in this expression of loss. Given the unequal set of economic relations between staff and customers that I have discussed, it is all the more remarkable that the staff is engaged as much as it is in the communal ethos of friendship, caring, and support that characterizes the experience of so many customers at Julie's.

Social support has been defined by gerontologists as interpersonal transactions that include affect, aid, and/or affirmation.[41] Affect includes expressions of liking, admiration, respect, or love; aid refers to transactions that provide information and practical assistance; affirmation denotes expressions of agreement or acknowledgment of the appropriateness of some act or statement of another person. Social interactions at Julie's suggest that support in all three forms is offered and received in a routine fashion by shop participants through a number of different mechanisms. These mechanisms variously provide social support and consequently feelings of social connectedness and self-worth to the participants.[42] They do this through a pervasive and ongoing emphasis on relationality between and among Julie's women.

When gerontologists and other social scientists search for sources of support for the elderly, they need to be more imaginative in envisioning alternatives to kin, neighbors, and friends. Like other contemporary people, they and their subjects of study are guided by classical Greek views of friendship. A more expansive view of friendship reveals that care, support, and self-worth for older women are available at Julie's International Salon from their "beauty shop friends." If these can be found in a neighborhood beauty salon, where else might we look? And once we find alternative but unintentional communities for older women, how can we nurture and sustain them?

CHAPTER TWO

The Witch in the Mirror

Feminine Beauty and Its Imperatives

All her life she had been held upright by an invisible fluid, the notice of other people.

—Doris Lessing, *The Summer Before the Dark*

My grandmothers represented two distinct feminine "types" in the years that I was growing up in Chile. Grandma Ella, a Russian-born immigrant, was small and round. She made her own clothing, simple and unglamorous, usually dark in color, as was appropriate for a woman her age. She wore her hair in a short, rather severe cut, combed back and secured on each side of the head by a small, dark comb. She indulged in several feminine conventions, however: Occasionally she dabbed a drop of cologne—a gift from my aunt—behind her ears and on the inside of her wrists; she used red lipstick to liven up her otherwise unmade-up face; and she wore tiny gold earrings.

By contrast, Grandma Ana, an immigrant from Germany, displayed a far more developed vanity in her self-presentation. Her clothes were more fashionable and reflected her superior economic position to Grandma Ella. She also wore fine jewelry, including a large gold ring mounted with rubies that was a favorite of her two granddaughters (my sister, alas, inherited it). I expect that occasionally she had a permanent done on her baby-fine hair. She polished her nails and, graced by beautiful skin, she wore lipstick and no other makeup.

When these women immigrated to the United States in their sixties, their styles changed only marginally. Both grandmothers came to wear more colorful clothing, since, as my family observed after we came to this country, even old ladies need not wear dark colors here.

My mother was thirty-nine at the time of our arrival. She had worn only lipstick in Chile. She had begun to wear eye shadow and mascara the year before, modeling after other women in Buenos Aires, where we lived for some months. It took her some time to adapt to North American styles: Blush, for example, came years later. But very soon after our arrival she began putting her hair in curlers, a practice new to her. It was my responsibility, I still vividly remember, to get up extra early each morning and "do" her hair before she left for work: teasing, combing, and spraying it. Now in her early seventies, she goes to the beauty shop only a few times a year, eschewing the weekly visits of other women of her generation as not being "me."

The foreigner's experience is immensely helpful in exposing the social construction of culture. In a very simple way I can dig into my past and compare my mother's and grandmothers' self-presentations to those of the women at Julie's International Salon; they certainly started out in very different ways. In my mother's case, at least, I directly witnessed her conversion to an American definition of femininity, one similar but not identical to that of second-generation Jewish women. Such transition is discernible in a more dramatic form in the experience of European Jewish immigrant women—Julie's customers' mothers and grandmothers—in the late nineteenth and early twentieth centuries. The shift from Eastern European towns and cities to urban America called for major changes in self-presentation: in hair styling, clothing, shoes, and hats. Many Orthodox Jewish women, for example, were pressured—by their husbands, by their families, and undoubtedly, for some, by their own inner needs—to give up the *sheitel*, or wig, traditionally worn by married women. In order to fit in America, they had to embrace American definitions of feminine appearance, which at that time included long hair swept up on top of the head and the wearing of fashionable hats. As Barbara Schreier puts it, "[T]he immigrants quickly learned that in America decorative hats were more than an accessory; they were an essential component of the feminine toilette." The same was the case regarding bodily shape. "The solid frame of many Eastern European women," writes Schreier, "was too unmanaged for popular taste. . . . [A] woman with full breasts and solid hips appeared large rather than curvaceous, and she could be ridiculed for her 'Jewish figure.'" Many Jewish women hence turned to the use of the corset.[1] In short, for Jewish women of that period the body and its representation revealed success or failure in the process of Americanization.

It would not be an exaggeration to suggest that for many contemporary American women, feminine identity is likewise importantly, perhaps centrally, signaled by the body. Appearance takes on a critical role in the life of the woman, and, before that, the girl child. Consequently the acquisition and maintenance of femininity—female gender identity—requires continuous and unfailing attention to the body as an instrument of self-presentation.[2] The linking of physical appearance with femininity is not a new development. Women's beauty, and their preoccupation with it, has been a recurrent theme in Western thought. Jean-Jacques Rousseau (1712–1778), for example, viewed women and men as essentially different. He argued that the body needs to be cultivated before the soul by both men and women, "but the aim of this cultivation is different. For man this aim is the development of strength; for woman it is the development of attractiveness." Mary Wollstonecraft (1759–1797) took issue with Rousseau's essentialist view of femininity and rejected the notion that concern with appearance is a woman's natural inclination; rather, she argued, it is learned: "Taught from their infancy that beauty is woman's scepter, the mind shapes itself to the body, and, roaming round its gilt cage, only seeks to adorn its prison."[3]

While the imperatives of masculinity call for men's striving toward mastery and competence, femininity demands of heterosexual women that they tend to their bodies in order to attract men.[4] Men's identity is thus culturally nurtured toward self-development; women's identity, in this and other ways, is geared toward pleasing others, and hence to being under their control. Herein lies a fundamental imbalance in the power dynamics between women and men.[5]

The twentieth century represents a change of degree, not of kind, in the connection between beauty and femininity, insofar as commercial interests have frankly exploited this link in the present century.[6] Between the late nineteenth and the early part of the twentieth century, for example, the use of cosmetics in the U. S. moved from "marking the prostitute and the aristocratic lady" to being understood as "respectable and indeed necessary for women's success and fulfillment."[7] Kathy Peiss holds the cosmetics industry responsible for "revising definitions of female beauty into ideals that could only be achieved through cosmetics. . . ." Furthermore, "the cosmetics industry foregrounded the notion that one's 'look' was not only the expression of female identity but its essence as well."[8]

In the United States, widespread concern with beauty fashions—from hair to clothing to cosmetics—came to be popularized with the development of national markets and mass media beginning late in the nineteenth century, coinciding with the rise of consumer culture. As Susie Orbach puts it,

> The advent of the department store, the woman's magazine, the participation in mass culture and . . . the process of assimilation of immigrants from pre-industrial cultures, are factors that have coalesced to create an enormous pressure on women to identify their interests with the clothes and bodies of the mannequins and movie stars. . . . The impact of movies, television and mass culture in general has created a population responsive to imitate and take up the received images of femininity.[9]

Stuart Ewen and Elizabeth Ewen argue that the film industry was especially influential in the development of new images of femininity. Films served as important agents of Americanization for immigrants and their daughters: "Movies were manuals of desire, wishes, and dreams. . . . Out of De Mille's movies came a visual textbook to American culture, a blend of romantic ideology and practical tips for the presentation of self in the new marriage market of urban life."[10] Obviously movies served to establish ideals of beauty for American-born women as well.

Since that time the number of venues for the display of feminine images has increased dramatically, for example, through modeling, advertisements, television, and most recently, music videos. Concomitantly, the so-called beauty industries, capitalizing on women's appearance and the need for its ornamentation and improvement, have become huge financial successes. In the United States today, for example, there is the "33-billion a year diet industry, the $20-billion cosmetic industry, the $300-million cosmetic surgery industry. . . ."[11] Femininity as we know it, then, is not a "natural" endowment of women. Rather, it is a social construction motivated, in good measure, by power relations and financial gain.

As I have suggested in passing, normative feminine looks are not unchanging; in fact, different periods define feminine imperatives differently around such variable categories as ideal weight and height; hair color, length, and styling; cosmetic use—subtle or dramatic—or its absence; fashion styles; the display of glamour and sensuality or their masking. A perusal of fashion magazines, such as *Vogue*, through various decades of the twentieth century would reveal alternative images of ideal feminine beauty. The only constant in this instance would be women's imperative to look attractive for the men of their dreams.

Participants in this study have accommodated especially well to the dominant beauty ideal of the white, middle-class culture of a given time period. Consequently, in this chapter I assume that their experiences speak for many other American women similarly situated. Given the omnipresence of this ideal in popular culture, no woman living in this society can easily escape it. However, alternative experiences and evaluations of the feminine self are reported in communities that present women with other ideals and norms, as, for example, among lesbian groups and in the African American community.[12]

Going to the Beauty Shop

Concern with hair styles—as with fashion in general—was the province of the elite throughout much of Western history . Hair styles were generated in the courts of Europe and then copied by the well-to-do.[13] Women's (as well as men's) styles came and went: hair braided or worn loose; use of hair pieces in elaborate styles or natural hair pulled back from the face into a modest bun at the nape of the neck; wigs or natural hair powdered to look like wigs; hair styled in curls or smoothed down, close to the head; fanciful styles worn high on the head, and austere, severe looks, with the hair concealed under cloth.[14]

The beauty salon is a modern institution. Hairdressing has a long history—it is often mentioned in the literature and portrayed in paintings of many ancient cultures. And while barber shops for men have existed since classical times, there has not been an analogue for women until the nineteenth century.[15] In America, beauty shops—at first called "bazaars"—seem to have grown out of hair importing businesses in the 1870s and 1880s. Lois Banner writes that these shops resembled stores rather than the small establishments we are familiar with today. Sometime before the turn of the century, hairdressing salons were introduced by department store owners by enlarging the "ladies' parlor," which had been used by women to try on dresses and to rest.[16] Neighborhood hair salons arose in American cities in response to the new vogue of short hair for women early in this century. According to Susan Brownmiller, "once a woman was free of the coil at the nape of her neck, it became her urgent mission to seek out new ways to feminize her head."[17]

The beauty salon is one place, among others, that assists women in attending to their appearance: by setting its standards, by maintaining it at an acceptable level, and just as critically, by improving it. In these ways the beauty salon serves as an important tool in the creation and maintenance of femininity.

In the last chapter, we saw that the communal nature of Julie's International Salon serves to provide support of all sorts to the older women who congregate there. Sometimes this support is offered to address needs unmet by women's family members or the society at large, such as the need for attention, companionship, touch, comforting, and visibility. In these ways, people who populate Julie's may be acting in opposition to the practices of the general culture, which by and large erases older women from public view. In this chapter and the next one, we turn to ways in which the beauty salon collaborates with the larger society in imposing and sustaining visions of appropriate femininity. The salon, in this case, does not resist cultural imperatives; rather, it advances them by promoting culturally acceptable features of feminine representation.

During one of my regular visits in the period of participant observation, I spot an impeccably and elegantly dressed woman sitting on a bench, awaiting her turn with Jeannie, her beautician. A retired schoolteacher in her eighties, Merle comes to the beauty shop because "I am following in my mother's footsteps. . . . My mother was always careful that way. My sisters and my aunts looked nice and well-groomed." Consequently, "the beauty shop is part of my life, like going to the grocery store."

Likewise, Shelley, also in her eighties and a regular customer, tells me that she has always come to the beauty shop and that her mother did so in her later life, adding that her mother also had a cleaning lady, even though they did not have a lot of money. So Shelley "kind of expected" to have a cleaning lady and to go to the beauty salon. Reva's mother also went regularly to the beauty salon, and, hence, so does she.

Some women have unmanageable hair and feel the need for professional care. Clara, for example, who dislikes beauty shops because she considers them a waste of time, feels nonetheless that she must go, for if she washed her own very curly hair, "I'd look like an old Shirley Temple." In like manner, Marny has "kinky" hair and as a child had it straightened in beauty shops catering to a black clientele. As she puts it, "My whole life I've been in a beauty shop. I've probably been in eight hundred beauty shops. I've never been without [one]. . . . I stop at nothing for this hair business."

Most women who visit Julie's on a regular basis started patronizing beauty shops only as adults. Frequently this practice began in young adulthood, at the time they were entering the work force. Young women who worked "downtown" in shops and offices may have decided, as did Sadie, that now that she was "making a few bucks," she could afford to get her hair done: "So why shouldn't I have it done? . . . I always wanted to look right." Clara started going to the beauty shop in 1945, now that she had a "maternities" shop and could afford it: "I used to go every week because I felt I had to look well for my customers. There is nothing as bad as a slovenly looking salesperson, be she the owner or not." Harriet, who in her thirties began running a tavern, "didn't have time to monkey around with my hair or anything. So I had it done every week."

Martha, a high achieving professional woman, began getting her hair done as a young woman in order to fit in with her first husband's work cronies: "I really had to look like some of the other women he worked with." Later on, when she herself came to occupy a significant job—one with public visibility—she began her regular association with beauty salons because "I had to look somewhat authoritative." Public exposure also motivated Beth, who began going to the beauty shop in her forties, when she returned to work after raising her four children. An additional impetus devolves from the fact that her husband is a cantor, and hence by extension she is "out in public . . . and so, when you're out, they look at the husband, they look at the wife. To me it's important, and my hair looks nicer. That's why I indulge."

For other women the major motivation behind their visits to the beauty salon has been their husbands. According to Anna, her husband was a very good-looking man, sharper looking than herself, and "I always wanted to look my best with him. . . . I felt I had to look good for him." A different story is told by Sara: "One day Joe [her husband] said to me, 'You know, there's a young fella that eats at the same time I do in the restaurant. He owns a beauty shop just across the street. Why don't you go there?' I said, 'What for, I don't go to beauty shops.' 'Go in there,' he said, 'See if you like it, the way he does your hair. Maybe you'll start going to beauty shops." A more dramatic recollection of how Sara began her routine beauty shop visits emerges in the ensuing dialogue between her and Joe that I witness in their apartment:

Joe: When I worked, I used to come home late in the evening, while Sara was finishing her cleaning, since she watched her 'stories' during the day.

Sara: Well, I worked a couple days a week, so my time was limited to my cleaning days. I used to wash the floor on my knees.

Joe: Hair with the curlers, with the rollers.

Sara: And cold cream on my face. Well, I never knew when he would come home.

Joe   [walking in the house at that time]: And I says, "Oh, my God," I says.

Sara   [recalling his statement]: "Don't ever look like that again!"

Joe: "I don't want to ever come in the door and see you like that. I work with fifteen or twenty pigs, where I work, and they *worked* all day. You get your hair done, and I want you with makeup on, and dressed decently, and I can sit there and look at you." And after, I think, Saturday, she started going to the beauty shop.

We see here that the urge to "look right" or improve one's appearance via beauty salon care was nurtured in these women by a variety of external influences: role modeling by mothers, the expectations of work and public settings, and the husband's desire for his wife to look a certain way. In all likelihood, Joe and Sara's situation reveals the additional influence of upward mobility in shaping the husband's changing expectations of his wife's self-presentation.

Developing a Feminine Image

Self-awareness about feminine looks makes its appearance early in a woman's life. In fact, self-evaluations regarding physical acceptability enter a girl's consciousness in a variety of ways. One of these is undoubtedly conformity to peer group standards and practices. My own daughter was relatively unconcerned with her appearance until she reached the age of ten or so, when she occasionally arrived from school complaining that she was fat, an objective absurdity insofar as she was a thin child. More recently—at thirteen—she mournfully observed that she was too skinny. She has also become concerned with her hair so that today she seldom goes anywhere without hairbrush in hand. Yet she mockingly reports the exaggerated preoccupations of some of her female schoolmates who complain about "bad hair days" and broken nails. Nonetheless, I frequently overhear her conversations about hair and clothing with her own school friends.

During intensive interviews I ask the participants in this study to look at pictures of themselves as young women in order to recollect their youthful self-evaluations. Two patterns emerge in this process of photo-elicitation, patterns typical of how these and many other American women experience femininity. In the first pattern, most women report that they thought of themselves as pretty in their youth, but mainly because others—relatives, boys, and then husbands—provided such evaluations. In the second pattern, competition emerges as a central ingredient in the constitution of a "feminine" self.

Speaking of herself at age twenty, Beatrice declares, "Oh, I was very proud of the way I looked. I had lots of admirers. A lot of them.... I always thought of myself as pretty. Even now. With my husband's help [chuckles].... In a room he'll say, 'You're the cutest, the prettiest. Who has that figure?' He says that to me, all the time." Clara was "a very popular girl" with "a terrific sense of humor." I ask if she thought of herself as pretty or attractive. "Well, you know," she replies, "when you date a lot, and the young men that you go with think that you're pretty, you suddenly become pretty, whether you're pretty or not." Clara directly concedes here that her self-evaluation was shaped by others' perceptions of herself, an astute social psychological observation applicable to other participants as well.

Sylvia, who was born in Europe, declares, "I never was pretty. No. But, what should I say? The boys wanted me, OK?" Furthermore, her grandmother thought she was pretty and would compare her with one of her aunts, whom Sylvia found to be very pretty. Hence her grandmother "was kind of proud of me. My father was proud of me." Lucy did not feel pretty at age twenty "because I was very fat. But I knew I was pretty because everybody told me I was pretty. But *I* didn't tell me I was pretty." Laughing, she adds, "However, I never suffered from an inferiority complex."

Sara did not feel pretty either, but neither did she think she was ugly. She recalls going to see a movie, where her date made her feel uncomfortable because he could not take his eyes off her. He admitted to staring because, as he put it, "I think you're beautiful." She herself had never thought so, and her mother confirmed this suspicion by telling Sara that "I wasn't beautiful, but I was attractive. So I believed her. I thought attractive was even more important than being beautiful." Dori's experience was different, as she thought of herself as pretty. But it is similar in that she immediately qualifies this evaluation by saying, "When I went to [college] I won a beauty contest." The same dynamic obtains for Beth, who thought she was pretty as a young woman because "people told me I was attractive."

In short, we repeatedly see that women's developing sense of their bodily selves is strongly shaped by the way they are perceived by others. As Naomi Wolf sees it, "What little girls learn is not the desire for the other, but the desire to be desired."[18] Consequently, the search for attractiveness encourages a kind of passivity on women's part,[19] in the sense that they aim to become objects of male desire, not subjects themselves. We will see that this tendency is not limited to women's youthful years but continues to affect the time and attention they devote to their physical appearance throughout their lives.

A significant number of women recollect feelings of competition and sometimes of inferiority in comparisons they made between themselves and their peers. In her no-nonsense way, Harriet tells me that she felt "average. I didn't think of myself as a beauty. I felt that there were a whole lot of people better than me, but I felt I was average."

Marny makes a noncommittal and somewhat contradictory statement in her self-evaluation: "I don't think I was pretty, and there were girls that were prettier than me, but I was pretty." Alice also felt ambivalent about her looks. Asked whether she thought of herself as pretty or attractive in her youth, she responds,

> You know, that's a good question because I did and I didn't. Like Jorie [a friend] was tiny, and I wanted to be tiny. . . and I loved the way she dressed, because she was all foo-foo, and I wanted to be all foo-foo, and I couldn't, I was too tall. And so I always thought she was cuter than I, everybody else was cuter than I was. I was not the cute one. Everyone else was. . . . But I loved all the girls. I didn't care because I thought they were darling, too. They couldn't help it if they were darlinger than me.

More painful than her sense of insufficiency vis-à-vis her friends is Alice's memory of her nonsupportive mother: "She went with me to do all the shopping, because she told me I didn't have very good taste. She kind of cut me down, you know. She didn't tell me I was darling or pretty or anything like that."

Edie felt jealous of her beautiful cousin. "I wasn't that bad, it's just that I didn't know what to do with myself." Likewise, Anna thought her sister was cute, but not herself. Reva recalls always feeling too big: "Big, broad. I was a broad, big woman." She felt self-conscious, as there were "cute small girls, and you felt very klutzy." A similar experience of inadequacy is recalled by Shelley: "In high school I was on the plump side, and I had a very dear friend, who is still my dear friend. She gave me a complex: that I was fat. She and I would go to a party together and I'd come home to her house to sleep, and her father would say, 'All the boys wanted Reizel [her friend], didn't they?

They liked her best.' She was an only child of sixteen years, and I realize now that this was terrible for me."

Teri cannot remember how she felt about herself in her youth. She knows she cared about her looks and her clothes, taking after her mother in this regard. When she looks at photographs from her youth and middle age, she does not see an attractive woman there, as I do. In one of these she stands with a good friend. Affirming that she thinks her friend is definitely attractive, she asks me, "Don't you?" "What makes her attractive, but not you in that picture?" I retort. Teri sighs deeply. "She had the prettiest teeth of anybody I ever saw. White, white, white. And I said, 'What do you use on your teeth?' She had the whitest teeth, and when she'd go and put lipstick on, they were just gorgeous. I used to tell her, "You know what? If you weren't such a good friend, I'd hate you [laughing].'"

Comparison and contrast: familiar dynamics for many women in twentieth-century American society, central elements in the construction and maintenance of femininity. These dynamics do not cease in youth. They prevail in women's experience well into old age. As Julie tells me with some frustration, more than one customer needs to be told, during each weekly visit, that she is the prettiest woman in the shop. The picture that emerges is one in which the feminine self is developed through a vigilant and sensitive response to ever-present external assessment: from parents, boyfriends, husbands, friends. The skills needed to create the feminine body are developed both through cooperation and competition with other girls/women: cooperation, insofar as techniques and fashion consciousness are learned from mothers and girlfriends; competition, because the attention women get from all quarters—teachers, family, friends, and men—depends in large measure on how their bodily appearance stacks up in comparison to others: real people, professional models, and media images of femininity.

What we see in incipient form here is the problem of female subjectivity and women's agency, a problem that women encounter in childhood and must confront for the rest of their lives. This problem, to which we will return, raises the question of whether women can truly define who they are and how they present themselves to the world given the expectation that they meet definitions established by others. Another way to put it is to ask whether women can act as moral subjects, truly free and able to make choices about self-representation, in a socio-cultural environment uncongenial to such freedom for the "fair sex."

Appearance and Vanity

While I'm "hanging out" at Julie's, I grab every opportunity I get to ask customers why they go to beauty shops. "To look nice," says Bertha. "To look good," answers Alta. "To look neat," asserts Leah. "To look right," offers

Sadie. Frequently I sense a note of impatience if not incredulity in the respondent's voice, as if these reasons were self-evident, shared by one and all, and hence not worth discussing. I need to probe further, to encourage reflection by suggesting we know so little about women's own experiences and motivations. Customers struggle to move beyond their naturalized conceptions of reality in order to clarify what they mean by "looking nice" or "looking good" or "looking right"—and why this is important to them. I am struck by the general absence of awareness, let alone feminist analysis, of the sexual politics or power dynamics encoded in women's feminine practices.

Some women say they go to beauty shops because their hair is hard to manage, as we saw earlier with Clara and Marny. Others suggest that their beauticians do a better job than they can, or that now they can afford this service. Still others confess they are lazy and would prefer someone else to do the work. The ultimate purpose of the trip to the beauty shop is no different from those who want to "look nice" or "look good." These women are simply providing reasons as to why the hairdresser can best accomplish the goal of enhancing their appearance.

Why, then, is appearance—"looking good"—so important? Here are some typical answers: "For self-esteem." "For my morale. It's a good boost." "It's therapeutic: If my hair looks right, then I feel right." "Maybe we feel we are more attractive." When women expand their responses, their reflections generally fall into two interconnected categories: the first pertains to the significance of appearance insofar as the woman is the object of someone else's gaze; the second reveals the discourse of vanity.

"Why do we find it so important to look a certain way?" I ask Sylvia as we sit at her dining room table eating sandwiches for lunch. "We want to look good," she tells me in her accented English. "We want people to point at you: 'Take a look how nice she look [sic]. Take a look at the beautiful dress. Take a look [at] her figure and everything.' That's life, OK?"

Beth's experience of being noticed encourages her vigilance about her appearance.

> I get compliments. I do. Not that I'm conceited, but someone will say—or say to my husband—"You have a pretty wife." Or people at work: "Oh, you're a pretty lady." You know, it's nice. I don't look in the mirror and say, "I'm pretty," but it's nice to hear. And they notice what I wear at work. They say, "You should be a model." . . . And they notice the cologne I wear. . . . But needless to say, I don't look in the mirror and say, "I'm pretty." But if you get a compliment, it's nice. A woman likes to hear a compliment.

Alice also pays close attention to how she presents herself in public: "I think of people when I get dressed to go out. I want to look nice for them, so they'll have something halfway pleasant . . . something halfway decent . . . to look at, rather than some frump. Well, don't you?"

Speaking of the cinema, Laura Mulvey has called the cinematographic tendency to display women for the gaze and enjoyment of others—particularly men—a woman's "to-be-looked-at-ness."[20] The term may be applied to the status of women in society as well, since in our culture men typically look at women as objects of desire, and not vice-versa. As a result, the "to-be-looked-at-ness" nature of a woman's experience prepares her to be ever at the ready for being observed, looked at, appraised on the basis of her appearance. Women's need to be attractive pertains to their learned need to be found desirable—by their husbands, lovers, or friends. There is a power imbalance implicit in this situation since those who do the looking have the capacity to pass judgment and define the acceptability of the looked-at.

Customers often link their interest in their appearance with the notion of vanity. When I ask Clara why she goes to the beauty shop, she says, "Well, to look as nice as I know how." This is very important, she claims, because "I have a great deal of vanity. I do." A bit later she adds,

> God help the woman who doesn't have vanity in her. Because she's going to look like a frump. . . . I think it's up to every woman to look as good as she knows how. First of all, if she has a husband, why not keep him alert and entertained. To be able to say to you, "Oh, how pretty you look," instead of being accustomed to you with the curlers and the toilet tissue around your head when you go to bed at night. Yech! If I was a man, I wouldn't want to be with anyone who looked like that. Really, really. You know.

Later on, Clara amplifies her thinking by saying that "there are probably very few women who have no vanity, absolutely no vanity at all. And those are the people that really look like frumps. They don't even try, they don't even try to make a personable appearance. And I think you ought to. Why should my daughter be ashamed of the way I look? Why shouldn't she be proud of the way her mother looks?" Clara seems to be suggesting that it is the woman's obligation to meet acceptable standards of appearance—"personable appearance," as she calls it. Failure to do so has several implications.

First, the husband is bound to be disappointed, if not repelled, since he ought to be able to look at a presentable wife. This scenario is reminiscent of Joe's insistence that at all times he wanted to see Sara "decently" dressed, with her hair done and her makeup on so "I can sit there and look at you." Second, a woman's neglect of her appearance will render her a "frump," a term also used by Alice and others, which, according to the *New Shorter Oxford English Dictionary*, means "an old-fashioned dowdily-dressed, ill-tempered woman."

"Dowdy," in turn, suggests "a woman who is shabbily, unfashionably, or unattractively dressed."[21] In short, a woman lacking vanity will not only be unfashionable; she will be decidedly unattractive, a feminine failure. Third, the woman's loved ones—like Clara's daughter or Sara's husband—will feel ashamed in her company. A woman's lack of effort to look "as close to perfect as I can"—as one customer puts it—or to look "her best"—as most women define vanity—shames her and those around her. Her unwillingness to take responsibility for her appearance discredits her, and by extension, dishonors her family. The woman's body comes to reflect her character—a theme we will come back to. She is judged to be either virtuous or morally suspect. Attention paid to one's appearance is thus not simply an aesthetic preference but a moral imperative. Attention to appearance has a substantive content in this context: It does not mean clean clothes and neatly combed hair, as my grandmother displayed. The body must conform to certain specific conventions, which include use of makeup, styled hair, and fashionable clothes. My own Grandma Ella, a good and nurturing soul if there ever was one, would undoubtedly be judged to be a frump by those who have internalized the dominant ideology of femininity. Along with that judgment would come assessments of her very worth. Thus aesthetic judgment comes to be laden with moral meanings at times. It would not be my grandmother's *given* looks that would necessarily come under judgment; rather, her character would be evaluated negatively for her perceived failure to *improve* her body. She would be judged irresponsible in this regard, and hence unvirtuous.

This ethical dimension is readily discernible in the following account. Sara is telling me that she was "never that vain." In contrast, she suggests that "I always wanted to look well." This reminds her of the only fight she had with her older sister, a woman well along in years whose failing health led Sara and her husband to find her an apartment in the same building where they resided.

One day I ran into her, and she looked like she wanted to be put into a coffin. That's how terrible. Not a drop of lipstick, nothing. I was very angry. And I said to her, "When you go out, I want you to put a little makeup." "How can I put makeup? What do I care? Nobody cares." And this and that. So I thought to myself, "I'm never going to be like that." I wouldn't allow myself to be. So when I go outside . . . to the beauty shop on Friday, I dress myself and put makeup on and I want to feel that it's the best I can do. If it's not good enough, that's nobody's fault. But at least I feel secure that I did the best I could for my appearance, for my self-enhancement. My sister taught me a lesson, may she rest in peace. And besides, it's the old adage, "Smile and the world smiles, laugh and the world laughs with you, cry and you cry alone." And I don't want to cry alone.

Sara is deeply aware here of the social implications of conforming to or rebelling against cultural norms, and she self-consciously chooses to conform, as she doesn't want to "cry alone." She recognizes that her sister made a decision to cut herself off from social expectations by her conviction that "nobody cares," a decision that enrages Sara. So she chooses conformity for fear of marginalization, but also because she believes it is her *obligation* to do the best she can for her appearance. Like most women at Julie's—and surely many other American women—Sara has internalized mainstream middle-class definitions of femininity.

The failure to wear makeup, to have one's hair looking neat and "done," or to look "the best one can" is a source of shame here, and elsewhere. It exposes the self as an unimproved, "naked" body. I am reminded of efforts made by feminists in the 1970s—myself among them—to break once and for all with some of the perceived oppressive practices of femininity: using makeup, shaving legs and underarms, styling the hair, wearing hose, dresses, and skirts. For most of us many of these efforts failed in the long run. The display of hairy legs and makeup-less, washed-out eyes felt too exposing of the unadorned body. Such unimproved body parts were experienced as shameful and defective because they failed—by far—to meet extant images and embodiments of femininity constantly entering our consciousness. After all, these images—whether in magazines, posters, television, or film—assume that the female body is incomplete or flawed as is. They continually advocate the need for "makeovers," improvement, enhancement, and correction of body parts. And the images themselves suggest solutions for the fixing of the body insofar as they represent ideals to strive for. In the case of commercial ads, the prescription for correction is, of course, made explicit.

During photo-elicitation, my photographic skills sometimes leave something to be desired, and I retake the photo. I am interested in likeness, not in studio-quality work, but whether I take what I consider to be a very good facsimile or a very poor one, the responses frequently suggest disappointment if not bewilderment. Sadie expresses concerns that form part of a fairly common pattern of response. Looking at the first Polaroid photo, she exclaims, "Oh, God! My head is on the side. That's not a good picture. And I didn't smile or anything. I had my head to the side here." And addressing her image in the photograph, she adds, "Oh, God, you're ugly!," as she breaks into self-mocking laughter. I take three different pictures; she is disappointed with each one in turn. Her perception that her head tilts to a side is especially worrisome to her, as she considers that ugly. She blames herself for this. "That was a bad habit." She maintains that judgment even after I suggest that perhaps she has some arthritis in the neck, a condition for which she received some physical therapy in the recent past. The last Polaroid is judged to be a bit better: "At least my head is a little straighter," but "[it] shouldn't have

turned at all." Apart from her focus on the angle of her head, Sadie's attention is drawn to her hair, which to her looks unacceptably flat in one shot and
overly dark in another; to her facial look in general, which may be explained
by a recent significant loss of weight; to the fact that she did not smile; to her
mouth being open; to her nose looking too long. Her concern about her nose
generates an explanation, so as not to be misunderstood: "I'm vain. But I'm
vain because I want to look nice. It's not that I'm crazy about myself or anything." Lest we think Sadie is exceptional in her vanity, and comical to boot
in her litany of imperfections, let's turn to the experience of other women
examining their contemporary images.

Shelley says of the first picture, "Oh, my mouth is open." I explain that she
had been talking to me when I snapped the shot. "I'm talking. That's no good.
You don't want that." When I take the second shot, she comments, "I like that
one better, even though you can see my hump. . . my dowager hump."

Anna: "My hair looks terrible. It's sticking up and I'm not used to that."
Sara responds by saying, "Oh, oh, no! Horrible. Horrible. Absolutely horrible. First of all, where does all this hair come from. . . . Look at the hair on
the side. . . . Awful. Oh, my God. Look at the size of my nose!"

Harriet: "Look at my mouth, Jesus! . . . I really don't like what I look like
here. I feel I have too many pouches here and I don't do anything about it."

Alice, when showing me a photo taken at age sixty-four, remarks, "Well, I
sure had a pot. Look at that. I did, too. I can remember just getting into the
bathing suit. And if I can be candid, I should have used—worn—a little more
of an uplift. Wouldn't you say?"

Edie, when seeing the first Polaroid, exclaims laughingly, "Oh, my God. My
eyebrows are terrible!" While she likes her hairstyle in the second photo, she
points to her chin in the picture and asks, "Why is it like that? I can't stand it!"

Merle has a similar response. She first acknowledges the likeness of the
photo ("Well, that's me") before adding, "The one thing that looks awful is
the chin. Not the chin, the neck." She is commenting on the loose folds of
skin around her neck.

What all these women have in common is their identification of a body
part as insufficient, inadequate, embarrassing, shameful, or otherwise unacceptable. The recurrent tendency to break their image apart reproduces
advertising's propensity to isolate female bodily parts in order to sell merchandise that will improve or make desirable that part needing servicing:
from clothing to hair products to makeup to body fat or flab. This tendency,
while exploited by contemporary capitalism for the sake of profit-making, is
not new. According to historian of religion Margaret Miles in her book,
Carnal Knowing, representations of women in the Christian West have often
broken their bodies into parts. In a chapter disturbingly entitled "'Carnal
Abominations': The Female Body as Grotesque," she writes, "I will . . . argue

that, because of woman's affiliation with the quintessentially grotesque events of birth, sexual intercourse, and death, from the collective male perspective of the public sphere, the most concentrated sense of the grotesque comes, not from exotic but distant monsters, but from the figure 'female.'"[22]

The association of the female body with the grotesque or with evil, more generally, has an early provenance. The ancient Greeks saw reality in dualistic terms, whereby that which was good was opposed to that which was evil; in like manner, man was seen in opposition to woman, the soul as the opposite of the body, reason as the opposite of the emotions, and so on. The association of men with reason and women with the emotions, assumed in much of Western thought, was already present in ancient Greece.

The wholesale association of women with the body and men with the soul or spirit came into its own with the Christian Church Fathers, who lived in the first six centuries of the common era. These architects of Christianity merged Hellenistic ideas with the ascetic mood of their times. The body and all its inclinations were to be suppressed and controlled in order to serve God, who existed in the realm of the spirit. Women's unique physical experiences—menstruation, pregnancy, birthing, lactation—became identified with their very being. These experiences are all quintessentially bodily matters—absent in the experience of men, who were already seen as normatively human. By contrast, women are Other. In consequence, women's physical nature predisposes them to evil—they turn to the material rather than the spiritual. Such views of the sexes were used to justify male control of women in all facets of life.

Added to these dynamics, and especially condemning of women, were the evolving interpretations of biblical passages in Genesis 2–3. These passages pertain to the creation of man and woman, and most centrally, to the eating of the fruit in disobedience to God, which in Christianity comes to symbolize the Fall. Eve becomes the prototype of all women in this act of sin. In this classic passage, the early Church Father, Tertullian (ca. 160–220 C.E.), addresses Eve as he links all women to her deed:

> *You* are the devil's gateway. *You* are the unsealer of that forbidden tree. *You* are the first deserter of the divine Law. *You* are she who persuaded him whom the Devil was not valiant enough to attack. *You* destroyed so easily God's image in man. On account of *your* desert, that is death, even the Son of God had to die.[23]

Like Eve, all women are seen to be morally weak, incapable of moral responsibility, not to be trusted. Furthermore, Eve's offer of the fruit to Adam is interpreted as a form of seduction. Eve's body, her "carnality," becomes the personification of sexual temptation, the body her principal tool of manipulation. Like Eve, women are corrupting because their bodies are "carnal."

These theological positions might be viewed by some as bizarre but mercifully outdated by now. Miles, writing of former theological preoccupations about woman's nature, suggests that we need to "remind ourselves that it is the figure 'woman,' not the actual women of everyday experience, that was under discussion." "Nevertheless," she continues,

> women in Christian societies were not unaffected by the public representation of "woman" as defective in body and mind. A perennial open question as to whether women were human beings with souls, surfacing repeatedly in learned debate and popular caricature, cannot have failed to generate hostility toward women and, for women themselves, problematic self-images.[24]

So when American Jewish women look at their images and find fault with this or that aspect of their bodies, they may be reflecting a certain degree of personal idiosyncrasy. But they are also revealing a Western, culture-wide phenomenon, namely, a centuries-long association of women's bodies with evil, imperfection, deficiency.[25] This realization is confirmed over and over whenever I discuss this topic with students in various courses. In a recent discussion in my "Women and Religion" course, the continuing impact of traditional negative judgments of women's bodies was again revealed. The class exploded with energy and intensity, with students waiting in line, as it were, to have their say. One attractive young woman shed tears of recognition when I named the difficulty so many American women experience in viewing their bodies as acceptable and good.

The Beauty Salon as a Tool of Improvement

Item: "I'm a beautician, not a magician" whimsically reads a bumper sticker attached to the mirror of Victoria's work station.

Item: A customer enters Julie's International Salon looking subdued. Julie asks her what's wrong. "I'm feeling blue. Everyone does sometimes." She then offers that she's come to the shop in order to feel better, to be "improved."

Item: Beatrice complains that the nape of her neck is burning when neutralizer is applied to her scalp to stop the action of the permanent fluid. Verena comes over to check, declaring that the skin feels cool. Beatrice still complains that it burns. Tongue in cheek, Verena retorts, "What do you want? You have to suffer to be beautiful!"

Beatrice's complaint is confirmed by Julie's own experience. I come into the shop and begin talking to Lucy, who is sitting near Julie's station. Soon Julie joins us; she is wearing a white plastic covering over her hair. She starts working on Lucy. Seemingly in pain, Julie abruptly announces, "I cannot talk." We wonder if it is something in her mouth. She tells us it is pain on her scalp from the permanent Helen has just given her.

Women come to the beauty shop to get their hair done. Many also get manicures. Some get pedicures. In all three instances women are attempting to improve or enhance their appearance, for as we have seen, they are expected to look their best, lest they be judged "frumps." If they endure pain in the process, so be it. That is the cost of looking "beautiful," or short of that, presentable to self and others.

Carmela and Blanche are sitting on the bench behind Julie's station, discussing the economic recession. Blanche says she's seen on TV that people are tightening their belts when it comes to "extras" like beauty shops and laundry cleaners. Carmela insists that the report pertained to "a different class of people [than ourselves]," adding, "I'd rather die than not get my hair done." To this Blanche retorts, "I look at myself in the mirror and I see a witch."

The "natural" woman as witch is not an image uniquely Blanche's; others use it as well. Parallel images are culturally available that identify the woman who does not invest in her appearance, who fails to "put on a face." She rebels against feminine practices, standing outside social boundaries—as did Sara's sister. Consequently she is frequently viewed as a misfit: a "frump," a "dog," a "bag lady." She might be seen, as one customer suggests, as having given up: She "might as well die right there and then."

These images and their labels communicate in no uncertain terms the revulsion inspired by the unimproved female body. They reinforce the cultural requirement that the feminine woman must be in disguise, insofar as the skin must not be "natural" skin, but skin moistened by cream, coated with foundation, colored by blush, brushed by powder. Her lips should sport lipstick, and perhaps gloss as well. Her eyelashes are to be curled and darkened, her eyelids colored with shadow, her eyebrows plucked, defined, and shaded. Her nails should be polished, her hair coifed. Her body ought to be draped in appealing fashions. The feminine woman is on display: Her efforts are intended, not only for her own gratification, but to be noticed, to be complimented, to give other people "something halfway pleasant to look at, rather than some frump."

In a study of the explosive appeal of cosmetic surgery in the United States today, the philosopher Kathryn Pauly Morgan writes, "What I see as particularly alarming in this project is that what comes to have primary significance is not the real given existing woman but her body viewed as a 'primitive entity' that is seen only as potential, as a kind of raw material . . ."[26] There is a difference between cosmetic surgery and the feminine practices I have been describing, of course, but I believe this is a difference of degree, not of kind. The same presupposition obtains: A woman's value in contemporary American culture is all too often associated principally with her bodily appearance, measured against idealized standards, and not with "the real given existing woman." This type of objectification diminishes women's personhood by devaluing other aspects of their being: It discourages appreciation—their own and others'—of women's inner lives and accomplishments by its pointed attention to physical looks, pressing many women to spend inordinate amounts of time, money, and energy in the elusive pursuit of public acceptability. In these ways the dominant beauty ideal harms women.

In this context I find especially apt the subtitle a student gave to her paper on the cosmetic industry: "The Externalization of Women's Identity."[27] The subtitle recognizes that under cultural constraints, women's sense of identity moves from internal, self-directed considerations to external, other-directed preoccupations with self-presentation. Sandra Lee Bartky identifies the principal source of these cultural constraints as the "fashion-beauty complex"— a system of corporations which set up norms for acceptable femininity through products, services, information, images, and ideologies. In doing so, this fashion-beauty complex leads to women's alienation from their bodies. As she puts it, it "produces in woman an estrangement from her bodily being. On the one hand, I *am* it and am scarcely allowed to be anything else; on the other hand, I must exist perpetually at a distance from my physical self, fixed at this distance in a permanent posture of disapproval."[28]

We are speaking about vanity, and Marny struggles to make sense of her experience:

I like to feel that I look good for myself. I spent a lot of time when I was younger looking in the mirror. . . . If I'm going somewhere, for reassurance let's check the mirror. . . . It's just to make sure my hair looks OK and I have a drop of lipstick on, and I'll notice, not that I look tired or old or young, but am I presentable? . . . It's gotten better. But at parties I'll get up and look in the mirror, but I don't know what I expected to see, but that I wanted to know if I looked OK. A lot of mirror business. . . . A lot of mirroring. Sometimes we'll be at a wedding or dinner party, and it's taking a long time, and it was so important that I was taking a look. Have you ever heard of such a thing, having to check yourself in the mirror? In the restaurant, out with the mirror, putting on a little lipstick. During a party, let's make sure that everything is looking OK. I don't know what I expected to see.

While Marny begins by suggesting that vanity entails looking good *for her-self*, she puzzles about her preoccupation with checking herself on the mirror, which belies an urgency to view herself as others see her. Here we find the feminine woman as the woman on display. As John Berger sees it, "from earliest childhood she has been taught and persuaded to survey herself continually." Arguing that a woman sees herself as men see her, Berger continues:

> She has to survey everything she is and everything she does because how she appears to others, and ultimately how she appears to men, is of crucial importance to what is normally thought of as the success of her life. Her own sense of being in herself is supplanted by a sense of being appreciated as herself by another. . . .
>
> Men look at women. Women watch themselves being looked at. This determines not only most relations between men and women but also the relation of women to themselves. The surveyor of woman in herself is male: the surveyed female. Thus she turns herself into an object—and most particularly an object of vision: a sight. . . .
>
> This unequal relationship is so deeply embedded in our culture that it still structures the consciousness of many women. They do to themselves what men do to them. They survey, like men, their own femininity.[29]

If women must conform to external standards of appearance in order to meet cultural expectations, to what extent are they the agents of their own decisions? The question is complicated, of course, by women's tendency to survey themselves as men do. How free, then, are they to make personal choices about their self-presentation? Susie Orbach provides us with a way of thinking about this that recognizes the way that the status of women as objects and their status as subjects are inexorably interconnected:

> Each woman has to find a way of being with and in her body that expresses both her oneness with the culture and her individuality. But this imperative itself is problematic, as women are encouraged to see their bodies from the outside, as if they were commodities. Feminine perception is informed by a devastatingly fierce, visual acuity turned on itself. It operates as a third eye. . . . The receptivity that women show (across class, ethnicity and through the generations) to the idea that their bodies are like gardens—arenas for constant improvement and resculpting—is rooted in a recognition of their bodies as commodities.[30]

The question of choice is critical here. To be sure, women are not simply "cultural dopes" who blindly follow cultural expectations and unthinkingly submit to the "oppressive regimes of beauty." Rather, women know "the routes to success in this culture—they are advertised widely enough—and they are not 'dopes' to pursue them."[31] If anything, they are astute for doing so, for the alternative is to surrender aspirations of marriage, successful employment, and other forms of social prestige. In other words, the pursuit of beauty and body improvement is a vehicle to women's power, and many engage in these practices with full self-consciousness. On the other hand, expression of choice, of individuality takes place within a rather narrow field of possibilities. So while there may be choice, say, between wearing blue or green or brown eye shadow, there is conformity about wearing shadow altogether. One wonders at the degree of coercion that is present in the decision to conform to this and other feminine practices. That women may have internalized this coercion does not negate its existence. It may simply support Michel Foucault's contention that power in modern societies does not only flow from top-to-bottom in hierarchies of control but is to be found in more diffused ways everywhere and nowhere, as it were.[32]

All that being said, however, we should not lose sight of the fact that women themselves frequently reap pleasure and joy from the processes of beautification. Herein lies one of the many contradictions in this area. When Beth tells me that "earrings are my hobby," for example, she is articulating a joyful playfulness in using her body for ornamental display. In like manner, Teri fondly remembers those youthful days when she would spend her lunch time hour trying on hats with a friend, just for the fun of it. At Julie's many women have thought about their motivations in grooming and hair care. More than a few conclude that at this stage of their lives, they engage in these activities, not just for the sake of external admiration, but "for myself," that is, for the pleasure they experience in the outcomes of these feminine practices. There may also be something to be said about the aesthetic concern for one's appearance being a form of caring for the body, much as good nutrition is an expression of responsibility toward physical health. In this regard women's attending to their looks takes on a positive moral dimension. Pride in one's appearance, earned by time and attention devoted to it, is a way of positively identifying the self with one's body; it may well serve as an antidote to the historical traditions and contemporary tendencies that alienate women from their bodies.

The process of bodily improvement at the beauty shop generally begins with a hair wash, lovingly and efficiently accomplished by Helen. In fact, she is a jack-of-all-trades who also sometimes sets women's hair, applies permanent and coloring fluid, removes curlers, periodically sweeps the floor, and occasionally brings coffee to customers. Quiet and self-effacing, Helen is nonetheless an important part of the beauty shop team. Many report that her hair washing is a delight they look forward to. This is an instance in which women who typically nurture others in their lives become the recipients of touch and nurturance themselves.

The customer then waits her turn with her beautician, who may cut, set into rollers and comb, set and perm, set and color, or blow dry the hair. Cost and time spent at the shop depend on the combination of these services and others, such as nail care, a customer gets during a visit. Most women routinely get a "wash and set," although some get their hair blow-dried instead, which takes a shorter time to do but generally does not remain in place as long. Permanents and coloring require the use of smelly unguents and fluids, periods of waiting for the permanent or color to set, and more washing to remove these special agents. Setting solution is applied after the hair is put in curlers; the customer then sits under a hair drier for a period of time—half an hour to an hour, depending on the amount and thickness of the hair. Often customers get their manicures or pedicures while sitting under the drier. The last stage involves getting the hair combed. This procedure necessitates the use of foams or gels, moisturizing agents in the case of permed hair, and lots of hair spray to keep the hair in place.

"I spend a lot of money there," says Martha when we discuss expenses incurred at Julie's. At the time, a wash and set cost $11, blow-drying $14, a hair-cut $10. Coloring—otherwise referred to as a "touch-up" and required every four weeks—ran $12, a manicure $8. Permanents, which generally are needed every three months, were about $40; pedicures, needed every six weeks, ran $20. Not all women use all these services. Most consider these prices to be quite reasonable, certainly competitive, and worth the investment. Shelley tells me that taking everything into account, "I would say my beauty parlor bill a month adds up to about $100." Recognizing the high price tag, she adds, "I'm earning money, and I can have my hair done. I suppose I could do it if I wasn't earning money. Thank God." Leah figures she spends between $80 and $100 per month. I ask, "Do you feel that you deserve it?" "Yes, I do," she replies. "I don't play cards. I don't drink. I don't go out and shop till I drop—I buy what I need, you know." The investment is worthwhile because "I know that I'm going to look better coming out of the shop than I looked going in."

Not surprisingly, women's differing financial status emerges in this discussion. Julie believes that in some cases the choice of getting a wash-and-set over a blow-dry is dictated by finances, as the former is less expensive and the hairdo lasts longer. Beatrice tells me that Verena would like her to have a permanent more frequently, but two or three times a year is all she can afford. While she finds the charge for a wash and set is "not so bad," she claims that for a permanent "they are very high. And it only takes fifteen minutes. Of course, it takes her time to put in these little rollers. But they're quite expensive." By contrast, Clara, who feels she is very well off monetarily, believes that "they're a little more reasonable than the average shop." She then says with some indignation, "My daughter [once went] to a place that charges a hundred dollars for a cut." "You're kidding!" I exclaim in shock, revealing my own socio-economic level. She replies,

> I am not kidding. . . . It's ridiculous. I would never do that—ever, ever, ever, ever, ever. Neither [my daughter] nor I. No. And the funny thing is both of us could do it [routinely] if we wanted to, financially. But for me it's stupid to throw money away like that. It came too hard. It came too hard. I worked too hard for it. I have great respect for money. And to just deliberately throw it away. What could she do for a hundred dollars? Really. Big deal. I don't know.

The women who patronize a beauty shop like Julie's must have the financial wherewithal to pay for the services they receive—hence in a sense they constitute a self-selected sample—those who can afford it among all those who would want to, but can't. When compared to other beauty salons, Julie's is on the lower end of the price range, reflecting a clientele who, though mostly on fixed incomes due to their own or their husbands' retirement, or their status as widows, relies on a combination of prudent spending and income-bearing investments. As the saying goes, "It costs to be beautiful." What are the costs, I wonder, to women who cannot afford to receive professional services once they enter old age?

The woman comes to Julie's in order to enhance her appearance. The very procedures designed to accomplish that goal, however, ironically strip her gradually of her public persona. On a Friday morning, early in my study of the salon, I observe Shelley virtually disappear behind layers of veils. First a dark plastic sheet covers her whole body—now dressed in a salon gown—including her arms. Then a white plastic bag is placed over her hair, which has become gooey and wet with coloring solution. She sits in a chair while the solution does its work, appearing to strangers as an anonymous, virtually unrecognizable being, stripped of all cues to her customary self-presentation. Such loss of public persona is no impediment to other customers, however, who at various degrees of visual anonymity themselves have no trouble singling out their friends for an amiable chat.

The beautician serves as the woman's consultant—a kind of beauty priestess, if you will—in all these procedures. The customer often asks her beautician whether she needs a cut, a perm, or a touch-up. The beautician also advises the customer regarding what hair color she's been using and may suggest a change. Most women accept the advice of the hairdresser but may give her small suggestions or reminders as to how she likes a particular strand of hair combed or cut. Some customers enter into routine conflictual encounters with their beauticians, often regarding hair color.

Such is the case with one woman, who in front of Julie tells me, "I need to take a Valium each time I get my hair colored." Later, in private, I ask her what is so stressful. She offers that "the only time we fight is when I get color" because it does not come out the same each time. Sometimes Julie has to do it all over again. Julie speaks to me about this situation at another time. Clearly she shares the woman's experience of conflict between them, but her interpretation is rather different. It pertains to Julie's perception of the customer as a demanding and sometimes unreasonable person.

Verena and a customer confess that they frequently fight. "What about?" I ask. "About hair, what else?" responds Verena. "She likes it one way, I another." The customer adds, "I fight with her. I love her. It's like with one's kids. We love each other but we fight." A bit later, referring to Verena, this woman joshingly declares, "She's my mother." The use of such familial language insinuates the intimacy of their relationship, even when fraught with tension.

As for manicures and pedicures, Svetlana is in charge of these feminine disciplines. An authoritative, no-nonsense, middle-aged woman from the former Soviet Union, she impresses me again and again by the mantle of competence and self-assuredness she wears at all times. Whether she speaks of nail color, the care of arthritic feet, or leg massage, you *know* Svetlana knows what she's talking about. She is serious indeed about her work. Assuring me that she never forgets her customers' nail color, she adds, "I might forget a name and a face, but I always remember the nails."

Not all customers get their fingernails polished at Julie's on a weekly basis. Some routinely do their own, others may occasionally get them done for special occasions, while a couple have given up this practice altogether. Many women respond that "grooming" is the reason they polish their nails. I ask Alice why she gets her nails done. "They're so dry," she responds. "And they're lined. And they're ugly. They're strong, but they're ugly." Evelyn also believes her nails look ugly without polish, especially now that her fingers "are all wrinkled and crooked." Edie feels her nails look nice when they're polished. "Without it, to me I look like a slob." Dori gets her nails done because she can't do them herself—she's been a paraplegic with limited use of her hands since her thirties—and "it's part of being beautiful."

Anna and Shelley elaborate on these perspectives. Anna's initial motivation is to protect her nails, since without the polish they break or chip quite easily. But she also likes the look of the polished nails, for they make her hands look neat, giving them a "finished" look. "I don't feel that I have pretty hands," she explains. "I don't want to be embarrassed about my hands. . . . Nobody has ever seen me without polish. . . Hands and feet are not the prettiest part of a person's body and I feel that [the nails] should be covered." For Anna the unpolished hand is a potential source of shame, as it is also for Alice, Evelyn, and Edie. Polish improves on the ordinary nature of the nails and hands, allowing the individual to feel clean and attractive. As with hair fashion, the use of nail varnish is a historically conditioned development, and very recent, at that. According to Fenja Gunn, painted fingernails originated in Paris society and among the French elite who vacationed in the Riviera resorts. "It came to notice of the general public when film stars began to adopt the fashion."[33]

I tell Shelley that she has pretty nails. "I'm vain about my hands," she responds. And that is the reason she offers for getting her nails polished. "I like the way my hands look. . . . I've always had nice hands. For a woman my age, now, you know, they aren't too wrinkled. Not too veiny. And I'm vain about my toes. . . . I don't have bunions, and I don't have corns, and I have nice skin." As she compares herself with other women her age, Shelley feels gratified that her hands and feet look better than the norm. Polishing her nails adds to her sense of satisfaction because her natural endowments are thereby enhanced and worthy of the admiration of others.

A smaller percentage of customers get pedicures at Julie's every few weeks. Some women feel they don't need this kind of service, as they are still agile and are able to trim their toenails themselves. Others visit a podiatrist on a regular basis. Some customers choose to use Svetlana's services. She tells me that in Russia there are no podiatrists; it is people like herself who are trained to take care of feet, in a medical as well as a cosmetic sense.

Some customers readily acknowledge that pedicures are an indulgence they truly enjoy. As one woman puts it, part of the reason for getting a pedicure is to "relax, to treat oneself." Apart from nail care, Svetlana diagnoses certain foot-care problems, takes out calluses, and massages feet and legs. Other women insist that pedicures are not for vanity's sake but, as Reva suggests, "strictly for comfort. When you're this old you're not as agile. You can't pick up your toes." This situation motivated Teri to get a pedicure. In addition, she reports with a twinkle in her eye, her nails were in terrible shape, "some looking like they'd been bitten." Teri sounds offended as she recollects a remark another customer evidently made while Teri was getting a pedicure: "Getting pampered, huh?" "It's not pampering, it's a necessity!" she responded adamantly, stinging from the perceived inaccuracy of the comment.

There is a tension expressed here between necessity and indulgence that goes beyond the case in point. Some women view their concern with their appearance in terms of grooming alone. They interpret their weekly visits to the beauty salon as a commitment to hygiene and a desire to look "neat." Teri's heated claim that a pedicure is a necessity reveals such a view. On the other hand, other women experience beauty salon practices as moments of intrinsic pleasure and as forms of desired improvements, forms of elaboration or decoration of their bodies, going beyond what they themselves are able to do. Undoubtedly, for many women these motivations are mixed: They want to be well groomed and *also* to enjoy the process and the outcome of the practices of femininity offered regularly at Julie's International Salon.

For some, like for Teri, the tension is not easily resolved. Her defensiveness regarding her motivation for a pedicure suggests guilt. This response is rather usual for women, as Rosalind Coward notes: "There's another emotion which comes with pleasure, like a faithful dog that won't be shaken off. Guilt. Women know all about guilt—it's our specialty. Pleasure generates guilt, and that's bad enough. But even worse is the guilt that is generated when other people discuss our pleasures critically—guilt if we enjoy cooking, guilt if we like clothes, guilt if we go on a diet."[34] I might add: guilt if we get pampered, guilt if we are the recipients of care. What might be the meaning for a woman like Teri of getting some touch, comfort, and pleasure along with the functional business of getting her toenails cut?

Weighty Matters[35]

The preoccupation with weight, and being overweight, is ubiquitous today among women living in the United States.[36] Being overweight represents the clearest failure in the maintenance of an ideal femininity, that is, of a femininity defined by the dominant culture. I still remember a surprising and humiliating episode that brought this point home to me a few months following my immigration to this country. I was just fourteen, had started high school, and was making a successful entry into school life. I am standing with some friends, hanging out somewhere on campus, when out of nowhere my friend Janice's finger is pushing against my stomach, firmly pressing into my flesh. Not a word is spoken, but the message is crystal-clear: "You want to fit in here? Pull in your stomach. It is unseemly to display your gut." I had yet to learn at that time that teen as well as women's magazines devote considerable attention in every issue to features on dieting and weight control: "how to lose weight, or how to stabilize at a lower weight, how to manage food temptations, how to avoid eating 'bad' foods."[37] I am a quick study, however: I have been concerned about fleshy matters ever since.

At Julie's I am an evident feminine success, judging by the number of times customers applaud my slenderness—with a mixture of admiration and envy. Pam is my most avid fan. "How do you stay so thin?" is her frequent question, more rhetorical than not, I find out, when I offer an explanation that does not satisfy; it includes metabolism, genes, and some luck. I also add that I have a bit of excess stomach at present. She laughs at this confession on my part as she tells Svetlana, "She's so flat!" Another time, speaking to no one in particular as I stand around, she declares, "Not an ounce of fat!"

On another occasion I am getting acquainted with Alice, who is under the hair drier. Reva yells at her from across the room, referring to me, "Don't you hate her? Look how thin she is!" Alice retorts, "Yeah, I hate her. But she's also adorable!" This exchange takes me back to my childhood in Chile, where Grandma Ella is always telling me to eat more. Years later, in the United States, when I'm an adult and she an old woman, she is still pushing food at me, claiming I am too skinny (I am not). I do not resent it. I recognize that half a lifetime of deprivation and an alternate cultural standard that values a rounder figure have shaped in her a very different view of what is acceptable and desirable in feminine beauty.

We have seen that Julie's customers are often dissatisfied with, sometimes highly critical of, their physical appearance. Nowhere is this more the case than around the issue of weight, which is a popular topic of discussion. The most frequent comments women make during photo-elicitation concern their weight, most often the judgment that they look fat, less so that they look just right.

Beth has a generally positive body image. As we look at a contemporary photograph, she remarks, "I felt I looked nice," adding, "I didn't have the double chin, and the extra rolls all over, so I felt good, and I thought it was a good picture." Put on a diet by her physician due to a medical problem, Beth lost twenty-five pounds in the past year. Claiming she felt fine about her figure before then, she nonetheless says, "I didn't feel I was fat until I looked at my pictures," where she would note she was developing a little double chin and looked a bit heavier. Delighted about her weight loss and the fact that she can wear smaller sizes in clothing, she also adds, "And thank God, I lost my double chin."

Leah is a large woman who in her youth tried weight reduction pills, which made her very sick. She decided she would simply watch what she ate. Acknowledging that she was a size sixteen, she assures me that "I was always satisfied with the way I looked. As long as I was neat and clean and my hair was combed . . . and I had a nice dress on." She is now showing me pictures of her wedding to her second husband. She has told me of her long and unfulfilling first marriage, and the joy and happiness of her second. But looking at the photograph, what she sees first is weight: "I look so fat there," explaining that she was thinner but gained twenty pounds after she quit smoking. This bothers her "because I put the weight on."

Even for women who are self-accepting of their bodily shape and size, the feminine ideal of slenderness is never absent and often merely beneath the surface. As we have just seen, Beth felt fine about her figure, but now that she is thinner she feels much better. Leah claims that her large size is acceptable, only to feel disappointed in herself for having gained weight.

Sara is a slim woman who tells me that "weight I didn't have to lose." But she assures me that her figure was shaped by many years of exercise: "I didn't really lose weight, but I lost measurements, and that was important." Likewise, Beatrice, a petite woman, tells me, "I never got fat. And I never will." "Was it important to you—to look slim?" I ask. "It was very important to me, yes. Very important. I said to myself, 'I'm short, and the only thing I can control [is my weight].' That's what I said. I even say it now, while eating a candy bar, you know. And I'm going to do that, to the best of my ability."

The theme of self-control as the answer to the problem of unwanted weight is ubiquitous in these discourses. Reva has been a large person all her life. She recalls the pain of being called fat as a youth, "especially if there are some nice boys and you're *this* tall and they're *this* short"; she uses her hands to show the differential heights. Self-conscious later on about her large size, she tells me, "Naturally I joined Weight Watchers and took off a lot of weight." Today she is careful about what she eats: "If there is something I can't control, I won't have it in the house."

If size is to be controlled, the way to do it is two-fold: through food and through exercise. Failure to reach one's goals is an ever-present experience for most women. Marny thinks longingly of her figure fifteen years ago, when she embarked on a rigorous exercise program and "got fit. Not so much thin but solid and trim." "Staying trim can be done," she adds later, "if you dedicate yourself to it and have the discipline. With my business and everything else, I can talk about it and I can complain, but I'm not going to do it. I do the exercycle and that's just weekends, and that's as much as I do. I'm too lazy [to go to the gym]." In Marny's case her failure is identified with her lack of will: She is "too lazy."

Most women believe that their lack of self-control regarding food is the culprit, however. Blanche asks Svetlana if she has lost some weight. "No," the manicurist responds, "I think I look like a pig. I've been eating a lot this week." Shaina's doctor has told her she must "leave the table." She says she loves to eat and doesn't know if she can do it. Some weeks later I ask, "Did you lose weight?" She replies in the negative, adding that the outfit she's wearing is good for concealing fat. Anna claims she goes "up and down like a yo-yo" when it comes to weight, an expression other women offer as well. "I was never a thin person," she tells me. "Now I'm fat and I'm having a terrible time with it because I'm not a big eater. I have a very bad metabolism. I have a thyroid problem." A bit later she adds, "If I don't diet, I can't lose [weight]."

Here Anna provides a contradictory explanation for being overweight. On the one hand, she believes there are legitimate physiological explanations to account for it. On the other, however, she concludes that dieting is the way to deal with her extra weight. Since she is evidently not losing weight at present, she is to be held responsible: She has failed to diet—or to diet well enough. Otherwise put, there has been a failure in self-restraint: She has not adequately restricted or denied her hunger. These conclusions emerge as central tenets of femininity as I explore other women's bodily self-perceptions.[38] Most women, I discover, find themselves wanting. Their bodies are inadequate, and by extension, *they* are inadequate, for they fail to be thin enough.

Evelyn shows me a photograph taken when she was in her early fifties. Her first remark is, "See how fat I was, my stomach's sticking out." Alice shows me a recent picture. Her first comment, referring to other photos I have already seen, is "At least I'm thinner than the other two." "Is weight something that bothers you?" I ask. "Yes. It bothers me a lot. . . . I've been this weight for quite some time. And I would like to be a little thinner." Like other women I have known, Alice disliked the weight she gained during pregnancy: "Not that I was ashamed of it, but I figured the smaller I am, the less I show, the better I feel. I didn't want to be huge, with a big stomach in front of me."

I wonder if women's preoccupation with weight tells us something, not only about changing cultural aesthetics and expectations about the look of the female body, but also about the appropriate use of space culturally assigned to women. Women move in space in ways that are different from—far more constrained than—men.[39] They also sit and stand in ways that make the figure look smaller in space, in contrast to men, who are expansive in how they position their arms and legs. Women's bodies seemingly need to take less room, and this might be explained, as Brownmiller argues, by "a feminine esthetic that usually denies solidity by rearranging, accentuating or drastically reducing some portion of the female anatomy or some natural expression of flesh."[40]

I'm exploring with Shelley her feelings about her body. "I have always felt I'm fat, even though people tell me I'm not now. You know, I've always felt that I'd be happier if I was ten pounds less." She concedes that there is not much she can do about this, as she eats little and her metabolism is very slow. Her current figure, she explains, is a consequence of the changes to her body in her late forties and early fifties. "You will find that a lot of women put on weight. I weighed more then than I ever weighed in my life. . . . You spread. Your figure changes. Sometimes your weight doesn't change but your figure does." In this instance, this woman concludes that she can't help her current figure. While her incapacity to do something about it may diminish her guilt about her weight, her self-esteem suffers nonetheless.

I have taken a Polaroid photo of Sylvia. "I never was fat like that," she comments. "You think you're fat there," I say, mirroring her feelings. "Yeah, sure I am, I am fat." At another point she complains that she is "too small to be fat," wishing that she could be skinny, instead. Sylvia's sense of self is profoundly wounded by her inability to meet normative standards of body size.

Martha perceptively addresses this issue head-on. I am speaking with her as we sit at her dining room table. She believes that advertising is setting the standards of what is considered to be attractive, and thin seems to be the "in" thing. Which is really abnormal. Most people are a variety of different weights and built differently. Some are big-boned, and some are small, and so on. But if you can't fit into that size four or six or even two . . . But those are the standards we seem to have now. But they're artificial. Nobody really *looks* that way.

Martha identifies here cultural representations—media images—that homogenize women's real differences. In real life people's body shape and weight differ, but these images—almost exclusively provided by very thin, young, white models—erase such differences in idealized beauty. They encourage ordinary women to continually measure and judge themselves against them.[41] The consequence is that women like Anna, Sylvia, Shelley, and countless others fail the test and find themselves wanting.

A dramatic case in point is provided by Marny, a woman who confesses to feeling "shame and disgust" about her bodily shape and weight. In this account she takes turns implicitly comparing and contrasting herself, first, with women who stand outside cultural standards of acceptability, and second, with those who meet those standards perfectly. In both instances the intensity of her response reveals the deep significance that issues pertaining to weight carry for Marny's own self-understanding:

> When I was in [name of town], there were a couple of women who were obese, and I was appalled, and I wonder if this will mean anything to your research. I really was like, 'Oh my God! How could they let themselves get that way?' And they were youngish. They were well under fifty, and I thought, 'Are they that unhappy and insecure that they could let this happen?' It was nauseating. It is ridiculous to look like this.
>
> And I do remember the first time I was in Paris, I wanted to slap every French woman I saw on the street. They were all perfect. . . . They were all little and trim and perfect. No one had an ounce. . . . I said, 'What is this?' I was so mad, everywhere you turned around, they looked like you [Frida], and some of them were smaller. Trim, perfect, and all around and downtown. And there were tons of people, and I didn't see any fat people. I was very mad! [laughs]. So . . . it's always in the back of my mind. What are you going to do?

In the first instance Marny feels revulsion toward women who, in her view, allowed themselves to get fat. This represents a failure of will, a lack of essential restraint, the opposite of what women in this society are compelled to do. In short, these women are obese because they indulge in eating, thereby failing to curtail their appetite. These are not acceptable choices for women in this society. We are much more tolerant of men reveling in eating. But a gluttonous woman is perceived as disgusting. Women are culturally defined as those who should prepare and serve food to their men and their children, not those who should enjoy it. For the moral imperative calls for women's self-abnegation in this area.[42] Fat women may thus represent those who choose to transgress cultural norms, who act as free agents, who risk marginalization for the sake of their own agency. To find them repulsive reveals a profound embrace of socio-cultural expectations and hence contributes to the work of stigmatization.

In the second instance Marny feels resentment toward the French women because they are thin. She surmises that these women have greater discipline and will power, and, therefore, more character than herself. Like other moderns, Marny supposes she can discern character based on people's physical appearance.[43] As the obese women are seen as morally bankrupt, so the French women are perceived as virtuous, for presumably they have achieved their thinness through the faithful and hard work required by the ethic of self-restraint. Needless to say, I am suggesting that Marny's views represent widely held assumptions in the American dominant culture.

Two study participants represent real exceptions as far as their willingness to break with cultural weight expectations is concerned. Carmela enters the shop with a package of mandelbrot in hand. She places it on Julie's counter and proceeds to sit next to me on one of the "shampooing" chairs. She tells me of a recent visit to the doctor, who has told her to lose some weight since her cholesterol is high, as is her blood pressure. Her weakness is that she likes to eat "certain no-no's," like hot dogs. Turning toward me, she asks, "Do you know what would happen if I lose weight?" I venture, "Will you look drawn?" She responds that at her age her skin is not very bad. I suspect she is fishing for a compliment, for in fact she has lovely skin. Her skin looks this way, she explains, because of the layer of fat underneath. Lose that fat and you get a face-full of wrinkles, and *that* she is not ready to do. She concludes with a maxim to the effect that it is better to be happy and live a shorter life than live longer and feel awful. For the sake of a pretty, younger-looking face and the enjoyment of food, Carmela disregards the cultural imperative—and in her case the medical advice, as well—that she must be thinner.

Teri speaks frankly about the "fat gut" that she now has and concedes that she's never been on a diet, though now "I say I'm on a diet. You know, I try to eat less. I go along for two days and I'm real good, and then I fall by the wayside." Her physician has instructed her to lose weight, advice she does not take overly seriously because "I love food! Any kind. My husband used to say, 'Nobody would know what nationality you are by the food you eat.' Because I love all kinds." Later on she comments on her stomach. "I wish I didn't have it." Laughing, she adds,

But it looks like I'm not doing too much to get rid of it. . . . I think if I had lived differently I wouldn't have it, although I got the same shape as my mother. . . . She had a stomach as long as I can remember. And we used to make her laugh, and when she'd laugh, her stomach would [jiggle]. And you have no idea how many times I talk to her. I say, "Mom, take a look! [laughs]." History repeats itself!

Teri's deep well of self-acceptance—an attitude she has had her whole life— allows her to escape the cultural message that women must put controls on their consumption of food. She eats what she likes and as much as she likes. She is able, as well, to ignore the avalanche of visual images that daily engage other women in continual comparisons, self-devaluation, and ongoing efforts to repair and shape up their flawed and sometimes flabby physiques.

Weight consciousness has not always been at the center of American women's preoccupations. Concerns about slenderness entered popular culture only in the twentieth century,[44] along with other images of contemporary femininity. As the century has progressed, increasingly thinner bodies have become the norm for women. In the 1930s, for example, the smallest size typically stocked in women's dresses was a twelve or fourteen; by the 1950s, a fourteen or sixteen was generally the largest size available.[45] A generation ago, the average fashion model weighed approximately 8 percent less than the average woman. Today that figure is 23 percent less. In a recent study of body image, 75 percent of women aged eighteen to thirty-five believed they were fat, when actually only 25 percent were moderately overweight. At the same time, 45 percent of *underweight* women thought they were too fat.[46] The explosive rise of eating disorders—anorexia nervosa and bulimia— among women in recent years unmasks cultural pressures placed on *all* women: to restrict and deny hunger; to continually exercise self-control; and above all, to be slender.[47]

It is not only women who have been influenced by the media and mass culture. Society as a whole has been influenced, insofar as women's status, prestige, and finally, acceptability depend on the degree to which they conform to culturally imposed images and expectations. For, as Joanne Finkelstein, among other commentators, argues,

The body, like other consumer objects which represent prestige and status, has been transformed into a sign, a material commodity. . . .

The consumer ethic, the innovation of the department store, fashionability and widespread credit have heralded an era of the representational and exhibitionist. . . . The body has become a vehicle for displaying valued goods, and physical appearance, shape, size, prowess and so on are read by others as if they were signs of character.[48]

The availability of goods and services associated with twentieth-century capitalism, coupled with the omnipresent images of the mass media—daily brought into our very homes—undoubtedly contribute to the centrality assigned to appearance in evaluating the person. "That women are currently more vulnerable to culturally defined ideals of physical appearance is a reflection of their subordinate position," Finkelstein continues. "The status of men in industrialized societies is more closely attached to their labour value, and this can account for their physical appearance being of secondary value. For women, however, their status has been historically tied to fluctuations in cultural definitions of beauty, femininity and sexual seductiveness."[49]

This current state of affairs raises two significant ethical issues regarding the nature of our social order. The first relates to the moral status of women in this society. If a woman's worth is primarily judged by her conformity to external standards of appearance, what value is given to "the real given existing woman"? The second issue, connected to the first, pertains to the loss of self-worth and experience of moral failure of women who, though they try, are unable to meet normative ideals of femininity: They possess the wrong body type, the wrong weight, the wrong face, the wrong skin, the wrong hair, the wrong _____ (fill in the blank). Rather than blaming individual women for their failure to meet cultural standards or for their inability to come to terms with their limitations, what responsibility does society as a whole have to examine, evaluate, condemn, and change those expectations and practices that harm some, and militate against the well-being of all, women?

Jewish Looks

It is a Friday, soon after I begin doing field research at Julie's. I spend some time visiting with Svetlana and her customer, who is getting a manicure. The customer expresses some interest in the work I am doing, but she becomes truly engaged with me when she learns that I am Jewish. She is incredulous. Apparently I remind her of Victoria, one of the salon's beauticians, and hence she thought that I, too, was Greek. Similar exchanges occur repeatedly. "You are Jewish?" asks Shaina in disbelief. "You don't look Jewish." Pam joins the conversation, only to agree enthusiastically with Shaina. A few days later I am chatting with a woman regarding the neighborhood. She asks me if I belong to a local Catholic parish. After a pause, I tell her I am Jewish. She is surprised, she says, because "you don't look Jewish." A bit later that day I talk with several women as Julie sets Carmela's hair. One of the women asks me if I know a priest who taught at a Catholic university in the city. I respond that I teach at a different Catholic university. Somehow it comes out that I am Jewish. A chorus of voices responds, "You don't look Jewish!" Julie comes to my defense this time, legitimating my Jewishness by referring to the fact that I am married to a rabbi.

The theme of who does or does not look Jewish begins to emerge as an important one in this setting, often provoked by Jewish women like myself who do not seem to fit shared expectations. A dramatic expression of this phenomenon becomes evident when Julie trims the shoulder-length hair of a "thirty-something" blond woman—not a regular customer. Blanche remarks that Julie has given her a nice hair-cut. The woman proceeds to tie her hair into a pony tail. "With such pretty hair, why tie it back?" asks Blanche. "I cover my hair with a beret or a wig," responds the woman, signaling that she is a strictly observant Orthodox Jew. "What a shame," Blanche tells her, adding after a pause, "I understand you. I thought you were a *shiksa* [Yiddish for a non-Jewish woman]!" The woman laughs and tells Blanche how pretty some of her wigs are. Leaving the shop, she graciously turns to Blanche and says, "Thank you." With the woman safely out of sight, Blanche tells me how pretty the woman looks, "but like a shiksa." She then adds, "You, too." "Why do we look like shiksas?" I ask her. "I can't tell, you just do."

I begin to explore what "looking Jewish" means to people. Frequently the response is just as ambiguous and intuitive as Blanche's, as we will see. Eventually I develop a set of questions designed to probe, not only this question, but whether women think of *themselves* as looking Jewish or not, and what significance—if any—such self-evaluation might have for them. These issues are not necessarily related to femininity, which has been the focus of this chapter, but I believe they warrant discussion on two grounds: first, they pertain to the ways women envision themselves physically—hence the connection to appearance; and second, they interconnect with concerns about feminine beauty, inasmuch as ethnic women's looks are often evaluated from the perspective of the dominant culture's ideals. In this instance, Jewish women's understanding of their appearance must be seen within the context of a non-Jewish culture that has frequently denigrated and stereotyped them as members of an ethnic and religious minority. At times some of them, like other minorities, internalize stereotypes generated by the dominant culture. I have come to understand that women's ambiguity and frequent ambivalence in matters relating to Jewish looks—theirs or others'—bespeak their actual experience of anti-Semitism, their anticipation of possible bigotry, and/or the potential marginalization imposed on those who fail to meet standard images of feminine beauty. As American women are seen from the perspective of the male gaze, Jews and other ethnic minorities are judged from the vantage point of the dominant culture. Jewish women, then, are under "double jeopardy" in the public assessment of their looks: as women and as Jews.

Sara enters complex terrain when she begins to explore why she thinks I don't look Jewish. I am eating lunch with her and her friend in her apartment. She begins by commenting on my physical appearance. "It's your features and the way you are built. . . . Your nose is too small for a Jewish person." Her friend breaks in, "Most Jewish women are blondes and they're fat." Sara retorts, "They're not blondes by birth, you know." Her friend signals agreement. But soon Sara moves on to describe "your very being. First of all, this is bad to say, but it's a compliment to you, but not to us or Jewish people. You don't look Jewish. You don't act Jewish. You don't talk with your hands. You don't talk loudly. You're a gentle person, a genteel person. There are plenty of Jews that are the same way, but we don't know too many of them, as a rule." Sara's friend interrupts: "So we're stereotyping people." "It's true, it's true," responds Sara. Her friend continues, "But you know what? If you go among gentiles, and I've been amongst them, they talk pretty damn loud. And they use their hands." Here we find two Jewish women whose judgment of who looks Jewish is partly based on those Jews who populate their own world. They know they're banking on stereotypes when they universalize from their own experiences or when they use external images of Jews to characterize all Jews. Yet they do it all the same. They are also making a judgment of Jewish ethnic behavior of their generation—talking loudly, talking with one's hands—from the perspective of the gentile world, which they implicitly characterize as genteel. I wonder how much these characterizations speak, in a coded way, about tensions they may have experienced in achieving normative definitions of femininity.

To be perceived as "looking Jewish" in American society may well be experienced as derogation, as the language of some women reveals. Merle, for example, goes back seventy years to remember that she went to school "with a lot of non-Jewish kids, *but no one ever threw that up to me*, maybe because I was blond and blue-eyed. I don't know, but I was not dyeing [my hair] at any time. I've heard the expression, 'He looks so Jewish,' whatever you mean by 'looking Jewish'" (emphasis added).

Leah and Anna have similar reactions when I ask them whether they have thought about looking Jewish at any point in their lives. "I'll tell you," replies Leah. "I never gave that a thought. We were brought up to respect everybody's religion, whether they were black or whatever they were. My mother always said there is no difference; if we cut our finger, the blood is the same color. I was brought up in a Scandinavian neighborhood, and when I started going to school I went to church a couple of times. But I never gave a thought [to] me looking Jewish. Never thought about those things. People think about those things?" Likewise, Anna identifies concerns with "looking Jewish" with prejudicial judgments: "I hate those kinds of things. We never had that in our house." She spells out the ways in which her family of origin, and then her own, employed black workers and "never had a problem with it." She is sensitive to the way language can be used to stigmatize people and has therefore always refused to use derogatory words to refer to either blacks or Jews.

Sadie becomes agitated with this line of questioning. "Nobody ever took me for Jewish," she says, followed by a pointed question, "Why do you have to look Jewish or gentile or what?" Conceding that people do indeed make these kinds of judgments based on appearance, she concludes, "but they don't know what they're talking about sometimes." She recalls the time in her youth when she worked at a downtown store, selling hats. She told her boss that she would not be in to work on Yom Kippur. "He didn't give me an argument about it, but they all said, 'Oh, gee, we never knew you were Jewish.'" So Sadie's experience is that people always assumed she was gentile, not Jewish, "'cause my mother didn't look Jewish either." When I ask her what "looking Jewish" means to her, she replies with impatience. "That's a stupid thing for anybody to say, 'You [do or] don't look Jewish.' Some people have big noses, and that's, I guess, what they feel [when they say] you look Jewish or gentile. . . . Men, of course, don't look into those things. 'Do I look Jewish? Do I look gentile?' But I never made anything of those things. . . . Never thought about it." I ask her if she ever considers whether the older women who sit in the lobby of her building look Jewish. "Yeah," Sadie responds, "because a lot of them fight together." For Sadie, then, Jewishness is more about behavior than appearance. She does not seem aware of her own use of stereotype in her "reading" of Jewishness, however.

I am puzzled by these responses. These women grew up in a climate suffused by pressures toward successful Americanization, which included the desire to fit in, appearance-wise and more. They form part of a generation of women who often experienced anti-Semitic prejudice in work settings. I am puzzled, especially, by people like Leah and Sadie, who say they never *considered* whether or not they looked Jewish. Does this constitute denial? Self-protection? Resistance to the dominant culture's effort to label and hence control one's sense of self?

Only a few of the study participants think of themselves as looking Jewish. Shelley tells me she has experienced discrimination based on her appearance because "I look Jewish. . . . I think I have a Semitic face." I ask her what that means, exactly. "It is really hard to pin it down," she says. "Let me give you an example. I was in Cleveland with my brother and we went to a restaurant. . . . Everybody looked familiar because they were Jewish faces. I was in Washington, DC, and my son took me to a delicatessen, and everybody looked familiar. So there's a certain look. . . . It's the general appearance."[50] I tell her people often say I don't look Jewish. "You don't."

Evelyn says, "I look very Jewish. . . . What does that mean? I have the gentile definition of the Jewish look: a large nose. I don't know, what else does it mean? I'm short, I'm big in the bust, you know?" "Do I look Jewish to you?" I ask her. "No, not really. You don't." "So what makes us both Jewish?" I query her. "Some kind of unseen empathy . . . or rapport. Not even that. There's a sense of a brother who knows a brother. You know what I mean?" Though Evelyn accepts the gentile definition of Jewish appearance when she characterizes herself as looking Jewish, she in fact believes that Jewishness is internal.

Marny recalls that when she was in Israel, "there were people who looked very Jewish and there were people who didn't. . . . I don't know what [looking Jewish] is either, but you have a stereotype of a Jewish look." "How do you fit into that notion?" I ask her. "Myself?" she asks rather startled. "Do you see yourself as looking Jewish?" I continue. "Is that . . . something you think about?" Marny thinks for a bit and then responds. "It depends on who I'm with and where I am. I would say, I'm aware if I was to be in a situation where there were no Jewish people at all, and I sensed any kind of . . . prejudice, I just sort of would think that I must look Jewish to them. Yeah." While Marny does not really say that she would *feel* Jewish in that situation, she suggests that the situation might so define her.[51] In other words, she connects her experience as a potential target of prejudice with her bodily visibility as a Jew.

The women who believe they look Jewish all base their judgments on non-Jewish definitions of Jewish looks, frequently based on physiognomic stereotypes, like big noses. Undoubtedly many of them carry painful memories of their parents' and grandparents' experience of marginalization as Jews in their European places of origin. In *The Jew's Body*, a study of the representation of the Jew in nineteenth- and early twentieth-century central and Western Europe, the historian Sander Gilman explores "the anxiety of being seen as a Jew. Being seen as a Jew meant being persecuted, attacked, and harassed." He discusses in this context the development of the "nose job" as a surgical procedure, intended to address "the severe psychological damage done by the internalization . . . of the 'Jewish nose.'" Gilman concludes: "It is in being visible in 'the body that betrays,' that the Jew is most uncomfortable. For visibility means being seen not as an individual but as an Other, one of the 'ugly' race."[52]

Negative images of the Jew continue to exist in American popular culture today, although their capacity to disempower has been considerably weakened through legal interventions since Julie's customers were young. But their power to stigmatize continues. Whatever might be the "content" of looking Jewish—as we have seen, it is highly contested—what is at stake here, it seems to me, is the power imbalance evident in the relationship between the dominant and the minority cultures involved. For the dominant culture projects its own values, aesthetics, and perspectives as normative. As Gilman sees the Jews' position in European society, so Iris Young views members of minority groups—African Americans, Latinos, and sometimes Jews—in America: They are "rendered invisible as subjects, as persons with their own perspective and group-specific experience and interests. At the same time they are marked out, frozen into a being marked as Other, deviant in relation to the dominant norm." Young adds an important insight here when she writes that "victims of cultural imperialism cannot forget their group identity because the behavior and reaction of others call them back to it. . . . When the dominant culture defines some groups as different, as the Other, the members of those groups are imprisoned in their bodies."[53] Jewish participants in this study, whether or not they think of themselves as looking Jewish, are situated in this context of unequal power relations. Some buy into the dominant culture's definitions, others defy them.

The vast majority of Jewish women I interview report that they do not look Jewish, also based on non-Jewish evaluations of their appearance. Several assert that people see them as looking Italian. Sara, for example, says that "people have taken me, new people, newcomers, for Italian." Beatrice tells me she worked at a place for five years where they did not know she was Jewish, adding that it would have been a problem for her had they known. "I never looked really Jewish. I looked, they'd say I looked more Italian." Evelyn says that as a young woman she was taken for Italian or Spanish. Likewise, Harriet tells me that she does not feel she looks Jewish because "a lot of people have thought I was Italian." Undoubtedly, to be visible as a Greek, as a Spaniard, or an Italian is safer than as a Jew. I cannot blame them for welcoming such characterizations.

Other women are less explicit about which ethnic group they are associated with by others, but equally certain that they do not look Jewish given the experiences they have had through the years. Lucy, for instance, declares, "If anybody does not look Jewish, it's me." She proceeds to tell me how at graduation from her grammar school, her home room teacher asked her if she was going to the local Catholic high school. Lucy finds this particularly amazing in light of the fact that her maiden name was readily identifiable as Jewish.

Beth, who currently has a Jewish-sounding last name, is confident she does not look Jewish "because people have told me I don't look Jewish." Given her experience, she believes one cannot go on names to determine Jewish identity, but neither can one go on appearance:

> You can't say what looks Jewish. I mean, I deal with hundreds of [Jewish] people [at work] and in the *shul* [synagogue], or with my grandchildren, or when I go Israeli dancing. I mean, you know, one's tall, one's short, one's fat, one's skinny, one has a big nose, one had surgery and their nose is up in the air, and if all of them had surgery by the same doctor then the nose would look the same. So you really can't say a Jewish person looks like this.

Despite this view of things, Beth agrees with the general perception that I don't look Jewish. Perhaps this inconsistency can be explained by her observation that "Usually, Jewish people aren't, I would say, blond." (My hair is light brown.) But then again, she reiterates her conviction that you can't say what Jews look like because some are redheads—like one of her relatives—in her view also an uncommon coloring for Jews.

In their study of Jewish women in America, Charlotte Baum, Paula Hyman, and Sonya Michel investigate immigrant and second-generation fiction written by Jews. "This literature," they write, "abounds in examples of self-hatred among Jewish women. Those who 'looked' gentile were delighted with their good fortune. . . . This self-hatred among Jewish women was not without its external causes. As Jewish men imbibed Anglo-Saxon standards of beauty, they rejected Jewish physical characteristics."[54] If fictional literature tells some truth about the actual experience of people, then we gain an insight as to why some of Julie's second- and third-generation women seem so ready to dismiss the possibility they might look Jewish. In their youth the threat involved in looking Jewish may well have come, not only from outsiders, but from negative judgments internalized by Jewish men, and, by extension, by themselves, as well.

Some Jewish women, like Clara or Marny, who have naturally curly hair, have gone the route of ironing their hair, and later, of using liquid straighteners to do the job. Others have likewise experienced the rejection of those Jewish men who prefer to pursue the shiksa, stereotypically blond and blue-eyed. Members of other ethnic minorities have spoken eloquently about the pain of exclusion experienced by their failure to meet dominant standards of beauty. Toni Morrison's novel, *The Bluest Eye*, immediately comes to mind, with its poignant and disturbing portrayal of an African American girl longing to have blue eyes, like those of a white schoolmate.[55] These examples link in a direct way the dilemmas of feminine and ethnic looks.

Sylvia alludes to this link as she recalls a particularly painful experience from her youth in Poland. The offer of a baby-sitting job was withdrawn when the employer discovered, through a neighbor, that Sylvia was Jewish. Sylvia cannot understand the source of the anti-Semitism since she looked like a Pole. "Usually they say [that Jews] have long noses, right? And I didn't have it, OK? And [I was] blond and [had] light complexion, and this and that. I, well, didn't look Jewish. But I am Jewish through and through, OK? . . . I was very hurt that the lady does [*sic*] not take me to take care of the baby. Very hurt."

Clara developed survival strategies early on in life to cope with the widespread anti-Semitism of her youth. Raised in a gentile neighborhood, "I was the only Jewish kid in school until my sister started. And I grew up with the fact that I was called 'sheeny' and 'mousy Jew.' I mean, this was a terrible cross for me to bear.[56] And so, as I say, we were raised in the atmosphere of—I don't know what you would call it—racial discrimination?" Looking at a picture of herself as a young woman, she comments,

Well, I think I had a lot of guts. And I did some of the things that I don't know if I'd be brave to do now. Lying my way in so many areas. For instance, getting my first job when I was fourteen. I told them I was seventeen. Getting a much better job and telling them I was Italian and French because I knew that a Jewish girl could not get a job. . . . So I lied about getting the job. I became a secretary to one of the vice-presidents. And when I married, I left there. But not before I let them know.

This gutsy young woman confronted her employers by first having them praise her work performance during her years with the company in the late 1920s. Only then did she challenge them with this question, "'Then would it have made any difference at all if I had been Irish or Jewish or Hindu?' They said, 'Of course not.' I said, 'Then why the restrictions against the Jews?' They had no answer for me." Seventy years later Clara explains why her Jewishness went undetected. "You know, one Jew can always tell another Jew. But I had the brown eyes and the black hair. . . . I had very fair skin and could have passed for anything." Shortly after she left, she recalls, "the B'nai Brith started this business because there were so many organizations that didn't allow Jews to work." "So did B'nai Brith campaign against that?" I ask her. "Yes, absolutely. Absolutely."

Anti-Semitic experiences are not uncommon among the participants of this study for, as Leah puts it, "Every Jewish person has gone through that." These experiences vary in severity, however. Leah, for example, recognizes that once or twice in her life she has overheard anti-Semitic comments, but "I don't think it's ever been directed at me, but maybe in an offhand way." Others, like Sylvia and Clara, as we have seen, encountered work-based discrimination based on their Jewishness. While Clara chose to "pass" as non-Jewish in order to get a job she needed, Shelley refused to hide her Jewish identity. As she tells it, "I was looking for a job and I went to an agency, and they said, 'With your name we can get you all the jobs you want if you say you're not Jewish.'" "So they wanted to erase your Jewish identity," I note. "Absolutely," Shelley asserts. "And you wouldn't do it?" I ask her. "Of course not," she replies softly, adding that she had been an ardent Zionist in her youth, actively campaigning for the partition of Palestine. "And I wouldn't think of giving up my identity." Instead, she gave up the idea of getting a job through the agency.

Martha, who started out as a high school teacher, remembers her efforts to get her first job. "It was hard, you know. You knew you couldn't get into certain school situations." She recalls a wonderful interview she had with the head of the board of directors of a school district. She spent the rest of that day shopping and when she got home late, her mother reported that someone had come from the school board with contract in hand, ready for her signature. "So I got called the next morning and—apparently from talking to my mother—they realized that I was Jewish. They said they had another person they were interviewing. That was odd. . . . I was so upset."

More than one woman reports traumatic encounters involving anti-Semitic remarks. I ask Lucy, who claims she does not look Jewish, whether she has had any anti-Semitic experiences in her life. "Oh, ho, ho, ho. Would you like to pay for all the noses I broke, and all the glasses I broke? I also have a violent temper. . . . People would say things that they would never say had they known I was Jewish. . . . I'd hit 'em! My mother and father were forever paying for glasses. Whack!"

As the owner of a tavern, Harriet enjoyed the challenge of the work but had trouble with men's foul language. She remembers an experience involving a man who, upon discovering that Harriet was Jewish, told her, "Too bad Hitler didn't kill more of the Jews." Harriet's reaction was to throw a bottle at him, which missed him but got him out of the tavern in a hurry. She told the man's buddy his friend was never to come back or "I will kill him." Harriet tells me all this with a great deal of animation, obviously relishing the memory of standing up for herself.

Anna's reaction is very different. She recalls being at the beach one day when she noticed that a man had thrown down a lit cigar. She remembers her concern about children running around. "I said, 'You could have put that in the garbage can.' And he said, 'Why don't you go back to where you came from?' I laughed because he didn't think I was Jewish. He figured I was Italian. And I thought, "Oh, my God, how ignorant. . . . I [didn't] pay too much attention to it because my father told me, 'Consider the source, and ignore it.' . . . What are you going to do, fight?"

Whether or not these women think they look Jewish, or whether or not they have experienced deeply upsetting instances of anti-Semitism, virtually all have strong Jewish identifications. The nature of such identification varies, however. Only one out of eighteen Jewish participants in intensive interviews is strictly religiously observant. Married to a cantor, Beth adheres to the religious requirements of Jewish law. Her language is frequently peppered with Yiddishisms (such as "Kenahora!"), with references to God (as in "thank God"), and with allusions to Jewish holidays, most particularly, "Shabbos" (the Sabbath).

A close second is Shaina, a woman I frequently see at the beauty shop but whom I do not interview at length. Shaina tells me her husband is a "holy roller," her way of characterizing his level of observance. He wears "the black hat," she has to keep a strictly kosher home for him, and she does not drive on the Sabbath. Shaina's friend Pam volunteers that Shaina "does not even play cards on Friday nights." I ask Shaina if she was raised in an observant home. Pointing to Pam, Shaina says, "I was a shiksa, just like her." Shaina's use of irony is not uncommon; here it is masterful, for Pam in fact is not Jewish, while Shaina may have been nonobservant in her youth but certainly was culturally and ethnically Jewish.

Similar characterizations are offered by other Jewish women. Harriet, for instance, volunteers that "I am what you call a 'Yiddish shiksi.' Why? I never was much of a believer. I never run to the temples or observe special holidays. I observe them to a point, and I believe in my heart I'm Jewish, but I don't keep a kosher house." Dori lists a number of Jewish foods she does not especially like, suggesting that her housekeeper—who is not Jewish—"makes better matza balls than I do or my mother.... Like I said, I'm really not Jewish. I never went to Sunday school. The temple that we went to was so far away and we didn't have a car." Dori's view of being Jewish here suggests that it entails a religious commitment, unlike Harriet, who associates Jewishness with personal feelings of identification. Lucy's perspective is closer to Harriet's when she says, "To me Judaism is something that's in here" [pointing to her heart].

Reva does not really address the question as to whether she looks Jewish. But she insists that "I'm Jewish. I accept that I am Jewish. I am nothing else but Jewish.... I never denied that I was Jewish. I've always been proud to say I was Jewish." Beatrice was not raised in a religious home. Today she feels that "the older I get, the more I want to be Jewish." Although she and her husband are not members of a synagogue, some time ago she taught herself to light candles on Friday night. She also reads novels with a Jewish theme. She does these things because "I just want to belong to something."

The various meanings these women associate with being Jewish are consistent with those extant in the larger Jewish community, where Jewishness is not identified with a single characteristic. Jews do not restrict their association of Jewishness to a person's looks. The latter might serve an orienting function in a society in which identification with, loyalty to, and solidarity with one's own are especially important for the survival and flourishing of members of minority groups. Hence the assumption made by some that a Jew always knows another Jew or, otherwise put, "it takes one to know one." For most Jews, however—and for the Jews of this study as well—Jewishness entails a great deal more than one's looks: religious practice, knowledge of Yiddish or Hebrew, ethnic and cultural associations, personal feelings. All these entail choice, whereas physical appearance presents constraints beyond one's control.

Jewish looks are undoubtedly contextually evaluated. When I was growing up, I remember the tenderness and pleasure in my grandmother Ella's voice when she commented on a child's *yiddishe punim*, Jewish face. My grandmother's attitude was informed by the values of her Jewish world. In the multicultural society that my study participants inhabit, however, where appearance is evaluated on the basis of norms set outside the Jewish community, a "Jewish face" may well be the carrier, not of status or prestige, but its opposite, devaluation. It becomes a public marker of an identity not universally welcome. It may well render one as Other.

These Jewish women may thus find themselves in the midst of several dialectical tensions: between in-group acceptance of Jewish looks and its out-group rejection, between their experiences of inclusion in the larger culture and their experiences of exclusion, between their need to be full-fledged Americans and thus to conform to standard norms of appearance and their desire to affirm the particularity of their own ethnic group. These tensions might explain their general denial of looking Jewish themselves—or their disinterest in this question—and the aggressive insistence by some that I look like a shiksa, a term they do not typically use to characterize their own looks, for it would make them into in-group outsiders.

The discomfort many women seem to feel in describing Jewish looks and in identifying themselves with them may thus indicate a rejection, or at least a distrust of, ascribed characteristics of Jewishness, historically so frequently shaped by denigration and bigotry. Refusal to enter the discourse on Jewish looks, or ambiguity regarding its main features, may point, then, to a refusal to allow externally conceived images and their interpretations to define and control one. In this regard most of the participants of this study differ markedly from their tendency to embrace unquestioningly mainstream definitions of femininity. The latter is an understandable move, for it is conformity to these definitions that has assured Jewish women—as it did their immigrant mothers or grandmothers—a place of respectability and acceptability within the compass of American womanhood.[57]

Photos 1 and 2. Julie's International Salon as an unintentional community—beauty shop friends. *(All photographs by Caryn Chaden.)*

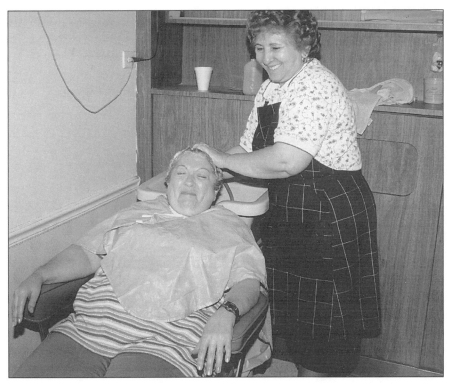

Photo 3. Enjoying companionship along with a delightful hair wash.

Photo 4. Working on one customer while another waits her turn.

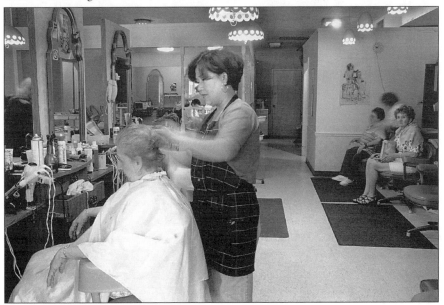

Photo 5. Applying color to a customer's hair.

Photo 6. Relaxing under the hair dryer.

Photo 7. Enjoying a manicure.

Photo 8. Setting a customer's hair.

Photo 9. Approving the finished product.

CHAPTER THREE

"What's My Alternative?"

Aging and Its Challenges

❦

Time marches on. And eventually you realize it's marching
across your face.

—Robert Harling, *Steel Magnolias*

Since my mother discovered, at age sixty-nine, that she had developed osteo-
porosis, I have become "religious" about doing physical exercise as a pre-
ventative measure. Three, or preferably four, times per week, I go to our
family room, stand in front of the television set, and do aerobics; or, to use
the parlance of my family, I do "Janes"—Jane Fonda's low impact aerobics,
that is. For months now, I have studied the commitment to diversity evidenced by the team Fonda has assembled to lead us into slenderness and car-
diovascular health: women and men, blacks and whites, thin and chunky (but
not too chunky). Apart from Fonda, whose age is difficult to discern, I have
looked in vain for age diversity. Virtually all the others seem to be in their
twenties. The message is clear: To be young is to be active; to be young is to
be healthy and sexy.[1]

These observations, and variations thereof, may be replicated time and
again by just being attentive to the many ways in which older people disappear from sight or, alternatively, are depicted in demeaning or trivializing
ways. This seems especially the case when it comes to older women. Think
of the dearth of older female characters on television or the movies, for
example. Or notice how frequently older women, when they are featured at
all, appear to be ridiculous or plain stupid in TV or radio commercials.[2]

A common attitude toward old age is revealed in a recent letter to Ann
Landers, that oracle of contemporary popular wisdom:

My son is a senior in high school and on the varsity football team. After a
recent game, we all went to a well-known fast-food place and the whole
team lined up at the counter.

When the server took my order, she asked me if I wanted the senior citizens' discount. (I am 54 years old.) I was humiliated to death and so was my son. You know how sensitive teenagers can be about their parents. Needless to say, I will never step foot inside that place again.

In my opinion, this was an invasion of my privacy and in the worst possible taste. If people want the senior citizens' discount, they should have the option of asking for it.

Please print this letter. Maybe if businesses see they are losing customers when their stupid employees embarrass the clientele, they will stop this practice.

Keep Age Out of It in Vermont

"Dear Vermont," Ann advises:

No customer should be asked if he or she wants the senior citizens' discount unless alone, since that question could be an embarrassment.

I see no problem, however, if the customer is unaccompanied. In fact, it could be viewed as a favor.[3]

Both writer and columnist presuppose an association between the incorrect perception of age and embarrassment (as in "I was humiliated to death"). More specifically, the server's great faux pas is seen to be the inaccurate attribution of *old age* to a still middle-aged individual. As participants in U. S. culture, we can safely assume that the writer would have experienced little offense, and more likely glee, if the server had *shaved off* a decade in guessing the customer's age.

"Aging" is a largely biologically determined phenomenon, but like any other human experience, it takes place within a social world. It is thus interpreted from the perspective of that social world in regard to its meaning, value, and significance. "Old age" is a socially constructed category, depicting, in the West, a late "stage" in the life cycle. Such a view is culturally specific, as anthropological research demonstrates: There is no agreement cross-culturally that chronological age is a significant or meaningful social category, or that life is a series of stages through which the individual moves.[4] Our current view of old age is rather recent, influenced by a modern industrial economy and capitalist-driven values.[5] It is variously defined, insofar as we lack clear, hard and fast definitions of what old age means. Increasingly we have come to divide the human life into the three stages of youth, correlated with education; adulthood, associated with productive work; and old age, connected with retirement, and hence, "unproductive" activities, such as leisure. Following this logic we frequently name sixty-five as the beginning of old age, an arbitrary number born of retirement policies developed earlier in this century.[6] Gerontologists, increasingly recognizing the differing experiences of people in their sixties and those in their eighties or nineties, have further subdivided the old into the "young old" and the "old old."

The anthropologist Barbara Myerhoff argues that the Western view of time—quantitative and linear, with a beginning, middle, and end—shapes a negative view of old age: "If time is understood as finite, then the close of life is an irredeemable tragedy, an irreversible loss."[7] This characterization may be correct in our own days because the religious world views that gave meaning to time and old age have ceased to grip the consciousness of most people. Despite the linear view of time of the ancient Israelites or medieval Christians, for example, old age was accepted by the Israelites because it revealed a righteous life and God's favor and by the Christians because it was seen as a preparation for death and eternity.[8] Thus the logic of linear time leads to tragedy in the absence of transcendent meaning.

How people use time also bears on attitudes toward old age. Harry Moody notes that since the seventeenth century Westerners have favored a life of activity over contemplation. Time needs to be filled with busyness for our lives to be considered meaningful. As a consequence, Moody believes, "Old age, like death, is an indictment of that fantasy of agitation that the young and middle-aged take to be the meaning of life. Old age appears only as a limbo state, an absence of meaning in life."[9]

These negative views of old age become exacerbated with rapid social change. In many societies of the past, the old were seen as the repositories of knowledge and communal know-how. The Book of Job expresses the view of ancient Israel in this way: "Wisdom is with the aged, and understanding in length of days" (12:12). In our computer age, we are less likely to refer to wisdom; instead, we talk about information. And information is now stored in more efficient ways than in the human brain; consequently, experience may be viewed as irrelevant, and the young come to be seen as the promise of the future.[10] Otherwise put, our society "values *tomorrow*'s knowledge, not yesterday's, and such a society stores and transmits its data on floppy disks, not in old people's minds and stories."[11] Hence as a culture we appreciate the future over the present, the ability to change our environment over our acceptance of it, the significance of becoming over being, of achieving over accommodating.[12] These value orientations result in the devaluing of older people "as belonging to the past."[13]

Undoubtedly contributing to this devaluation of the old is the association people make between old age and death. We constitute, after all, a society that aggressively avoids grappling with death at an existential level. As a consequence, older people elicit anxiety about younger people's own mortality.

There are a variety of ways to go about discerning contemporary cultural views of aging and old age. One way is to investigate images and assumptions available through the media, including films, newspapers and magazines, radio, television, and commercial ads; or to note the complete absence of any images whatsoever. Recently I chose a somewhat different approach. I asked about fifty students in two classes ("Women and Religion," "Values and Gender") to reflect on prevailing cultural images and assumptions about old age and the elderly that they had assimilated as members of this society. The following are the characteristics that students came up with; I list them without editing: frail, dependent, lacking in judgment, angry, unattractive, conservative, slow drivers, sickly, absent-minded, depressive, wise, cantankerous, cheap, non-sexual, forgetful, hard-of-hearing, overly traditional, lonely, domestic, inactive, having poor judgment, useless, crabby, whiny, ineffective, more religious (than the population at large), senile, fumbling, deaf, short tempered, slow, crotchety, nostalgic, needing attention, storytellers, childish (second childhood), mean, stingy, set in their ways, complaining, alone, stubborn, incapable, decaying, burdensome, experienced, out of touch, humorless, pitiful.

I then asked students to identify cultural associations with older *women*, specifically. This was their collective list: domestic (good cooks), nostalgic, interfering, out of shape, bitter, overbearing, frustrated, needy, stubborn, a liability, worn-down, gaudy, wrinkled, more vulnerable to attack, rambling, busybodies, hag, wicked, evil, nag, constant complainer, meddling, gossipy, worrisome, manipulative, martyr, advice-giving, grouchy, fat, "little old lady," bespectacled, moles, crooked, shrinking, widowed, helpless, tea-drinking, arthritic, bingo-playing, liver spots.

While I cannot claim "objectivity" for this method of data collection, we can rely on our own experience as a test of reliability for these students' perceptions. I believe we can readily arrive at the conclusion that older people in general, and older women, specifically, are depicted in stereotypic ways, often viciously so. As with other forms of stereotype, students were quick to offer that their own grandparents rarely conformed to these condemning qualities. In a society that privileges youth, material productivity, and physical attractiveness, to become old, but especially to become an old woman, is to enter difficult terrain.

I confront this reality head-on when I interview Evelyn, who is seventy-seven years old and atypical in some ways, perhaps because, as she tells it, she has always felt insecure. Some ten years ago, she tells me, she developed a condition called Bell's Palsy. It affects the nerves on the right side of her face, slightly pulling up her lip on that side, altering the aperture of the eye by a small amount; at least that's how it looks to this observer. She comments on her image in this way: "[Aging is] a metamorphosis, and to something you are not. You think you're something, you think that you're one thing, and then you look in the mirror and, 'Oh, my God, is that me?'" Here she is reading herself from her own point of view, recognizing a jarring discontinuity with her former image.

When Evelyn looks at a Polaroid picture I have just shot, she looks at herself in a different way. Her response is dramatic and astonishing, even in this edited version. I am ill-prepared for it. "Oh, God, I could cry!" she whimpers. "I look like a birth defect. Oh, God! I don't want to see it. . . . Oh, God, I'm never going out of the house again. How could I look so . . . I got to look like an animal, like a beast. . . . I can't stand to look at myself. I look so ugly! You cannot imagine what it feels like to look so ugly, so grotesque. How could that be me?" There is clearly some distortion going on here. I do not see what she sees. But I ask myself, What kind of moral order does Evelyn inhabit that causes her this kind of suffering? And is her response different in degree or in kind from those of other women in this study? These become central interests for me.

I turn to the ethicist William F. May to guide me in the pursuit of these interests. He suggests that the body has a three-fold meaning for a human being: 1) as an instrument for controlling the world, that is, "hands for working, feet for walking, tongue for talking"; 2) as a means of savoring the world, via our five senses; and 3) as a means of revealing ourselves to others: We not only *have* bodies, we *are* our bodies.[14] May's schema provides a helpful way for understanding the experience and meaning of old age for older women themselves. It allows us to examine women's aging around the loss of full physical health and its implications for their self-understanding as physical beings, to explore the gradual decline of the body and its implications for the enjoyment of life, to investigate the changing body and its implications for self-presentation and participation in communal life. Dividing these concerns into three areas is but a heuristic device. In real life, of course, they are inseparable elements of people's experience and identity.

The Body as an Instrument of Control

It is a Friday in May at Julie's International Salon. I am chatting with Shaina about her health. She is a large, handsome woman, assertive and attention-getting, a woman in her seventies. I comment that she looks better. Shaking her head vigorously, she tells me that she's had a new attack of Crohn's disease and she's experiencing side effects from her new medicines. She moves on to other things and I try to entice two other salon customers to participate in my study. I am telling them about my interest in older women. Shaina overhears me and loudly proclaims, in that characteristically acerbic tone of hers, "You could quote me that the 'Golden Years' are the 'Rusty Years.'"

Several months later, Harriet, a woman who is seventy-two, offers me a similar characterization of old age. She is a direct, witty woman, given to frequent comical turns of phrase. We are sitting at her kitchen table, where she speaks with some exasperation: "I never used to talk like this, but the way people say the 'Golden Years,' excuse the expression, but I say the 'Golden Years' are full of shit! That's what I say now; I never used to say that before. Because the Golden Years, if you can have Golden Years nice and easy and not have any aches and pains, fine. But how many people have that?"

The term "Golden Years" comes from a period in American history that gave meaning to the various stages—the so-called "seasons"—of life by associating them with the cycles of nature. During the seventeenth and eighteenth centuries, old age, like autumn, pointed to the chilling prospect of death; it was seen as a time of physical decline, on the one hand, but also a time of spiritual maturation in preparation for the greater rewards of the heavenly life.[15] For Shaina and Harriet the image of the "Golden Years" rings hollow, as well it should; in the absence of resonant culturally shared meanings associated with this expression, it is felt to be a mocking trivialization of the experience of old age, an artificial romanticization of a frequently difficult and painful time of life. These women's sentiments are echoed by Merle, a gentle, thoughtful woman of eighty-six, as she discusses her long-standing eye problems with me while sitting in the living room of her apartment. "Age is one of those things," she muses. "'A ripe old age,' they say, but we wonder how 'ripe.'"

A variety of physical ailments accounts for the discomforts of old age. Many women report suffering from arthritis. Clara, who at eighty-five is otherwise relatively healthy, reports,

> I have very bad arthritis in my legs and my knees. And now I find that it's getting worse as I go along, and I knew that it would be, even though I take anti-inflammatory medication. It definitely is getting worse. And I know that in the morning, when I get out of bed, I'm—I guess you could call it— a basket case. I actually hang onto the walls, until I get going, and I take medication, and I take a pain pill. And by the end of the day, I'm fine . . . as you keep going . . . the fluids begin to run in your system again, and you're OK.

Teri, a cheerful woman who is eighty-six and also struggling with serious, daily stiffness, concurs: "I push every morning to get out of bed. You sit on the edge of the bed and wonder, 'Am I gonna make it today or what? Get going, babe!'"

Evelyn reflects on her experience of growing old in another way. At age seventy-seven, she experiences a great number of physical discomforts. All the energy seems to have been "zapped" from her body; she feels tired just thinking of going out. "I have to force myself to take a bath, for God's sake. . . . 'Cause I can't lie in bed. I feel I gotta get out of bed." She reports terrible pain in her neck, hands, legs, and back. She speculates that she must have arthritis because "I hurt so bad. But the doctor has never diagnosed it. He says, 'Oh, you can't stand a little pain!' He's young, see. He doesn't feel it. No one can really understand what it is to get old until you've gotten old, you know?" A bit later she adds that her physician must be around forty-eight or fifty. "He can't understand what it feels like. I know I didn't at that age. And then you look at old people as though they're in the way, more or less, you know?"

According to gerontologists, older people frequently experience society's attitudes toward them through their interactions with their health care professionals. This is precisely Evelyn's experience. For her, the ailing body comes to be seen as the instrument through which the older person loses social significance. Shelley, an intelligent, thoughtful woman of eighty-two, tells me she has some trouble reading because her eyes begin to water. When she told this to her doctor, he just shrugged in a dismissive way. The optimist that she is, Shelley interprets this gesture in this way: "I guess [doctors] do that because they don't know what it is."

Some women are quite matter-of-fact about the loss of bodily control. Teri is simply being descriptive, not complaining, when she explains why she comes to the beauty salon for permanents and hair cuts: "I can't do that any more. I can't. I can't focus the way I used to. I can't get my arms up here. I can get them there, but I can't do anything with them." Other women comment on their propensity to forget words, to have stomach problems or cataracts, high blood pressure or high cholesterol. In short, as more than one woman puts it, "If it's not one thing, it's another."

The Body as a Means of Enjoyment

Our enjoyment of the world depends in good measure on our sensual experience: "the glare of sunlight, wine on the palate, the hum of streets, a fragrance of the breeze, and the corrugated feel of tree bark."[16] As the body declines, pleasurable experience becomes narrowed when eyes, legs, and stomach come to be less dependable or in some cases cease to cooperate altogether. Women in my study speak about three main areas where bodily decline has led to a diminution of joy in their lives: sight, food, and mobility.

Sight

Leah is a gentle, soft-spoken woman of eighty, recently widowed, and consequently quite depressed. We sit together at her kitchen table where we discuss how she can get back into life, reconnected after her loss. "I like to read," she tells me, "but I'm having a problem with my eyes now." It's glaucoma; apart from using daily drops, there's not much she can do about it.

Merle, who's had cataracts since youth, continues to experience eye problems. "I won't drive at night," she says. Fortunately her husband still does. A former schoolteacher, she now "can't read for any length of time. If I don't have the right amount of light, I can't read. I carry a flashlight." These limitations put a stop to her many years of volunteer work teaching reading in the classroom following her retirement. While on occasion she will still evaluate a child, "I can't make a practice of it. I'm not a young lady anymore."

Teri lives alone; occasionally she sounds plaintive about the lonesomeness of her situation. Today we are at Julie's, talking about hobbies. She says she used to do embroidery, but she can no longer do it, since "I can't see my finger in front of my face."

Food

Eating and sociability go together, of course. Losing the ability to eat freely feels like a double deprivation for some: one, the incapacity to enjoy foods they love and two, the inability to join friends around the dinner table. Shelley captures this double bind when she says, "I used to love going out; it means nothing for me [now] because I have to be so careful of what I order." In like manner, Sara tells me, "I'd like to live my life a little differently. I'd like to be able to sit down, either in my own home or in a restaurant or in a friend's house, and eat everything that's served to me, instead of picking and picking and saying, 'I'm sorry, I can't have this, or I can't have that.'"

Shaina resents the fact that she can no longer eat salads, a food she dearly loves. She is sitting at one of the beautician's stations when she tells me of her new bout with Crohn's disease. Anna, a Thursday regular and a food maven, quickly informs me that it was Shaina's own fault because she did not take care of herself. In self-defense Shaina explains her position, in typical self-mocking tones: "How much chicken breasts can I eat? So I ate a piece of cheese!" At a price, rebellion against the body is sometimes the preferred choice.

Mobility

Bodily decline may lead to special restrictions among those with specific illnesses and among the "old old." Shelley lives a half mile from the beauty salon. She used to walk that distance and enjoyed doing so. When she tried last summer, however, "I was so tired that I took a cab home. . . . I used to walk a lot. Now sometimes when I have to walk, I have to use a cane because of my balance."

Esther, a tall, statuesque woman in her seventies, lives a couple of blocks from Julie's. She reports with some pride that last Friday she walked there and then back home, leading her husband to assume that someone had dropped her off. She alludes to a problem with her legs but does not elaborate. I honor her privacy.

Merle tells me her problem has to do with her knees and the tibia bone. "I don't think I can walk," she says. "I have to walk a piece and have to sit." This condition now prevents her from enjoying cultural and musical programs she used to attend regularly. "The difficult part is the transportation," she explains. This is precisely what concerns Harriet, a widow living alone. She has a herniated disk and worries about renewing her driver's license next week since, as she puts it, "My car does my supermarket, my bank, the beauty shop."

Shaina is not alone in saying she used to be active in all kinds of organizations, but no more. I ask why not. She says she got tired of it. "What do you do with your time now?" I ask. "Go to the doctors and sit and relax." Evelyn and Harriet would concur in their tendency to stay put due to loss of energy and frequent experience of fatigue. In this regard these three women are not representative of most of the customers at Julie's, however, as most do not suffer from chronic or debilitating illness. If there is one thing I have learned at Julie's, it is that older people, like the young and the middle aged, are not all alike. I now know that Clara is right when she tells me, "See, there are so many ways of growing old, just as there are so many ways of children. You can have five children and each one is different, each one is different."

Responses to a Declining Body

To lose control and enjoyment of the world as a result of bodily change is difficult for participants of this study. However, as Clara says, not all people respond in the same way. Some resist older age and its losses with anger and resentment; some feel accepting. Some women might experience both attitudes. The experience of old age is not simple, I learn. It is full of paradoxes.

Resentment

At 64, Marny is a tall, handsome, sophisticated woman terrified of growing older. After cataract and hip replacement surgeries, she knows first hand the experience of physical decline. Her husband, two years her senior, wants to retire. Marny is adamantly opposed because "that's what old people do." She retells a conversation with a much younger friend as to whether she will have a fiftieth anniversary party when the time comes. Projecting herself into the year of her golden anniversary, Marny told her friend, "I don't want to have a party. My friends are old and sick and wrecked up now. I don't want to look at them." Half laughing, half serious, she continued: "I don't want to make a party for old people that can't walk, talk, or see, and they're in serious trouble." Then looking at me, she adds, "This sounds terrible but that's what I said to her." Armed with negative, incapacitating images of old age, Marny struggles to push away the reality of her own aging.

Sara is seventy-eight. She confronts her aging in this way: "I always said, 'I know I have to grow old.' I wanted to grow old, but I wanted to grow older and not old. And as far as I'm concerned, I've done both now. Well, I am doing both. I am older and old. Old because of my ailments." And this she resents: "More than my face, more than my appearance," she says intensely, "I think about my body. I resent it . . . that I am now paying for what I didn't have to pay for when I was young. I had no ailments then and I was very healthy. That's what I resent." It is not only the discomfort of her ailments that she resents; it is also the deprivation they cause her, for they prevent her from enjoying life in the way she used to.

For Harriet being old frequently engenders frustration. We are talking about her life when she was thirty-nine, over thirty years ago, when she was raising her children and taking care of her home. "Were you active in things outside the house?" I ask her. "Yeah, but now I can't even hold the [bowling] ball. I can't get my hand in the holes. . . . And now [if I walked in] high heels I would break my neck." Later on she says, "It aggravates me that I have to slow down and I can't do things that I used to do. Honest to God, I can't do half the things I used to do. . . . That's when I get angry at myself." "It's not your fault," I gingerly suggest. "I know," she says. "But when I think of all the things I'm missing that I could do and now I can't do. Like with my hand, when the light bulb goes out there." She points to the light over the kitchen sink. "Until I can do it, I got one foot in the sink and you should see me. Before it was nothing to me. Now I'm afraid to get on the ladder and when I get on the step stool, it's just not the same." Harriet is a woman who rages in the face of old age for she experiences her body as a betrayer.[17] Her resentment at her aging body may well reveal our cultural tendency to associate value with productivity and self-sufficiency and, consequently, to link loss of function with worthlessness.[18]

Shelley fights against old age on existential grounds. "I don't like being eighty-two," she says, "because I feel there are many things I can no longer look forward to. I always looked forward to things. . . . Most of the time I try not to think about it. I've got my head in the sand . . . because my life is coming to an end. [That's] exactly why."

Acceptance

Acceptance is the most usual response to bodily decline, at times accompanied by a note of resignation, a dose of home-grown maxims, and sometimes a hint of a cliché. It goes like this. Harriet says, "I take each day at a time because there's nothing that I could say and do that would change it." Teri agrees with this pragmatic attitude: "This is life. You know, you are born, you go up the hill, you get to the top, and then you go down. . . . This is the way life is. And you have to accept the good with the bad. And there is no sense in becoming bitter about it because that's not going to help." "You accept it," asserts Shelley. "I have a philosophy. 'You do what you gotta do.'" I ask her if there is internal change concomitant with changes in her body. "The only change inside is an acceptance . . . of everything," she says. "I don't fight city hall. I learn to let go. My philosophy is, 'So it isn't, so it isn't.' You accept limitations, where before I would fight against it."

Carmela, a spirited woman in her seventies, asks, "What's the option? There is no option." Then she tells me her mother's saying has been helpful in coping with her medical problems: "This too shall pass." Alice echoes this sentiment: "Tomorrow is another day." Leah simply asserts, "I just take it. That's part of growing older. I just take it as it comes." And Merle, commenting on her difficulties walking, says, "Like anything else, you have to learn to accept it and you do the best you can. . . . What's my alternative?"

There are no living role models for these women to emulate. Old age is increasingly lived out in uncharted terrain as people live longer than preceding generations and as social change, mobility, and cultural assumptions have transformed the social reality of the elderly. In short, these older women must find their own strategies for dealing with bodily decline and other experiences of old age. For many, what links them to the past are sayings learned from their parents in their youth.

Surprisingly few invoke religious resources in coming to terms with aging. However, some rely on their own internal insights to make peace with their situation, as does Reva, when she talks of the development of character in older age. "It doesn't come just like that," she says. "You mature and mature." While Reva does not associate this kind of maturity with religion, per se, I believe there is a spiritual dimension implicit in her view.

For those of us who are not yet old and who are healthy, understanding old age may only be possible through analogy.[19] I catch a glimpse of what accepting limitation might entail when, not long ago, I join my *havurah*, my fellowship group, to commemorate the Jewish holiday of Tisha B'av. This is a sad holiday—it recalls the destruction of the ancient temple in Jerusalem. We gather in a friend's backyard, chairs arranged in a circle. My friends light candles of remembrance and place them before them, also in a circle. Mournful singing commences, as does my asthmatic coughing. I move away from the candles to a corner of the yard, yet unoccupied, to no avail. My lungs will not tolerate the smoke released by the commemorative candles. I go indoors, painfully aware of my separation from my spiritual community. I struggle with feelings of exclusion, anger at my body, loneliness. I finally settle on a couch that leans against the back wall of the house. Only the wall and a large picture window separate me from the group. I pick up the prayer booklet, trying to join in, but I can't hear. When the group breaks into song, the sound, though muffled, is nonetheless audible. I sing along, alone yet connected. In between songs, I think about Julie's customers, who are teaching me about aging, and about how it must be for them, in greater or smaller degree, to become separated from the people they enjoy, restricted from activities that fulfill them, limited in their freedom to make choices.

Acceptance, I begin to see, is not a passive activity. It requires reflection and courage. It is a struggling of the soul to affirm what is yet possible, to let go of what is not. So when Merle says, "You have to learn to accept it and you do the best you can," she is referring to a spiritual process, the navigation from a realm of plenty to one of constriction and limitation. Penelope Washbourn comments on this process in this way: "Transcending despair and finding renewal even in the company of increasing limitation and suffering depend on risking ourselves. This is what religious people mean by faith—the experience of feeling ultimately accepted, whether by what we call God or the ongoing process of creative life."[20] Ultimately this process reveals a view of old age and death as part of the human condition, a perspective from which many Americans tend to recoil in this last decade of the twentieth century.[21]

Compensations

While acknowledging that physical aging brings about a narrowing of life in some respects, most study participants also identify concomitant positive changes in their inner experience. I have noted Reva's and Merle's reflections regarding what I see as a movement in the direction of spiritual maturing. Not everyone can put a finger on it, exactly. But Reva's view is that this is "a growing-up process besides the aging process." Lucy's thinking mirrors Reva's when she tells me that she's gotten better with age: "In every way. I think you grow as you get older. . . . What is important when you're younger, as you grow older you realize how stupid you were. . . . I think your perspective changes to a degree where you see how really dumb you are: things you worry about, choices that you make, should make, shouldn't you make." Speaking for herself, Sara says that she's beginning to be "more and more philosophical"; in fact, she speaks for many others when making this evaluation.

Some women identify emotional growth as most significant. Merle puts it this way: "I don't get upset over as many things as I did when I was younger because as you go through life you have experienced so many things that you can categorize your emotions." Harriet feels she can "put up with a lot of things I couldn't when I was younger. When I was younger I was a hellcat, and I would tell you off, one-two-three. Now I don't do that. I've cooled down to a point. I used to have a fiery temper." Beatrice concedes that "it's very difficult to explain your feelings," adding, "I'm glad I'm old, so I can have them [feelings]. You know what I mean? I'd rather be old and have them, than not. . . . I'm quieter. And I think I'm more forgiving of people."

Alice is now calmer, too. "I was always kind of an uptight, temperamental person. But then, I had the right to be, with the business and all. And I find I'm very low-key now. Things don't bother me like they used to. . . . Let the rest of the world do what they want to do. You do your own thing. You'll be better off for it." Here Alice points to the development of autonomy in her older age in a two-fold sense: She has fewer obligations, and she is no longer as dependent as she was on the approval of others. Many other women offer similar reflections. Clara says it plainly: "You get to the point where you say what you think." Martha agrees whole-heartedly that there are advantages to growing older: "Oh, definitely. . . . There is a freedom that you have. You don't have that many obligations. . . . You can probably, for once in your life, decide what you want to do." So while the body's decline often leads to limitations and consequent dependencies, the spirit, if you will, enjoys new freedoms.

Some women are pragmatic in assessing the advantages of older age. Sara names senior bus passes and dollar matinees, but finds little else of value. Sylvia, who worked very hard her whole life, often in highly stressful situations, says, "I wanted to retire, to be sixty-five, and to get a paycheck not working. I never had a penny not working, OK?" For Beatrice, getting Social Security "takes a lot of worry off my mind," and consequently, "that's a big plus." Other women talk about the development of inner contentment. When I ask Teri if there are any plusses to being older, she responds, "I can't tell you. I'm perfectly content in the way I am today." Marny tells me she now appreciates things she used to take for granted, realizing how lucky she is, for example, to have a loving husband. Anna's answer is the most pithy: The advantage is "that you're here."

Pride in their accomplishments surfaces when women talk about their personal growth. Clara tells me that she has been involved in a life-long commitment to learning. "You see," she says, "when you stop learning, unfortunately, that's when you stop actually living. You really and truly do. You really and truly do. There isn't any question of that. . . . And you know . . . I like myself because, at eighty-five, I think I've done everything in my power to make me like myself." Likewise, Beth tells me, "I've learned a lot. . . . I've accomplished a lot, I feel. And I've grown to be maybe a bigger person. Maybe better. Maybe I'm a better person than I was. I don't know." Modestly, she adds, "That's for someone else to say, not for me to say."

"Depth of character. You'll find that in older people," Reva promises. She is right about that.

The Body as a Means of Revealing Ourselves to Others

So far I have considered older women's experiences and attitudes toward the body as an instrument for controlling the world and as a means of savoring the world. In large measure they represent various ways of confronting existentially challenging situations in human life and hence open up for us alternative responses to fundamentally religious questions: the inevitability of aging, physical decline, and ultimately, death. Similar responses may very well have emerged had participants been men rather than women. But while loss of physical vigor and decline in health may be experienced similarly by both women and men, the aging body as a means of revealing the self to others has particular significance and consequence for women in this culture.

This is the case because bodily representation and self-presentation are a) shaped largely through cultural convention and social relations and hence are not inevitable, and b) they disproportionately affect women in this society. I want to know what happens to women's sense of self as they age. This query needs to be understood within a larger context, namely, the central role of beauty, femininity, and attractiveness in defining women's value in this society, which are issues I explored in chapter 2. Because women's worth is so frequently associated with their physical attractiveness, the normal physical changes that accompany aging—wrinkles, weight gain, hair thinning and graying—call into question women's social value and consequently raise ethical concerns.[22]

It is Friday morning and I'm keeping Marion company while her hair is getting colored under a kind of plastic shower cap. She is a recent customer at Julie's—for the past six weeks or so. I guess she must be somewhere in her late seventies. Little do I know that in five months she will die in her sleep, reportedly of a heart attack. This bit of retrospective knowledge adds poignancy to her already poignant words. "I want to get older," she says as she energetically uses her hands for emphasis, "but I don't want to *look* old." Needing to explain, she adds, "I want to get older because the alternative is to expire, and I want to *live*." She does not explain why she doesn't want to look old. Neither does anyone else, but just about everyone I ever talk to at Julie's International Salon takes it as a given that looking old is bad, looking young is good. This must be because these women are living in American society, where according to social psychological research, most people assume a) that attractiveness and older women are mutually exclusive categories and b) "What is beautiful is good, what is ugly is bad."[23] Since in this scheme older women cannot be attractive, let alone beautiful, they are often rendered morally unacceptable and subjected to negative stereotyping. Let us briefly recall some of my students' associations with older women: evil, manipulative, hag, busybody, wicked, meddling, interfering. This is hardly a catalogue of desirable virtues. Is it any wonder that an old woman like Marion doesn't want to look old?

In this study, older women's "reading" of their bodies is in constant tension with images of youth—their own, now past, or those of friends, acquaintances, or public figures like actresses or models. At Julie's my relative youthfulness is a recurring topic of discussion, as is the fact that I can wear my hair in the style I do because "you are young," or the shared perception that I'm lucky to look much younger than my actual age.

Lucy, an attractive, self-confident woman of sixty-two, moved to a suburb a good distance from Julie's. I ask why she continues to travel so far to get to the beauty shop. "It's comfortable," she says, adding, "and then I look around and everybody looks a lot older than I do." She chuckles and goes on. "It's like when you want to feel skinny, surround yourself with obese people, and then you look like a twig."

Marny recounts that friends are always telling her daughters "how much younger than so-and-so I look. I hear this a lot. I want to believe it and I love hearing it." Many women who feel good about their appearance do so on the basis of looking younger. Conversely, they feel bad if they don't. "Fortunately," says Merle, "I'm not too wrinkled." In like fashion, when we're speaking about facial lines, Sara tells me, "Well, fortunately, I don't have those." She attributes her good fortune to genes and to the prudent use of cold cream through the years. Then she adds, "About my appearance, I know I don't look my age. I don't act my age. That's why my age doesn't bother me." In making this judgment Sara reveals an implicit understanding of what a normative seventy-eight-year-old woman looks and acts like; age is not a problem because evidently, for her, her true age doesn't "show." Like other older women, Sara protects herself from potential age-based prejudice by implicitly accepting age-related stereotypes "in respect of other elderly women but . . . [by denying her] own old age; becoming old is then a misfortune that befalls other people."[24]

Whether a woman thinks she looks her age or not, she tends to *feel* younger than her chronological years.[25] "My body is going downhill," says Teri laughingly, "but I don't feel like my brain is yet." During one conversation I ask Sadie how she feels about getting older, and she responds, "I'm not getting older but younger at heart." Some months later, while I visit her at home, she tells me, "Believe it or not, I'm going to be eighty on January 1st. That's only numbers to me. I don't take it as age. My family, they all tease me, and I say, 'I'm young at heart.' That's the way I am, I can't make myself different."

When Clara looks at a contemporary photograph, she sees an old lady. "I really do. I see an old lady." I ask her how that feels. "Well, you know what I do? I just brush it off. It isn't me. Because the me is inside, here [pointing to her chest]. And I'm still younger than springtime." Adding that "You never feel old," Clara asks me, "And you know why, Frida?" To which she responds, "I think that the tomorrows, the tomorrows. Somehow life has a way of tomorrow, tomorrow, we're doing it tomorrow. And so you're looking forward, there's a continuity there. You're looking forward. It's never quite finished. It's never quite finished. . . . Because it seems like every day starts a new existence. Every day brings a new day with it. And if we didn't have that to look forward to, we'd say, 'What's the sense of going on?'" Here Clara provides us with a beautifully articulated phenomenological analysis of her inner experience. But in effect she creates a dichotomy between her body and her self. Her real self is internally situated, and must in some profound way be private, visually inaccessible to the world; she negates the body she presents to the world by saying, "It isn't me."[26] So the experience of having an older body is not only one of loss—loss of youth, of function, and of enjoyment; for some women it is one of denial as well.

Denial of physical changes takes many turns. Marny says that as long as "I'm not thinking about my appearance, I'm a very happy girl, and I don't talk about it." When she looks at herself in the mirror at night, with fewer clothes on, she'll say, "Will you look at this sticking out?! It's horrible." Edie takes her shower nightly, saying, "I don't want to look at myself." When she does, she exclaims, "My God, look at me!" What these women seem to be saying is that as long as they don't see their bodies, they feel fine, as their sense of self relies on internal experience; hence their desire to avoid their reflections in the mirror. Once the naked image is before them, however, the critical gaze comes into play, triggering the process of self-denigration.

I ask Frances how one comes to terms with one's face becoming lined. She jokingly replies, "Your eyes are better than mine." She then adds that not seeing well is what helps her deal with a changing face. To the same question Shelley replies, "You don't think about it. I see it in my friends, but I don't see it in me." When she looks at a Polaroid picture I have taken, she says she sees an old lady of eighty there, but not herself. The picture is an excellent likeness of Shelley. "Tell me about that," I say. "I'm amazed. You do not see yourself here?" "Evidently," Shelley responds, "in my mind I look differently. I'm better looking." A bit later she concedes, with some frustration in her voice, that "Of course I see myself, but that isn't the way I want to look."

Clara offers an interesting interpretation of this issue. Older women go to the beauty shop, she suggests, as a "facade" against the realization of their aging and inevitable death. She claims there is a certain amount of self-deception involved in women's visual self-evaluation, designed to stave off depression. For example, she reports reading that when looking at the mirror, people look from the eyes up, thereby neglecting to see the sagging face and other wrinkles.

The paradox of being old yet feeling young is poignantly demonstrated in the experience of Beatrice, an exceptional woman as far as her health is concerned. At age eighty-two, she proudly declares, "I'm in perfect health. I'm strong. My doctor says, 'You've got the body of a twelve-year-old.' I'm very strong," she repeats. "I always have been. Our whole family. Very wiry and strong." I ask her, "When you see yourself in the mirror, do you ever think about how old you look?" "Sure," she replies, "When I comb my hair, and then I put a little make-up on, I'm going to look as cute as I used to. And I do sometimes, 'cause of course they say, 'You're cute or you're nice' . . . in an older way, you know what I mean?" Chuckling, she concludes, "To me, I'm just as cute as I was before." But when she looks at a Polaroid photo I take of her, she reacts in this way: "Oh, I think it's horrible. . . . I really look old. Very, very bad. I look like a witch. . . . I really look old, old, old here. Do I really look like that?" I suggest we try taking another photograph. She likes the second one better because, as she puts it, with a chuckle, "[In this one] I'm not an old *kocker*" (Yiddish, *alter kocker*: old fart).

Beatrice has never felt old and she doesn't know why. I ask her what she thinks feeling old might be like. "I don't know. I have no idea," she responds, and then explains that her strong reaction to the first photograph may be explained by the fact that "I don't really feel older inside. And I look in the mirror, I don't really feel old. I know I'm older, 'cause I can see, but somehow or other, [my husband] tells me I look nice, I look young, I look pretty." When strangers react to her appearance, however, her certainty about her self-presentation via an aging body is unsettled. She recollects her experiences riding the bus to go downtown. "People will get up, you know. Younger people will say, 'You can have my seat.' And I say, 'Thank you, but you're tired, you sit down, you're tired, you're just coming from work.' And I say to myself, 'My God, I must look like I'm old.' To myself, I'm young, you know. See, I can't visualize myself as real old. I just can't. 'Cause I don't feel it. If I felt it, perhaps I would." She concedes that for her being old conjures associations with physical infirmity. In this she is not alone. As sociologists Arber and Ginn argue, for elderly people the word "old" does not refer to any particular calendar age,

> but to a state of decrepitude and feebleness. . . . What elderly people are denying is not their age, but a derogatory stereotype of incapacity and encroaching senility in which they do not recognize themselves or most of their peers. In a society which penalizes old age severely, a woman's efforts to avoid the appearance of ageing may be a rational response to the prevailing prejudice, a means of escaping the consequences of age discrimination.[27]

As women grow older, they acquire what Erving Goffman calls a "spoiled identity": Their old bodies come to stigmatize them.[28] In the dominant American culture, old age is accompanied by a loss of social status, manifested in a variety of ways, including social invisibility through the loss of respected social roles and the perceived loss of femininity.[29] When a woman gets older, she no longer fulfills reproductive or child-rearing functions. Nor is she considered suitable for purposes of sexual attraction or flirtation. This loss of status occurs in a cultural context where the woman's body frequently has been reduced to reproductive and sexual purposes. Because women are also culturally identified with their appearance, the old body in a woman becomes a totalizing representation of the self. To be perceived as "old" or to see oneself in that light is to identify the whole of oneself with the label. As Sally Gadow argues,

> "Old" is the meaning used to organize and interpret various phenomena; it is not the description of a self-evident state that individuals find in themselves. . . .
>
> The effect on the individual of social images of the body can be kept within bounds, since the body is only part of one's reality. . . . However, an attribute like "old" is intended as an encompassing designation of the person's entire being. An ascription that is meant to refer to the whole can be transcended only by the most severe measures: a young or timeless being is posited beside the old one.[30]

When I first began hearing women's claims that they felt young inside, I thought these claims revealed personal defensiveness, denial, or coyness. This shows my lack of understanding of older women's experience and their social situation. Now I can appreciate why I put off one of the women at the beauty salon. I learn about this from Julie when she tells me that yesterday I offended one of two women I was trying to recruit to participate in intensive interviewing for my study. I was explaining to them my interests in older women in light of the fact that we know so little about their experiences. Both customers were in their seventies. The nature of the offense, according to Julie, is that I should not have characterized them as "older." Astounded, I ask her what the woman wished me to say instead. "Middle aged," she replies. Julie is telling me all this while she works on a customer, who, after hearing our conversation, blurts out, "That's ridiculous!" That was my original reaction as well. Now I feel differently.

Clearly not all people internalize social meanings in the same way. Perhaps this customer is especially sensitive to the reductionistic nature of social labels like "old" or "older." The point is that total categories rob those who are labeled of their subjectivity, of their freedom of self-definition.[31] They objectify by converting the subject from a "Thou" into an "It," to use Martin Buber's felicitous terms.[32] Hence the tendency to claim a younger inner self alongside an older body may be interpreted as a form of resistance, not coyness or denial. In addition, there is a psychological need for continuity in one's self-identity throughout the life cycle. This need is heightened in older age in the face of both internal and external losses.[33] Self-identification with a younger self may be a manifestation of this need.

What happens in the instance when a woman acknowledges that she looks old? I am sitting with Reva in a small, cozy room of her apartment, enjoying a cup of tea. She tells me that when she dresses up and looks at herself in the mirror, she feels good. "But," she adds, "when I look at myself now, I feel old." What does Reva—or any other woman, for that matter—see when she looks at the mirror? She sees an image of herself, of course. But as she peers into the looking-glass, she sees herself from two perspectives at once. She sees herself from her own point of view, from her chronological experience of herself, finding both continuity and change in the image before her. But she also takes another reading of that image. She is seeing herself as others see her.

In chapter 2, I noted that women in this society tend to see themselves from the perspective of others—parents, husbands, friends—but most typically from the perspective of men. This observation is useful but does not go far enough in helping us interpret the experience of *older* women. When Reva looks at herself in the mirror and feels old, she is seeing herself from the perspective of men, as would a younger woman as well, but also from the perspective of a younger person. Hence she is twice objectified, or, perhaps more accurately in this instance, she partakes in the process of self-objectification in two ways: as woman and as *old* woman. As woman she is observed by the internalized male gaze. As older woman she is observed by the internalized gaze of youth. We spot here another unequal social relation, which, like the male-female relation, is a relationship of dominance-subordination. The image and its reading captures the social imbalance between youth and old age, especially as it pertains to women.

The preceding discussion points to the double objectification experienced by older women, first, based on the judgment that aging robs women of their central functions in society, namely, as reproductive agents and as sexual objects for the enjoyment of men—visual and otherwise; and second, as a result of the totalizing nature of the label "old" in a society enamored of youth, change, the new, and the future. Older women come to be known—and sometimes come to see themselves—as "old bags." And what is a bag but a shapeless, empty container, one which after use should simply be thrown away?

In such a technologically sophisticated and inventive society as ours, what resources are available to the aging woman to slow down, if not reverse, the appearance of old age? How can women deploy the pragmatic American spirit in the interest of finding relief from "oldness"? The beauty salon provides an ideal place in which to investigate these questions since, as we have seen, its primary purpose is the enhancement or improvement of women's appearance and hence their public image.

There is an agreed-upon assumption among the participants of this study that to look good is to feel good, or at least, better. Merle, for example, suggests that going to the beauty shop and getting one's hair done is good for one's mental health as well as one's appearance. In this vein, she adds, "A bit of makeup . . . makes you feel a little better or makes you look a little better. When you do that you feel better." In her assertive way, Clara declares,

"There is no question that when we look better, we feel better. There's no question"; she thus fights inertia and forces herself to get moving, despite her arthritic pain. In like manner, Sadie proclaims that appearance is the most important thing to a woman because "if she looks good, she feels better."

Many women push themselves to continue their investment in good grooming because of their fear of "letting themselves go." A friend had told Teri, "Oh my God, it costs you a fortune with your hair." To which Teri replied, "What am I going to do? Just let myself go because it's going to cost me a fortune? If I cannot afford it then that's something else." Reva tells me she wants to age gracefully, not let herself go, "by keeping our appearance, by getting up in the morning and we have nothing to do, but still at the end of the day my hair is combed." I ask her to clarify what she means by letting herself go. "I'd feel like I would lose my will of living . . . and what would you have to live for?" For Merle some people don't take care of themselves when they get older; they "allow themselves to just go," doing nothing about keeping their hair. Carmela feels that the attitude a woman takes about her appearance is critical. She is grateful that the first thing she does in the morning is to take a shower, never lounging around in a bath robe. That's the worst thing you can do, she argues, meaning that you give up and "let things go." Hence she adds, "I wouldn't think of not coming to the beauty shop."

Thus an important strategy for Julie's customers in combating older age and its dangers—physical, emotional, and social—is to maintain continuity with the past. For in refusing to "let go," these women are affirming a link between their present experience and their past behavior and image. They wish as best as they can to retain a semblance of feminine beauty, now compromised by the marks of aging. They are also affirming their membership in a continuing social community by conforming to social expectations regarding acceptable self-presentation, as when Teri explains why she goes to Julie's, now that she can't put up her own hair: "So I'd look like a human being." Finally, a refusal to "let go" has existential overtones, for it suggests one's unwillingness to give in to despair, depression, or inactivity.

Together, these interpretations suggest women's desire to maintain a measure of control and choice over their lives at a time when most of them experience some loss of control through physical decline and illness, the death of relatives and friends, and/or changes in physical appearance. Thus Shelley, speaking for herself and friends of her own age bracket, asserts, "We feel that our hair is very important, and it's the one thing we can still do something about. I can't do anything about the wrinkles; I can't do anything about the . . . liver spots." Perhaps this was also a motivation for one of Julie's longtime customers who from her death-bed requested that Julie come to her home to do her hair the day before her death.

Another typical prescription at the beauty salon is to dye one's hair in order to conceal old age and hence "look better." Many women agree with this prescription and follow it. Clara, for instance, asks, "Why should I look older than I have to? Really?! Gray hair," she continues, "does make you look older; there's no question of it." Alice once tried going "natural," but she quickly concluded, "It aged me ten years." Evelyn tells me that her son, who lives with her, wants her to quit coloring her hair, but she resists: "I think I look so old now that if I let it get gray I'll look ten times older. . . . I am old, I have to admit that. But I don't want to be old. I want to be young. At least about sixty." Shelley, on the other hand, colors her hair because it is important to her husband that she look the youngest in their circle of friends. She says her mother was gray from the time she was thirty-seven, whereas "I'm not because my husband chooses me not to be gray." I ask her what she would do if her husband did not demand she do so. She does not know because she can't predict whether or not she would like herself gray, but "sometimes I think it's a nuisance to get it colored."

Bertie says she likes to look her best, and graying hair would not look very good at work because "it would make me look old." The subtext here hints at the penalties that women pay in the workplace for looking old.[34] Harriet acknowledges that going to the beauty shop to get her hair colored is at times a burden for her, but she pushes herself because "You got to do it or you'll look like 'yik.' . . . I don't want to take the chance," she says, laughing. She then turns serious and adds, "I'm afraid. You know, I have enough problems, and I look bad as it is. . . . Without makeup I look like death warmed over." Her fear, of course, is motivated by her anticipation of social unacceptability and hence rejection.

The stigma associated with looking old is well demonstrated by Ida's experience of some twenty years ago. Now in her seventies, Ida then worked in a women's clothing store. One day she answered the phone and spoke to a customer who, acquainted with the store, wanted to determine who Ida was. Was she the owner, another worker, or "that old woman"? Ida's hair was naturally dark, with a dramatic streak of gray in front. "That comment stung me to the quick," Ida says. Her immediate response was to get her hair dyed blond, a practice she has continued ever since.

I can identify with Ida's feelings when, a couple of years ago, I stand with my daughter, then eleven, in front of our bathroom mirror. "You have such a pretty face," I tell her, inadvertently, spontaneously lapsing into a feminine practice. Then as I put my face next to hers and look into the mirror, I add self-mockingly, "You look just like me." She responds spontaneously, as well: "You're old, you're ugly." I know these are the words of a child, of my child, with all the baggage that carries, but they sting nonetheless. I do not have recourse to hair coloring on the basis of gray hair to fix her perceived connection between aging and unattractiveness, as my hair is not yet visibly showing gray. But I can see the issues that await me down the road.

While coloring the hair is the way to go for most older women at Julie's, not every color will do. There seems to be general agreement that older women do not look good with dark hair. Clara, for instance, insists that old skin and dark hair don't go together: "It doesn't, it doesn't, it just doesn't. . . . The skin is not young. . . . The look is not young. So how can you have black hair on an older face? You know that that's not normal. . . . It just doesn't go with it. It just doesn't go with it." Anna agrees when she says, "Dark hair looks bad on older women; it shows all the wrinkles." Verena, an experienced beautician, attempts to clarify this for me in the following way as I try to make sense of what Anna is saying: "What is desired is to take attention away from the face. Dark colors call attention to the face"; hence dark hair is anathema for older women.

At another time I overhear Verena giving advice to a customer on a related topic. She says the customer looks better with a permanent because "there is less face and more hair." In other words, the less we see of the older woman's face, the better. Coloring the hair light or getting permanents are devices intended to distract the observer from seeing the woman's face, a face with tell-tale lines. I keep my thoughts to myself, but to me the implications of this line of thinking are frightening. Does Verena reflect a generally held attitude about the undesirability of seeing the older woman's face? And if so, does it suggest the assumed undesirability of seeing the older woman at all? As far as I'm concerned, this is a prescription for virtual invisibility.

At Julie's some women, a minority to be sure, allow their hair to go gray naturally. These women almost exclusively have salt-and-pepper hair or display a head of completely white or "silver" hair; both these options are considered to be attractive and a stroke of good luck. Some women who color their hair would prefer to wear it natural, were it attractive, but they complain that instead their hair is "mousy" and makes them look old. A few women suggest that they would like to have the courage to let the hair "go natural." Leah, for example, says that she would like to do this for "health reasons" and also in order to "grow old gracefully." The latter notion suggests accepting one's aging, as demonstrated by Marny, who has considered letting the hair alone because "I like the idea of everything being natural. I think it would look very soft. . . . When you force trying to look young, you look pitiful, clownlike. . . . What's the cliché? 'Growing old gracefully.' I would like to think I could manage it. I think I would appear wise, but my biggest problem is the emotional part of it." By "emotional part" she means coming to terms with the reality of looking older in a society that disempowers the older-looking woman.

As the gerontologist Gari Lesnoff-Caravaglia puts it, "The determination of a woman of age to appear young is not born of vanity, but the knowledge that power lies in youth."[35] And considering that "women are old as soon as they are no longer very young,"[36] it makes very good sense that women would, in their own self-interest, attempt to slow down the appearance of age. Though understandable from the perspective of survival, I find this form of conformity to social expectations to be worrisome because it leaves unquestioned the premise that women's self-worth and well-being must be centrally attached to their appearance. It is ultimately bound to fail because a woman cannot do enough to ensure that she looks young enough to garner respect and visibility.

If hair coloring is one way to conceal the aging process, what about other interventions, like cosmetic surgery, a practice that has grown by leaps and bounds in American society in recent years? After all, as Clara puts it, there are some beauty shops in the more affluent parts of this metropolitan area where one would find "everything done but tummy tucks." Perhaps this is the case in some quarters, but not among the women who populate Julie's International Salon. Here cosmetic surgery is rejected by all the women I interview formally and informally, although the reasons for the rejection vary.

One group of women would consider undergoing cosmetic surgery were it not for their fear of untoward consequences and the concomitant loss of health. Leah, for example, is accepting of other women's choices but rejects surgery for herself: "If [women] feel it's a necessity and if it's going to help them, then go ahead and do it, but to go ahead and do it, do they think of the harm? What if it breaks down? You're worse off than you were before." Sadie is more adamant: "I think these women are nuts," she declares. "What they're doing to their bodies and faces . . . I don't want to touch my face. . . . You can't take your skin and just play around with it. . . . It wouldn't be healthy for the body or my face. . . . Why monkey around with your own body?" Marny says that though she certainly wants to look younger, "I would never consider a face lift. . . . I'm afraid. . . . I think there's a lot of charlatans out there. I don't trust or believe them. I kid my friends who have face lifts. I'll say, 'If God could give me a guarantee . . . that I wouldn't look worse. . . .' It sounds unnatural to me. I mean, if you've lost it, you've lost it." Here Marny links fear to her judgment that the "unnatural" is unacceptable.

This judgment is shared by others. Clara says she would not consider surgery because getting lines never bothered her. "Who cares?" she says, adding, "If I haven't at this point accomplished more than worrying about my lines, then it's just too bad." In fact, she judges women who are overly concerned about their looks in old age as narcissistic. Teri responds with bewilderment at the very idea of cosmetic surgery. "Even if I could afford it, Frida," she tells me, "I wouldn't spend my money for that. This is life. This is the way it's supposed to be and you're just going against your being."

Arguing that it is unnatural to interfere with life's course, she points to her legs, which run heavy in her family. "But this is the way I am," she exclaims, "and this is the way I'm going to stay. I tell you, you can go and have all that fat pulled. . . . No way. For what?" Laughing, she adds, "Here I am, take me. What you see is what you get!"

Teri, Marny, and others reject cosmetic surgery, in part, because they consider it "unnatural." Yet other feminine practices, like make-up, hair styling, and hair-coloring, also technically "unnatural," are regularly employed by them. A major difference, of course, is the irreversibility and high degree of invasiveness of surgical procedures. Teri's rejection of cosmetic surgery is also based on a profound sense of self-acceptance. She may well fit the profile drawn by numerous studies that suggest that "the less completely a woman has conformed to the conventional ideals of domestic femininity, the more likely she is to age with pride and independence, maintaining a positive self-image in later life."[37]

Anna reveals a similar sense of self when she says, "That's fine for them [people who have surgery]. . . . I would die first." I ask her why. "I'm me. . . I don't feel it's important to me." Both Teri and Anna, in their own ways, seem to be asking, explicitly and implicitly, the same question, a question that to them seems rhetorical, needing no answer or clarification: "For what?" Other women raise this question too, but for them there is an implied answer.

Harriet feels she has had too many noncosmetic surgeries already. Besides, she says, "I think at this stage of the game, why am I going to make myself beautiful, for what?" Martha tells me that sometimes she thinks about cosmetic surgery, but given other physical things going on in her life, she would not want it. As she reflects further, she concludes, "No, not at all. And what would be the point of it? My husband is getting older, too." Shaina is watching herself in the mirror at Julie's when she says that her daughter, like herself, is developing "chins" and is looking into cosmetic surgery. I ask her if she is, as well. There's too much going on medically with herself, she tells me. Besides, "Who would I do it for? I'm married." In a similar vein, Beatrice informs me that "Jane Fonda had everything done, from top to bottom. . . . To me, it's silly. Of course she's an actress, she might need it if she wants to keep going. But what do I need it for? I'm not looking for a man." These reflections confirm the notion that many women view themselves from the perspective of the male gaze. They seem to be saying that the purpose behind cosmetic surgery and its concomitant younger look is to please a man, whether husband or not. In the very act of rejecting cosmetic surgery these women reveal the processes of internalized objectification at work.

These women's age may account in part for their rejection of surgery. Today many women have cosmetic surgeries in their forties and fifties. The cost of these procedures has declined with technological improvements, leading to large numbers of people seeking such interventions. It remains to be seen what will be the attitudes and experiences about these matters of currently middle-aged women, like Shaina's daughter, when they become older themselves.

Some women, like Teri and Anna, reject cosmetic surgery because of an acceptance of themselves as they are; they are therefore less likely than others to engage in self-objectification. In some cases self-acceptance in the face of aging is articulated through a positive valuation of wrinkles. Martha recognizes that she has lines in her face, and she comments, "I think they are character lines. I don't really see that they're necessarily detractors." Lucy says of her facial lines, "I earned every one of them. Are you kidding? I would love to get rid of them. Would I love it enough to do something about it? No. . . . There's really nothing uglier than someone who is in their sixties and wants to look like they're in their forties and doesn't realize you can't fool Mother Nature. . . . You must accept it. Hey, this is what it is."

Reva is on the same wave length. Speaking of her wrinkles, she says,

> I earned every one of these, and I figure these are my stripes. My service stripes. Now, I camouflage them, I cover them up. . . . I look at some of these women who have had face lifts, like June Allyson. . . . It's ridiculous; her face looks like a girl of sixteen. Now, the woman is in her seventies, and you can see her face is all puffy and all that. . . . My lines will come and that's all. . . . You just take every day as it comes and be grateful for things that come. I count my blessings for the good things; the bad things, you can't help them.

These comments by Martha, Lucy, and Reva suggest that our culture furnishes older women with at least one positive reading of the older body to counterbalance the more copious and usual negative associations with it. In this instance, wrinkles are seen as marks of accomplishment, as "service stripes" or "character lines."[38]

Other customers reveal widely held cultural values when they criticize other older women: those who cross some kind of boundary regarding age-appropriate looks. Marny, for example, argues that "You don't have to dress like an old lady, but you shouldn't dress like a teenager. . . . Some women look ridiculous. I want to cry for them. It's sad. Who are they kidding?" Teri's judgment is even harsher when she criticizes older women who wear very short dresses when their "legs are like so. [She holds her hands wide apart to signify ample girth.] You make a fool of yourself." Then, with her characteristically hearty laugh, she adds, "Two-ton hussy in this little tiny thing!" Sadie addresses her concerns in this way: "I never put too much make-up on. I think a lot of these older women are putting on too much make-up. It doesn't look good at all." Clara agrees when she criticizes an eighty-year-old customer's make-up and black hair coloring. "It's sad, it's sad because she's an old person. You could wipe the makeup off. You know the Japanese geisha girls? This is what she has. It's white and red and dark blue and black. And then she has her eyebrows made black, when she dyes her hair. And you see people like that. . . . There's all kinds of people." Fannie used to dye her hair a reddish color, but as she got older she switched to blond, explaining, "I did not want to become one of those old women with red hair and a face full of wrinkles. Have you seen them? It looks awful!" Teri gets her hair colored a very light blond. At one point she asked Verena, her beautician, if she should not darken it: "Well, I'm getting older, and well, I got lines in my face and I think maybe it looks kind of floozieish. You know, my hair may be too light." Verena disagreed and Teri has remained a blonde.

The broad picture that emerges from these views is a complex and disheartening one. On the one hand, women feel pressured to look young as long as possible, for *looking* old reveals the dirty little secret that one *is* old; that is a devastating admission when it comes to social acceptability and self-esteem, not because of how these women live their older age—most are active and vital—but because of the cultural stereotypes that abound and that they frequently have internalized. Looking old transgresses contemporary ideals of feminine beauty, thereby denying women one of the only forms of social power and affirmation available to them. It is the individual's responsibility to prevent such transgression: The woman who looks old, who "lets herself go," is seen as unvirtuous in this regard as well as potentially depressed. Hence older women are encouraged to rely on practices that promise improvement over the unimproved face and body. Some of these practices are of course in continuity with those of younger women, as well.

On the other hand, measures taken to appear younger must be carefully selected lest one give away the carefully crafted but appropriately hidden strategies of age disguise. Thus, coloring the hair is acceptable providing it detracts from, rather than highlights, facial wrinkles. It must look natural, not artificial, for it is considered ridiculous when it departs too much from common-sense reality, as in the case of older women wearing pitch-black hair, practically a natural impossibility among older white women. The same careful choreography of self-presentation obtains regarding dress. Look youthful, but not too youthful, for you might give away your desperate need to stay looking young: "Who are you kidding?"

Ageism

A significant literature has emerged in recent years documenting the presence of age prejudice—ageism—in the way older women are represented and treated in American society. Some of this literature is written by specialists, some by older women themselves.[39] For example, Baba Copper, who belongs to the second category, draws a distinction between aging as a physiological or psychological process and ageism, a kind of "social aging": "Aging is a real process, which takes place differently in each individual. Ageism, on the other hand, is a constriction that rearranges power relationships, just like any other kind of discrimination or prejudice. When one ages, one may gain or lose. With ageism, one is shaped into something that is *always* less than what one really is."[40]

We have seen that some ageist attitudes are internalized by women—customers and staff alike—and embedded in the discourse at Julie's International Salon. Two interrelated themes have repeatedly emerged in this study of older women's bodily experience. The first reveals pervasive cultural associations of aging with decline and old age with stigma. These associations frequently lead study participants to fear, deny, or cover up bodily manifestations of aging and old age in an ongoing effort to look younger and hence "better." The second theme suggests that physical appearance is a chief measure of women's worth throughout the life cycle. This view perpetuates the cultural elevation of youth, inasmuch as youthful ideals of attractiveness serve as the norm against which all women are evaluated, both by others and by themselves.

Implicit or explicit negative associations with aging and old age are expressed when talking about all kinds of things. Early on in the participant-observation stage of the study, I am at Julie's, speaking with two women about why I wear my hair short. I tell them that after years of wearing it long, I had it cut in order to look more mature—and hence more authoritative—in the classroom. We discuss my actual age today, and they express great surprise, and then approval, about how young I look. One of them asserts that surely it is better for my students that I look young, while her companion nods emphatically in agreement. "Why?" I ask, frankly confused. "It is better for them to look at a young face than at a 'baggy' one. Students will have greater respect for you that way." That evening I append the following reflections to my field notes:

> The level of internalized ageism and projection of negative self-images connected to aging was truly disturbing to me here. This was one of the first times I recall being aware that being considered young-looking—along with the approval that that connotes—is ageist, and that I've been enjoying this attention for years. . . . But realistically they may be right. Looking older has significant costs for women in our society. Maybe they are correct when they say a younger-looking face will reap greater respect than an older one.

I also come to realize that I am guilty of ageist behavior, not just attitudes, when on another occasion I see an old woman sitting at Julie's station. She looks different from virtually all others here, as her clothes reveal a time long past: thick cotton stockings reaching above her knees and a kind of artless shirt dress over a round aged body. I feel resistant to approaching her, partly because it often takes so much energy to start a discussion with someone new, but also because she does not look "with it." This is a response I do not feel proud of, but at least I note it and mobilize myself to strike up a conversation. I hear customers expressing concerns about her age and using the term "old lady" to characterize her. One woman asks rather loudly, "Is she cookoo?" while rotating her index finger near her temple. It is clear, then, that other women label her, perhaps as a way of distancing themselves from her and feeling better about themselves. I discover that the woman is hard of hearing, and there is some memory loss in evidence. But she is also a person with a powerful story to tell, if one is patient—a story of survival during the Second World War in Greece, of gifted children, of artistic development as a painter. "Don't judge a book by its cover," I think to myself. How easily we do so with the elderly.

I decide to explore the question of ageism directly during intensive interviews. Martha, who is sixty-seven, tells me she recently had her first such experience when, while visiting a medical clinic, two young women professionals "talked down" to her. She experienced annoyance at this attitude given that "it was new to me to be treated as if I were an old woman." She also confesses feeling surprise and annoyance when her husband told her she "did not look the part" of the high-powered professional she had been before they met. We begin to talk about the connection between sexism and ageism in that comment, and continue to do so when Martha remembers a moment at her synagogue when she was serving as a discussion leader. After the program, she recalls, the rabbi addressed a question to her husband, not to her, about the topic under consideration. The rabbi's action rendered her invisible, along with her expertise in the matter.

This feeling is familiar to Evelyn, who believes that our society is not very tolerant of older people. "There have been occasions when I have felt—unless it was in my mind—I have felt . . . prejudice . . . like I was a nonentity, was passed by, like I wasn't there." It's hard for her to pin it down, but this happens, for example, when she is ignored after asking a question at a store. It is this experience of marginalization that leads her to seek service from African American sales clerks, if possible; she assumes they will empathize with her marginality. Evelyn also notices an ageist attitude in her daughter. "I want to tell her something and she will listen to me about halfway" and then gets distracted by other members of her family. "And so I just drop the subject."

A similar intergenerational tension exists for Sadie. I ask her if people treat her differently now that she is older. "Um, you know who does? I'll tell you who does. The younger generation. They feel that they're so smart and we're stupid." I ask her to give me an example. She recalls the time her son told her friend that he had gotten a promotion. He had not informed Sadie, and this caused her to feel painfully slighted, her sense of importance in her son's eyes terribly diminished. As an outsider here, I'm not in a position to evaluate whether these experiences are reflective of Evelyn and Sadie's growing older, or whether they represent tensions in parent-child relationships that have been present all along. But from these women's perspectives, they pertain to their age.

A more explicit association with age is evident in this account by Leah. "I was over to my grandnephew's house . . . and I was there quite a while and puttering in the garden. And he says, 'You're getting too old to do this digging. Come on.'" "What did it feel like to you when he said this?" I ask her. "I feel that I was capable of doing what I was doing, you know?" Leah is stung by the condescension she sensed from the young man—his assumption that he knew better than she what she was able or eager to do. But Leah is not vindictive. Instead, she plans her future strategy: "Next time he wants some help in the kitchen, I'll hand him the dish towel and say, 'I'm getting too old for this!'"

Some women believe that old age is not all bad as far as other people's responses are concerned. Sylvia, for example, says that "some people don't pay attention to you because you are old. And some give you respect. Respect. I feel that way, yes. . . . Yes, it depend [sic] on the person. It depend on the background." Harriet obviously identifies with the respect side of things: "As a matter of fact," she says, "Either it's me or I'm noticing it more now. [But] you go into a place, I don't care if it's a store or restaurant, and someone holds the door for you. And I see it more now than I did years ago. And I always thank them. You should do that for somebody all the time." Whether the opening of doors is necessarily a gesture of respect born of equality, however, is questionable. It may express several other things as well: a kind disposition (helping someone physically weaker); a social convention (opening doors and offering seats to the elderly and the disabled); and/or a patronizing attitude. As Copper puts it in regard to younger-older women relations, "Although old women often receive deference, I seldom experience a feeling of real respect from others. Almost never do I sense that I am being approached by a younger woman in the spirit of acceptance, learning or wonder."[41]

Reva does not believe she has ever experienced prejudice related to her age, but she concedes that the media often portray older women in an unfavorable light: "Some of those movies, when I look at some of those movies, and especially when they show the Jewish woman. And they make them such *yentas* [Yiddish for busybodies]. And they're ugly. And the way they speak, with the 'haccent.' We don't speak like that." Lucy also denies experiencing directly any form of ageism. She believes that the way older women are portrayed in the media "is not really the way it is. I think they're portrayed the way the media would prefer you to perceive." For Reva and Lucy, then, the problem is with the representation of older women; however, in their estimate, such representation has had no negative consequences for themselves.

Other women, like Sara and Merle, say that they know that some women experience invisibility and stereotyping, but that this is not part of their personal experience. Still others suggest that it's the older woman's own attitude and comportment that might well determine how she is treated. I'm discussing ageist behaviors and attitudes with Alice. "Have you experienced any of that?" I ask her. "No," she responds, "because I can put on an air that'll freeze 'em. And . . . if you go out, you present yourself well, they have no reason to look at you." "So it has to do with attitude and demeanor, the way you present yourself," I say. "Absolutely. Absolutely. Pretend you have class." I interpret what she's said in this way: "So you devise a strategy to be taken seriously." "Sure. Oh, yes." In like manner, Clara responds emphatically when I ask her if she encounters ageism: "No, no, no! No, I do not. I do not. And the answer is, there are certain people—I know even among my own people—that command respect. By their demeanor, by their deportment, and by the way they carry themselves." By contrast, she adds,

> there are people who do not carry respect. . . . Now I know some of my contemporaries speak very much out of place, silly, stupid, inane things. They make inane quotations that bore people. . . . And so the younger people recognize that. And then they say, "She's an addled old lady." . . . They may not remember that twenty years ago you were as sharp as could be. They remember you today. Today is the day. And I find a lot of my contemporaries do not command respect.

Clara is saying that the only thing people see in those circumstances is the "addled old lady," failing to recognize that the woman's current self-presentation does not signify all she is or has ever been. Commenting on "the way in which modernity partitions each human life into a variety of segments," the philosopher Alasdair MacIntyre writes, "So both childhood and old age have been wrenched away from the rest of human life and made over into distinct realms. And all these separations have been achieved so that it is the distinctiveness of each and not the unity of the life of the individual who passes through those parts in terms of which we are taught to think and feel."[42] In short, MacIntyre provides a historical interpretation of why, when we see an older person, those of us who are younger may only see her age, a point not too different from that made by Gadow about the reductive nature of "oldness."

I tell Clara I recently noticed an older couple at a reception who were left to themselves, seemingly ignored by the others at the table. I wonder whether this happened because they are older. "Well," Clara says, "by the same token, why didn't these older people speak with you? Why didn't they start the conversation? They're the ones who could have almost had control of the table, through their experience of a long life." In other words, Clara believes it is up to older people to take the initiative. "I should be more sure, I should be better versed than you. I'm not talking about book learning. I'm talking about world learning. . . . And I should be able to contain . . . to maneuver that table." For Clara, then, attitudes toward the elderly are well deserved as they correspond to older persons' individual behaviors—people saying inane things, on the one hand, or commanding respect and taking control, on the other. Clara speaks from her experience as an exceptional and exceptionally secure person who is able to contest social norms as most others cannot. She and Alice, both, are aware that the trick to getting respect is to stage a successful level of confidence in public: "Pretend you have class," says Alice. "Contain . . . maneuver that table," advises Clara. The need for such strategy belies a deeper truth, however: Such staging is necessary because simply being yourself, as an older woman, is insufficient to ensure respect.[43] Alice and Clara have found successful adaptive behaviors, on an individual level, to cope with what I see as a significant social and ethical problem: the loss of status, dignity, and respect on the basis of an older body. Religious and philosophical ethics alike hold that respect for persons is a minimum requirement—a *sine qua non*, in fact—for any form of positive social relation. It should be a given, not something people have to earn because of their age. In this regard ageism is like racism, sexism, or anti-Semitism, all of which diminish the person's dignity on the basis of criteria extrinsic to personhood. In the case of older women, of course, ageism and sexism go hand in hand. In the instance of *Jewish* older women, Jewishness and Jewish looks—which we considered in chapter 2—may well contribute to their disempowerment as persons.

Recall Evelyn's dramatic reaction to seeing her photograph described at the beginning of this chapter. She is mortified when she sees the effects of aging and Bell's palsy upon her face. Her reaction leaves me rather shaken, so I discuss it with several people, including an older woman uninvolved in the salon and several friends and colleagues, in order to gain a better under standing of it. Their interpretations include calling her response "extreme," "theatrical," "pathetic," and "neurotic." None of them see it as reflective of a distorted social order. It is viewed simply as an expression of her own inca pacity to be mature. In other words, it is seen as her problem.

The tendency to personalize the problems of the old deserves serious scrutiny. The early feminist maxim, "the personal is political," was aimed at recognizing that women's struggles were not simply limited to individual lives but revealed women's shared burdens imposed by a sexist society. Women's troubles needed to be understood and addressed in a systemic way. Likewise, Copper argues, "It is useful to analyze the state of mind which makes 'natural' and hence mandates oppressive behavior toward old women. This behavior is not noticed—it is the usual way people act without thinking. Age segregation, youth chauvinism, youth/beauty worship, age passing, revulsion for age—all express ageist attitudes which are 'natural,' hence invisible and politically inaccessible."[44] They, too, need to receive analytic attention, ethical evaluation and critique, and social action in a systemic way. To blame Evelyn for her response is, first, to belittle or trivialize her pain and to fail to see that her response may be different in degree, but not in kind, from that of many other women. It is also to disregard the practices that keep women's energies unrelentingly engaged in the pursuit of bodily attractiveness for the sake of public acceptability and psychic self-preservation. Finally, it is also to ignore what is truly "neurotic": the cultural valuing of youth, and of youth alone, and the consequential injury to the self-worth of countless women who live into middle age and beyond.

CHAPTER FOUR

"The Cheese Stands Alone"

Women in Relation to Work, Caring, and the Family

ஜ

Nursing does not belong to a man, it is not his province. A sick child is always the mother's property, her own feelings generally make it so.

—Jane Austen, *Persuasion*

There is no question that during the months that I regularly visit Julie's International Salon, the subject of families and family life is, hands down, the favorite topic of discussion. Conversations might entail a current bulletin on a spouse's condition, plans to attend a grandchild's graduation or wedding, the customer's hosting of the Passover seder meal for the extended family, or reminiscences about one's parents. For most customers of this beauty shop, life's satisfactions seemingly revolve around familial connections.

Beth, for example, tells me that she has had "a meaningful, happy life." "What would you say is the source of that meaning?" I ask her. She responds immediately: "My good parents. I have a very loving brother and a caring sister, a wonderful husband, and four—thank God—devoted children. Two daughters, two sons. Two wonderful sons-in-law. And my beautiful grandchildren. That's my family: my husband, my children, my grandchildren are my life. They mean everything to me."

Harriet pauses to consider the question of life's meaning. Acknowledging that "that's something hard to answer," she adds, "I think I was a pretty good mother. I don't say I was the best, but I was a pretty good mother, and I always tried to be reasonable with my kids, also with my husband."

Reva waxes philosophical: "I've had a beautiful life. Heartaches, problems, things that ran smooth. . . . I am one of the very fortunate people. I can go ahead and say I had a beautiful childhood and a beautiful marriage, and thank God, I got here so far. Happy, yes, I'm happy. Unhappy, yes,

I'm unhappy. Contented, yes. Discontented, yes. But you have to have an even keel." A bit later she attributes her sense of meaningfulness more directly to her familial relationships, adding, "It was very close, very close. And giving of yourself is very important. You know, it's not, 'What can you do for me?' You have to say to yourself, 'You're there to back *them.*' I sound like an old lady, don't I? Oh, my goodness gracious!"

By contrast, when I ask Sara whether she's had a meaningful, fulfilling life, she responds with an unhesitating "No." "No. I wouldn't say that I was unhappy, but [my life] wasn't fulfilled, it wasn't meaningful. . . . The fulfillment wasn't there because we had no children. And no grandchildren."

Except for Reva, all of these women have had considerable employment histories. Reva herself has found great satisfaction in volunteer work for at least a decade. Beth earned a college degree after her children were grown and currently holds a professional position. Harriet owned and managed a tavern for some twenty years, beginning twenty-six years after her marriage. Sara did office work, either full-time or part-time, until her retirement. I point this out to suggest that family evidently takes precedence over paid work in determining life satisfaction for these women. In this way, they probably reflect the experiences of most women of that age in this country, but also the Jewish emphasis on family many grew up with. This is not to say that women did not enjoy their employment outside the home. On the contrary. For many who left their jobs when they started their families, those jobs still elicit powerful, meaningful, and sometimes nostalgic memories.

Paid Employment

Virtually all the women I interview at Julie's International Salon were employed prior to marriage in a range of occupations: office work, retail fashions, teaching, sales. Only a few earned college degrees before marriage; most finished high school, but some took jobs before graduation, frequently out of economic necessity. Some of the older women were married during the Great Depression, others shortly thereafter, yet others during and following the Second World War. Pregnancy, if not the wedding, signaled the end of most women's employment lives, at least until their children were grown. Theirs was a time of sharply divided gender roles in American society, and such roles were viewed as polar opposites. Masculinity was identified with the breadwinner role, femininity with domesticity. Capturing the cultural ideal of the time, Dori says, "When I was growing up, a woman didn't work. It was not expected of them. It wasn't part of your fate." Only by thinking retrospectively does she add rather wistfully, "Now I think I really would have wanted to be a lawyer."

A very common narrative emerging out of my interviews tells the pleasures and fulfillment of the work world experienced by women and the frequently abrupt break from it. Anna was married during the war and for the next three years continued doing office work while her husband was in the service. Then he came home.

> I was working for a company and [my husband] came in; a cousin of mine was working there too, and he came in to say "hello." He came into my boss' office to say, "This is her last day." And he never let me go back to work. The only fights we ever had were when I said, "I'm going to go to work," because we certainly could have used the money, and he wouldn't let me go to work. It was a sore spot with him, and he wouldn't talk to me for a couple of days.

Sometime later her husband started his own business, with the office at home. "I was his secretary. So I really was a working lady. Never got paid for it, but I worked all my life." "Was that satisfying to you?" I ask her. "Yeah, because I had a very wonderful husband, and it didn't matter what we were doing, as long as we were together." Later, however, Anna reiterates ongoing tensions with her husband about work: "He would get very closed mouth, he would get very uptight if I talked about working, yet I *was* working." "Today women get paid for their work," I suggest. "That's right," she replies emphatically. "I used to argue with him. He'd say it wouldn't pay to pay. I guess with the income tax, I don't know, I never understood that."

Teri worked over fifteen years for a major insurance company, beginning as a "little clerk" after two years of high school, leaving as an office manager at age thirty-two, when she got married. "Did you enjoy working?" I ask her. "Oh, I loved it. . . . I didn't want to [quit], but my husband made me. Not because we had so much money. . . ." Her husband essentially bribed her into quitting, given her resistance to his wishes. He planned a vacation trip with Teri's sister and brother-in-law, threatening to go without her—two months after their wedding. "That's how I quit my job. Went to Mexico, on a shoestring. We didn't have any money!" "When you had to quit the job," I ask, "were you angry or resentful?" "No, uh, I missed it very much." "Did you sometimes think about going back?" I press her because I sense her mixed feelings. "I loved it. Yeah. But I never went back." "So you didn't go back because you felt your husband would not approve?" "That's right, yeah." "How did that feel to you?" "Uh, it didn't make any difference. If that's the way he wanted it, fine."

Teri's eyes widen, her voice rises enthusiastically, and her whole demeanor pulses with energy when she talks about her work life. To me this suggests a more complex picture than her last comment indicates: "Uh, it didn't make any difference. If that's the way he wanted it, fine." In my view this statement represents an adaptation to a seemingly no-win situation for her. It does not reflect a *happy* acquiescence to the expectations of contemporary gender roles mirrored in her husband's wishes. In like manner, Anna's ongoing struggles with her husband over the issue of her employment reveal the frustrations experienced by women who don't challenge the system but who are not at peace with it, either. There is an unspoken questioning here of those long-ago choices, now made from a retrospective vantage point several decades later. Both these women are now widows. Their sense of loyalty to their deceased husbands is palpable. Probably there are boundaries they are not willing to cross in judging some of the power dynamics in their marital relationship.

Quitting jobs they loved to meet their spouses' expectations is part of other women's experiences, as well. Beginning in high school and until her marriage at age twenty-two, Reva taught "speech, elocution, the old dramatic art" at a studio downtown. She always loved drama and in the course of her work she discovered that she was "a born teacher." But she concludes her story in this way: "Of course after I got married my husband didn't like the idea that when he came home from work I had to give the children lessons. He wanted quiet. So after that, I didn't bother." "Of course" in this narrative suggests the degree to which Reva internalized cultural norms. It assumes a taken-for-granted, shared perception of how things are or should be.

Sadie worked in fashions from the time she graduated high school to the time she got married, some eighteen years later. She did not continue working after marriage because "My husband didn't want me to work. . . . I loved it. I wish I could . . . go to work today." Shelley adds further information regarding her husband's motivation in this matter: "I was working and he hated it because he was doing very well [financially]." A man's social prestige was contingent on his ability to support a non-employed wife. Notions of masculinity and femininity were therefore interconnected. A successful husband was defined, in part, by an economically dependent wife. So no matter what the satisfactions the wife might enjoy from her work, as most of the women indicate, or the financial need of the family, many middle-class women were pressed to relinquish their interests and desires for the sake of their husbands'. In Reva's case her husband's need is identified as a desire for quiet after a day's work, an extension of the idea that the man's rightful place is in the marketplace and his home is his castle—a *refuge* from the work-a-day world—not to be contaminated by the hustle and bustle of that work world (his wife's, in this case).

Not all participants in this study fit the preceding picture, however. Women's educational level, childbearing history, and social class influenced their work histories. The three women with college degrees at the time of marriage—Merle, Martha, and Lucy—did not stop working outside the home, though Lucy cut down to part-time employment for a period of time. Martha never had children; Merle and Lucy were involved in the now more typical juggling of family and careers among middleclass women. These women were economically independent, and that probably contributed to their self-directedness in determining the course of their work lives. Four additional participants—Beatrice, Sara, Leah, and Sylvia—the first two childless, the last two mothers, also worked throughout their lives, motivated in large measure by economic need. Social class, therefore, dictated employment decisions in their case, a picture consistent with the experience of working-class women since the nineteenth century.

Clara represents an interesting mix of these approaches to work life. At age fourteen, only one year into high school, she got a full-time job as a typist in order to help her family when "things were very, very bad financially." She worked at that and "better" jobs for several years until, after marriage, she became pregnant. While raising her two children, she and her husband saved some money, as "we were looking for a business." Clara's cousin suggested they open a "maternities" shop, but

> I didn't want to. I had been a secretary. What did I know about buying and selling? But my husband was the type of man who was very adventurous when it came to business. I was [visiting] in [an East Coast city] at the time with the children. He comes in, and he said, 'You're in business, do you know that?' I said, 'What?' He said, 'I rented a shop. You're going into the maternity business.' I said, 'I know nothing about it.' He said, 'You'll learn.'

As it turns out, Clara's husband was right. She learned the various skills of the trade, became highly successful, and grew to love the work. Nine years later, Clara's son had joined the business, which by then had expanded into many stores and been shifted from maternities to uniforms. At that point, Clara reminisces,

> I dropped out voluntarily because the manufacturers all knew me. . . . They were calling me [all the time], and I didn't want that for my men. I felt that *they* should be the leaders. And so I said to them, "You know something, I am going to retire. I like my luncheons, and I like my organizations, and I like my card playing, and I want to be with the [grand]children." And I dropped out. Because I felt *they* should be the important issues: my son and

my husband. I didn't want to be there because all those years in maternities, [the manufacturers] all knew me, and I didn't want that. I didn't want that. It does something to a man. Definitely. Although my husband was very, very proud of every, any accomplishment that I accomplished. Still, I didn't want it.

I ask Clara if she has ever regretted retiring at that point because she has told me of the excitement and pleasure she derived from this work. "No, no, never," she responds. "Never, because I was not truly a professional woman. I wasn't. I did it out of need." "So it wasn't hard to give up that excitement?" I know I may be projecting, but I still think this is a fair question. She replies, "No. No. It wasn't. Because I gave it up for a better reason than my keeping it. I gave it up for, actually, the men in my life. And it wasn't hard because I had so many other interests. . . . But I was never left out of the business. If there were really decisions to be made . . . well, we were very thickly knit." She means here that she was always consulted in those decisions.

In Clara's mind her success at work somehow diminished the success of her men. There is an implied zero-sum gain here: If she was known by the manufacturers—if they asked for her and not for her husband or son—"it does something to a man." This implies that his self-esteem is injured if he is not "the leader," the "important issue" in the work environment, especially if his wife or mother is, instead. Clara opted to do the right thing: "I gave it up for a better reason than my keeping it."

What kind of moral universe does Clara's decision reveal? It seems to me that it supports the dualistic division of labor, alluded to earlier, between masculinity and femininity, man's rightful place in the public world of work and women's appropriate place in the private world of home and family. Notice that such division is not dependent on whether women can *in fact* successfully cross over into men's space, since it is evident that Clara did so, initially "out of need." Clara's world was so constructed, however, that her decision to withdraw is viewed by her as a gesture of love and caring. She intended her decision to be seen as an expression of generosity and nobility, not to be expected from a man, but somehow fitting for a woman. Recall Reva's view that "You have to say to yourself, 'You're there to back *them*.'"

Another way to view this issue is more directly along power lines: Men have power over the public world of work; women have control over the private world of home and family. Traditionally this division of labor has been seen as separate but equal. Known in nineteenth-century America as the two-spheres division of gender roles, it was operative in slightly dif ferent form in Eastern European Jewish culture, as well. Men, but not women, had access to the worlds of study and public worship there, while women were responsible for home and children, and, frequently, for making a living, as well. While these were separate worlds, they were not really equal since social status accrued much more to male than to female activities.[1] Likewise, in American society, the worlds of home and family have been devalued ever since work and home came to occupy different spaces with industrialization. Here, too, we tend to see the public world of paid work, still conceptually associated with men, as far more significant than the frequently unseen world of housekeeping, childrearing, and caring in general, still associated with women.

To apply these ideas to Clara's narrative, her decision suggests that she, like other Americans, internalized the sexual division of labor—along with its social valuations. She relinquished her place in the public arena of business to allow her men to reap the social benefits therein, such as recognition and status. She was content to pursue private activities she found rewarding because in the balance she found her men's needs overriding hers. She could find satisfaction in her own sphere. They needed to find it in theirs.

According to Susan Moller Okin, the gender inequalities of the marketplace do not disappear at the threshold of our homes. In fact, in *Justice, Gender, and the Family*, she argues that in American society, the family often is an important teacher of injustice because it socializes children to perpetuate male over female power. Okin writes: "Given the emphasis our society places on economic success, belief in the male provider role strongly reinforces the domination of men within marriage. . . . the fact that a husband's work is predominantly paid gives him not only status and prestige, both within and outside the marriage, but also a greater sense of entitlement." She goes on to say that "it is clearly the case that the possession by each spouse of resources valued by the *outside* world, especially income and work status, rather than the resources valuable primarily within the family, has a significant effect on the distribution of power in the relationship."[2]

A case in point is Reva's having to stop giving elocution lessons when her husband expressed a need for quiet when he got home. Or take Shelley's experience in the years she was raising her children and was not employed outside the home:

> As active as I was in organizational work, my husband used to be home at five o'clock, and he liked his dinner when he came home at five. And I'd always leave the meeting before anyone else. "So, he'll eat a little later" [a

friend suggested]. I said, "No. He chooses to eat then; then it will be ready." My mother taught me that when your husband comes home, you and your children have to be clean and neat, and the table needs to be set.

In both cases the man as provider takes precedence over the woman as housewife, mother, and volunteer worker.

Okin's perspective might help us understand why some husbands made decisions regarding their wives' work lives that appear unreasonable from a contemporary egalitarian position. We have seen that in many cases the husband insisted that the wife quit her job at the time of marriage or soon thereafter. Harriet went through a similar pattern, leaving her workplace to raise her three children for many years. We are sitting at her kitchen table as she reminisces:

> I stayed at home and my husband had a business of his own . . . an auto blast business. Then all of a sudden he says to me, "I want to buy a tavern." I said, "What do you need a tavern for? You have a business." He kept saying it, so I said, "Do what you want and don't bother me." And one Saturday I come home from the beauty shop and my younger son says to me, "Dad called and he wants you to call him at this number." So I called and I asked for him, and he says, "Come on down. I just bought a tavern." I went down, and I says, "Who's gonna run it?" And he says, "You."

I contain my incredulity as I ask in a tempered tone, "So he didn't consult you?" Harriet's simple answer is "No." She adds, "And that's how I got into the tavern business. I didn't know the first thing about it." This reminds me of Clara's husband's purchase of a maternity shop, despite the fact that she had objected to that sort of business. These cases do not involve the husband's opposition to the wife's working, but, rather, his decision that she do the work of his choice. When it comes to issues of paid work, then, the husbands of many women exercised control in the relationship.

Women's Work of Caring

With paid employment not an option for many of the women I interviewed, their work lives came to revolve around domesticity. Women's involvement with home and family reveals a dimension of their lives popularly obscured from public appreciation: their work of caring. As we saw in chapter 1, caring is a broad term, connoting, in Barbara Andolsen's words, "an ongoing pattern of actions that are designed to create and sustain positive relationships among human beings. The one who acts from a stance of care responds to the one-cared-for in a fashion that minimizes harm, comforts and, to the extent possible, increases opportunities for growth and joy."[3]

Women's work for home and family—the work of caring—is, decidedly, work. Household work includes meal planning and preparation, grocery shopping, and entertaining; house-cleaning such as vacuuming, dusting, scrubbing, wiping, dish-washing, toilet-cleaning, bed-making, floor-washing and waxing, laundry washing, folding, and ironing, window washing, general pick-up and straightening, garbage disposal; minor and major repairs, decorating, painting; paying bills; purchasing miscellaneous products and household items; and so forth.

Childrearing involves major skills and energy output: feeding and changing infants, running after toddlers, reading stories, singing and teaching songs, playing, shopping for clothes, doctor and dentist visits, tending sick children, helping with homework, library visits, shopping for school needs, taking children to various activities, making birthday parties, going on outings to parks, museums, picnics, disciplining, and so on. None of this includes the more ephemeral tasks of providing a supportive and loving environment for the child.

In fact, as the philosopher Sara Ruddick convincingly demonstrates, mothering should be thought of as a practice that places major demands on the mother—for the child's preservation, growth, and social acceptability. "To be a mother," Ruddick writes, "is to be committed to meeting these demands by works of preservative love, nurturance, and training." These tasks analytically organize the activities ordinarily associated with mothering, listed above. Preservative love acknowledges children's physical vulnerability and the mother's need to respond to it in order to secure the children's survival and enable them to thrive. Nurturance involves addressing the child's need for emotional and intellectual growth, recognizing that children are "complex and needy beings." Finally, training is a demand made by the mother's social groups, requiring that she train her children to be acceptable, that is, in accordance with group ideals.[4] Mothers respond to these demands with deliberate thought; their responses are neither easy nor automatic.

A parallel argument regarding women's cooking responsibilities is advanced by sociologist Marjorie Devault in *Feeding the Family*. According to Devault, feeding the family involves, not only food provisioning and preparation, but giving careful consideration to nutritional, economic, and interpersonal needs and to gustatory preferences.[5]

These descriptions of work are readily validated experientially by women who have "kept house" and raised children. Yet our society does not give adequate credit for the work that women do for home and family. In fact, frequently this work, which is often exhausting and never-ending, is rendered invisible by not being acknowledged as actual work. The irony here is that this work is essential on several grounds. Childrearing, for one, contributes directly to the reproduction of society's labor force—that is, the next generation of workers. Childrearing practices create emotionally healthy and productive individuals or the converse. And a clean, pleasant environment and regular, prepared meals lead to psychological well-being and emotional equanimity in addition to meeting survival needs. All of these tasks contribute not only to the quality of the child's life, but also to that of the husband. The wife is instrumental in facilitating his life in the paid work world, even when she herself is employed.

In light of the importance of women's caring work, then, why is it culturally devalued? I can advance several explanations. First, it is unpaid work. Our social values are shaped by a capitalist economy whereby that which commands a price is seen to be worthy. Since we do not pay for women's work in the home, that work in effect becomes viewed as nonwork.

Second, related to the first issue, women's caring work takes place in the context of home, the private domestic world, which becomes invisible and insignificant when compared with where the real meaningful social action is seen to be happening: in the public world of business, the corporation, and the factory, the halls of academe, the centers of government.

Third, women are socialized into caring for others from an early age. Sylvia tells me, "I was raised to take care of others." I ask her where she learned this. "At home, at school, everywhere." This socialization is frequently mistaken for women's *natural* inclinations to nurture and to put others' needs before their own, to be willing to do the work no one else is expected or prepared to do. It may be more accurate to say that women may have little choice as to whether they will do this work or not, given their uneven access to power when compared to that of their spouses. None of this should distract us from the necessity of this kind of work: It is essential work, it needs to be done. The question here is one of equity and justice. We must ask, Who is doing the caregiving, and on whose terms?

Fourth, much of the work that women do is physical, bodily work. While thought informs a great deal of it, the actual observed work is physical—whether it involves comforting a child, cooking dinner, or scrubbing the toilet bowl. In Western thought, as we saw in chapter 2, the bodily has been viewed as inferior to the intellectual and the spiritual, needing to be kept under control. Not coincidentally, women have been associated with the body, men with mind and spirit. Therefore, women have been devalued. The diminished value of women in this society thus accounts in part for the diminished value of their work.

Fifth, some of the work of women is emotional work, e.g., calming a frightened child or helping a husband deal with defeat and insecurity, and emotions are suspect in our philosophical and cultural traditions. Emotions are to be underplayed in the serious world of work. They presumably show weakness. Not surprisingly, professions that revolve around emotions—such as the clergy or the psychotherapeutic professions—frequently come to be seen as culturally feminized.

The centrality of work for home and family for Julie's customers emerges first during photo-elicitation. I ask study participants to show me photographs of themselves at various stages of their lives: youth, middle age, the present. We talk a good deal about issues of appearance and self-understanding. But I also ask some very open-ended questions: Who were you then? What was your life like? If you didn't know the woman on the picture, what would you say about her? In previous chapters I have discussed some of the women's responses to these queries. Here I want to lift out an emergent theme related to their lives within their families, namely, the work of caring. As women look backward and forward in time, caring work typically has included housekeeping, feeding, child-rearing (for those who became mothers), and care of husbands, ailing parents, and other relatives.

Most women enjoyed the work of caring for home and family. Sara and her husband, who had lived for many years in her crowded parents' apartment, moved to their own apartment after her mother died. "I was happy to be my own *balabusta* [Yiddish for good housekeeper]," she exclaims.

When her children were little, Dori was involved in an accident that rendered her partially paralyzed. Yet as the children were growing up, she would help them with their homework, also taking responsibility for family finances—writing checks for all the household bills.

In her early years as a wife and mother, Evelyn delighted in home and children: "Those were good years because I was so absorbed with taking care of [the family], of keeping the house clean. And I was thrilled with the house. Having had nothing in [my childhood], I thought this was a mansion. This little bitty ol' house. And I always wanted the meals to be perfect." She delighted in her baby son: "I was so thrilled with him. . . . And I was so proud to take him to the park. . . . I don't think I thought of myself very much then. I only thought of him." Later on she would spend time and energy planning her two children's parties and baking special birthday cakes for them.

The notion of not thinking of oneself, but only of those one cares for, is common. The other's needs—whether husband's or child's—take precedence over one's own: "It's not, 'What can you do for me?' You have to say to yourself, 'You're there to back *them*.'" At times this orientation takes on a strongly self-sacrificial dimension. Anna characterizes her life in her forties in this way: "It was the same running [as earlier in her life]. I have always been a running person." She juggled caring for an ailing mother and taking care of her husband and daughter, in addition to the secretarial work she did for her husband. "I was a very busy lady. Nothing for myself, always for others." "How did that feel?" I ask. "I don't know. I'm happier that way. If I can't be doing something for somebody else, I feel depressed." "Do you enjoy doing something for yourself?" "I never have. I don't understand it." This reminds me of my Grandma Ella. In my family ethos, she was seen as rather saintly for her self-giving ways—continually doing for her family, seldom a thought for herself. I no longer see this as saintly. I see it as a loss of subjectivity for women socialized into traditional domestic roles: others' worlds and wills always taking precedence over their own. In the process women renounce their own wills, their own needs, their own desires. At times they cannot even identify them.

Carol Gilligan observes such a tendency among women—a tendency to identify goodness with self-sacrifice and to deny the self when assessing their moral responsibilities to others. She argues that as women develop morally, they come to include the self in considerations of moral responsibility.[6] In short, they come to care for themselves as well. One of Julie's customers captures this move for me when she says, "I always used to do for others. Now I do for myself."

Women in this study either enjoyed being full-time wives and mothers, or they were pressed to juggle these tasks with the demands of paid work. When Sylvia looks at a photograph of herself at age forty-three, for example, she explains who she was then: "A mother, a wife, a working mother, OK? Always I'm working. . . . I never had time. I was working twelve hours a day, and then I had the jobs in the house." She did not have much time to devote to the children, but she did so more than her husband. And she had no time for socializing, which pained her deeply. Born in Poland and a survivor of the Holocaust, Sylvia's experience of always rushing through her life in America was nonetheless redeemed by the sense that here "I had a future. I had a future." Sylvia's deep need for friendships went unmet, given her demanding life. After long hours at their store, she—and mostly she alone—had to attend to home and family. Despite the contemporary agitation for greater equality in the household between working husbands and wives, current patterns in the division of household labor have not changed significantly from the time Sylvia was juggling work and home. For example, in *If Women Mattered*, economist Marilyn Waring cites a 1984 survey that shows that "72 percent of American women do most of the house cleaning, 75 percent cook most of the meals, and only 40 percent say their partners share equally in taking care of the children."[7] Men whose wives are employed do not put significantly more time into household work than those whose spouses are housewives.[8]

Lucy admits that she had a hard time being a full-time mother. "When I was twenty-seven, I was getting really nuts, boredom, unbelievable boredom. I thought I would lose my mind. I went to Girl Scouts, went to Campfire Girls, the whole business." A restless and energetic woman, Lucy got herself a part-time job as a private investigator while her children were young. In this regard she is an exception because many women were strongly committed to staying at home to raise their children and enjoyed the experience.

Beth's children went to a Jewish parochial school. She tells me:

> I would've needed to work because ... expenses were very high. But I didn't. I felt I had my children, and I should be home with them. And I was there. When they needed to go to the library, or "Ma, I need a new pencil, I need a new workbook ... I need this book for tomorrow morning." And for a while I wasn't driving. So I learned to drive, and so then I was more independent. . . . I was very happy with them, and I grew up with them, and they grew up with me, with us, and it was very nice.

Shelley expresses similar sentiments when she says, "I don't think a mother should work full-time. . . . I made it my business to be home to make dinner. I came home before [the children] came home. No matter what time they came home, I made a meal for them. You know you work at relationships with children. It is not a given. It's a struggle. And it's a struggle with the husband."

Clara has an interesting attitude toward childrearing, an attitude shaped in contrast to her own upbringing. She tells me,

> I made a success of my marriage. My husband was a very happy man. We were a very happy couple. My children were very happy. . . . We were just talking about it the other day, what a happy childhood they had. There were just the four of us, and every Sunday was children's day. They could do whatever they wanted to do. And usually it was a picnic. And if it rained, it poured, we had that picnic. . . . We never disappointed them, if it was humanly possible. And they grew up with that feeling. They didn't have that disappointment. You know, my mother, God bless her. It could be sunshiny, and if my father said, "Let's go to [a park] and we'll rent a rowboat, and

we'll take the children." "It could rain," [my mother would answer], "it could rain by four o'clock." My mother was a pessimist. I'm an optimist. And, so, there lies the difference.

Teri also alludes to the emotional work involved in raising a child. She recalls that her daughter

was a little hard to handle sometimes, and I'd say to her father, "I don't know why she hates me" [laughing]. . . . When she was little, he'd come home from work and I'd say, "Oh, God, what a day!" He'd say, "Yeah. I had a bad day too." I got smart. I never told him anymore. Because whenever I would say, "Oh, what a day!" or "I had a bad day," I thought, "Sympathy I'm not gonna get from him. So forget it!"

Teri's story communicates the experience women frequently have that their caring work is not given its due, that it is not taken seriously as "real" work, certainly not when compared with socially authenticated work, that is, paid work—the husband's.

For women who did not have children, the expectation that they care for others' needs is by no means absent. Martha arrives at Julie's quite exhausted one day, after having had some thirty people over to dinner the previous night. She did all the cooking and is now almost done cleaning up. When she married her third husband six years ago, she joined his large family clan. I ask if she enjoys all this. She says, "No. It's a lot of work, but it's expected of family and I don't want to break the tradition." Some months later, when I interview her at home, she tells me, "It's difficult. . . . There's always something going on. Right now we have another niece who's getting married . . . and I'm involved in the bridal shower, posters . . . that we're sending out, invitations, and dealing with this thing and that thing, and so on. And we'll have guests in this house for the wedding." She concedes that sometimes she enjoys this involvement. "Yeah, to some extent. Not always. It is a lot of work. Every year they're here for the holidays, there's a lot of work. . . . There's a certain amount of wear and tear." I ask, "And the ethos of the family is that you cannot say no, that you have to participate in these things?" "Yes," she replies. "You're expected. You're expected." The demands that Martha responds to come from her husband's family. She's expected to respond, I suspect, because that's what women in families do; they are responsible for "this thing and that." In the words of Jane Addams, this represents the "family's claim" on women's time, resources, and energy.[9]

Sara sounds exasperated when she tells me that though her husband has a heart condition, "He doesn't take care of himself. He's here because of me. Because I'm his wife. And I say that without any vanity or any pride. It's just a statement of fact, that's all. Maybe if we had children, maybe I wouldn't have had so much time to take care of him." Note that Sara does not question her obligation to care for her husband. It's simply a question of how much time she has to do it. Her exasperation has less to do with her doing this work, I believe, than her implied view that her husband's neglect of his health is a threat to them both.

Beatrice is also childless. Speaking of her husband, she says, "Oh, he depends on me so much." She recollects a conversation she had with her doctor about her husband. "'I have a husband that depends on me,' I said, 'and I have to take care of him. God gave me this to do.'" She then adds, "I feel this is my mission, I really do. 'Cause I had loads of boyfriends. Gorgeous guys. I had so much to choose from. And somehow, in my mind, [he was] the guy who was really good to me. He is so good to me." Later, she tenderly captures her caregiving in this way, "I treat him like a little baby. I say, 'Come here, _____ . Come here. How are you today?' He has constant headaches. . . . He complains once in a while. I'll tell him, 'Go take a nap, dear,' 'cause when he takes a nap, he can't feel it." Beatrice is saying, in so many words, that it is her purpose in life to care for her husband.

From their middle age to the present, virtually all the women in this study have undertaken familial caregiving responsibilities beyond the scope of childrearing. This has typically included caring for adult children, for ailing parents and other relatives, and for husbands—well and ill.

Sadie recently went to help one of her daughters when she gave birth to her first baby: "I was a great help to her this time, and she couldn't get over it. Sometimes I think that your own kids don't know what you can do [laughs]. Really." Sylvia occasionally baby-sits for her grandchildren as a way of easing her children's lives. Likewise, Lucy says, "I [baby-sit] because it helps our kid. That's the reason I do it, not for self-fulfillment or anything else." Dori frequently responds to her adult children's needs for money and home-cooked meals, while Shelley routinely provides emotional support for her middle-aged, married sons: "My sons always feel that I'm there [for them]. To this day, I laugh. If they have something that's troubling them—they don't feel well or something comes up. Now this is a fifty-two-year-old and a forty-five-year-old. They call Mommy." These examples should question the uncritical and blanket assumption frequently present in public policy discussions that older people constitute only a drain on social resources. They suggest, instead, that many older people—certainly many older women—make significant contributions, financial and otherwise, to their families.[10] This can also be seen in caregiving to ailing parents. This practice, often stretching into years, is virtually universal among the customers that I speak to.

Clara and her husband supported both her parents for a period of time because her father had a heart condition and was unable to work. After he passed away, they supported the mother in her own home for some ten years before her death. In similar fashion, Merle tells me her mother outlived her father by fifteen years: "She was a widow all those years and she lived alone. And then I guess the last few years she wasn't too well and we didn't think that she should live in the apartment by herself. So we managed to get a lady, like a companion, to take care of her." In both these cases, the care given is indirect: Clara and Merle were involved instrumentally in their mothers' care. As Joan Tronto would put it, they were "taking care of" their mothers by assuming responsibility for their need and determining ways to respond to it.[11]

By contrast, many other women were involved in what Tronto calls actual "caregiving," directly meeting their parents' need for care. This kind of caring actually involves physical work.[12] Sadie brought hospital beds into her living room so she could take care of her parents when they were bedridden. "They were my parents and I was there for them. . . . My mother and father never had to go to a home because I was there [for them]." She expresses some resentment that her siblings did not do their part. I mirror her feelings. "Sounds like you wanted . . . to take care of your parents when they were ill and other people in your family who could have helped didn't." "I felt they could have," Sadie responds. "I felt that way but I never said anything. I never said anything. What for? It was my house and I was capable. I could do it." A keen sense of responsibility, not fairness, drove Sadie's caregiving.

In like manner, Blanche discusses with Julie and me her responsibility toward her mother. She is sitting at a station while Julie combs out her hair. Blanche took care of her mother, who lived with Blanche, for the last four and half years of her life. During that period, her mother had four strokes, which sometimes rendered her irrational: "When her blood flowed she was aware. When it didn't, she wasn't." At times her mother did not recognize her. When Blanche would sometimes ask her, "Why do you hate me?" her mother would reply, "I don't hate you. I love you," obviously oblivious of her behavior. Blanche seems to take pride in telling us that "not once during those years did I ever tell my husband when he came home from work what I'd gone through with my mother. Why burden him with that? He thought everything was fine. He thought my mother was wonderful." Though at some point she hired someone to help her with the work, Blanche typically put in a twelve-hour day in caregiving, mostly staying around the house.

I ask Blanche how she dealt with her feelings. She becomes indignant. "Feelings? I don't believe in feelings. It was my obligation [to care for my mother]!" I pursue the point by asking her if she talked to friends who might sympathize and give her support. "There is nothing to talk about," she responds tersely. "They would have told me to put her somewhere, and I did not want to hear that. I don't believe in talking about my personal feelings, about complaining." A bit later, more pensively, she adds, "You *are* your mother." Addressing Julie now, she asks, "You know what I mean, right?" As Julie nods, I want to know what Blanche means by this. She says, "Because you came from her." "Would you feel the same about your father?" "Yes."

Blanche's sense of responsibility in caregiving seemingly devolved from a commitment to reciprocity. Since her mother gave birth to her, she owed her very existence to her, and the least that she could do was respond in kind: by giving all of herself for the mother's sake. For Blanche this appeared to be a lonely endeavor, a burden not to be shared with husband or friends. Why should her husband be burdened, too? There was a kind of strength, however, that Blanche derived from doing this work alone. Perhaps she felt this was a test of her moral courage: Could she meet her moral obligations unassisted? Could she disregard her own exhaustion, sadness, and pain for the sake of meeting her responsibilities to her mother?

Obligation seems to be the principal motivator in the caring work of Merle, Clara, Sadie, and Blanche. Other women indicate that they were also motivated by their emotional closeness to their parents, by their own enjoyment in being around them. "I had a wonderful mother," Anna exclaims, "and in the last years of her life she was quite ill. She was at [her own] home, but she had oxygen. I went every day, and I did her hair. . . and I cut her hair for her, and her nails were always done." After her mother's death, Anna's father moved in with her family. She speaks warmly about that time in her life, when he participated in her family's life. "I sleep well because my conscience is clear. I took good care of them. I took good care of them. We were good friends, besides [being] parent and child. Absolutely no problem."

Teri presents a similar picture. After her father's death, Teri's mother spent winters with Teri and summers with one of Teri's sisters for a number of years. "Mom was a delight to have, though. . . . She was something else, you know. I enjoyed having her. And I think she enjoyed being here because when it was time to go off to my sister's, she said, 'Do I have to go?' . . . She was funny."

When Sara was in her forties, her parents were not well. "I was always concerned about them and with them." But care is more than a disposition or an attitude. It also involves action: "When my father had to go to the doctor, I took him. My mother, unfortunately, had to go to the hospital by ambulance. I was the one that went in the ambulance. So my life only changed because I had more grief then, and I also had more anxiety then." I ask Sara if her siblings were also involved in caring for her parents. "No. They couldn't handle it like I did." She explains that she, and not her sisters, was on top of her parents' medical needs. Her parents were ill for a long time, a matter of years, "as long as I can remember. . . . My mother finally took to her bed altogether. And then I quit my job. Who's gonna work? I mean, somebody has to work in the family." Sara also tells me of times she took care of her sisters when they were unwell. "It sounds like you've often had to be in the role of caretaker," I reflect. "Always, from the time I can remember, from the time I can remember." "Has that felt like a burden to you?" I ask her. "No, no, no. . . . No, I never felt [that]. No way. My parents were too good. Too good to me. They deserved the best care they could get." Here again is a statement that assumes reciprocity in the act of caregiving. Reciprocity, of course, was not literally in place in the actual caregiving situation under discussion. Sara's parents were dependent on her; they were the vulnerable parties in the relationship. Yet in the history of their relationship, her parents got what was coming to them: They deserved it. Her emotional closeness to them precluded her from experiencing them as a burden. She was simply returning their kindness. Her sense of responsibility to her parents becomes contextualized within a relationship of mutuality. This is not obligation rooted in external, abstract rules. This is responsibility born of relationship and fueled by affection. "Discretionary" motives—such as affection and emotional closeness—to use a term current in family studies, often accompany "obligatory" motives in caregiving.[13]

Sara did not experience caring for her parents as a burden, as I have noted. But through the years she has wished that she were not so alone in her caregiving responsibilities. Her mother, it seems, miscarried when Sara was a few months old. "I don't know how they found out, even, in those years, but she was told it was a boy. And to this day, I think to myself, 'Oh, what I could have done with a brother. To take the responsibility off my shoulders." A bit later, referring to her husband, she says, "I used to think he was wrong. He never worried about anything. To this day, he doesn't worry. 'Cause he always said to me, 'You worry enough for the two of us.' And I always resented that, too. I would say, 'Well, take a few problems off my hands!'" For this woman, as for Blanche, caregiving is a solo act. But for Sara being the lone caregiver is the result, not of some moral test she set for herself, but of the unwillingness of others close to her to share responsibility.[14]

The fact that Sara, alone in her family, quit her job to care for her mother is also noteworthy, as it represents a pattern for American women that has serious financial repercussions. Data from the 1982 National Long-Term Care Survey, for example, show that 11 percent of caregivers—typically women—left the labor force to provide unpaid care; 40 percent of them had been unemployed for two to four years, while a little over a third had been out of the labor force for five years or more.[15] Even if the caregiver can afford at the time to do this kind of unpaid work, she will be financially penalized later, when she is retired and most likely widowed: Her Social Security and other retirement income will be substantially reduced as a result. While this situation may not be applicable to some of the women of this study, who did not work for pay most of their adult lives, it is an issue that is beginning to affect more and more women. It is contributing to the increasing patterns of poverty currently observable among older women in this country.

Similar patterns of caregiving emerge when we look at women's more recent tending to ailing husbands. Leah, for example, was unhappily married for forty years to a difficult man: "To begin with, he gambled; that made it bad. . . . He was antisocial. People would come to the house and he would lock himself in the bedroom. . . . Then he got kidney trouble, and then he developed a bad heart." She nursed him through many years of illness. "I felt sorry for [him]. I really did. He was kind." I sympathize by saying, "It was a rough life for you." "Yes. My mother always said I could do better, and 'What do you need him for?' I stood by him because I felt that was the right thing to do." Leah subscribed to a formal principle of moral obligation here: doing what is right. For Harriet the obligation is implicit, as she does not elaborate on her motivations for taking care of her husband when he became ill with cancer. "I did it alone. My children weren't here. I used to drive him for chemo and radiation. I used to take him every day. I used to take him and help him get dressed. . . . He couldn't walk around. But it's one of those things. You can't help it." It's important that we attend to the physical dimensions of this work in addition to the emotional ones; they are considerable.

In Anna Quindlen's novel, *One True Thing*, the protagonist is a twenty-four-year-old woman who discovers her mother has cancer. Her father urges her to move back into the family home and take care of his dying wife. She suggests an alternative course of action—that he take a sabbatical from his teaching job. He immediately answers, "It seems to me that another woman is what is wanted here."[16] She capitulates. Her father has banked, of course, on the assumption that women can somehow do this painful, arduous, physical job better than men, presumably because women are naturally nurturant. But what, specifically, makes driving, dressing, bathing, and feeding a desperately sick person a gender-specific job? I would say economics and power tied to cultural conventions. As I indicated earlier, the West has a long tradition of devaluing women, and, concomitantly, their work of caring. I have also suggested that women are socialized to serve and care for others, and that this expectation probably emerges far more from women's lower status in society than from a natural predisposition in these directions. As Paula Dressel and Ann Clark argue, "Who cares for whom, in what ways, under what circumstances, and to what end may be grounded in power relations that become mystified within the family and essentialized as 'women's caring nature.'"[17]

The fact that men typically earn more than women results in the expectation—from family members as well as employers—that women rather than men quit their jobs to care for the ailing, as the economic repercussions for the family are seen to be less dire in this way. Research suggests those men involved in eldercare tend to engage in instrumental functions—such as making phone calls or paying bills—whereas women do more bodily, expressive functions, including feeding and bathing of care-receivers.[18] Of special interest, however, is the fact that husbands caring for older, ailing spouses tend to do all functions. The gendered nature of caregiving should not obscure its concomitant class-based dimensions. Families who can afford it frequently hire working-class women at low wages to care for ailing relatives before they demand that male relatives do the job.[19]

Sadie is showing me pictures of herself with her late husband. I comment that they make a handsome couple. "He was a doll," she replies with obvious delight; then, more pensively, she adds, "And I hated to see him go. I took care of him completely when he was sick. He had Parkinson's. . . . And I was sick about it because morning, noon, and night I was with him. Because he was a very sweet man. He really was." Sadie's love for her husband is palpable in this communication, as is the fact that that love, nourished by his sweetness, propelled her devotion to him in caregiving. Perhaps it would be useful for us to think about what might be called "the dialectics of care,"[20] insofar as familial caring takes place within a relational context. Even though one partner in the caring dyad is more dependent on the other, that does not mean that the motivation for caregiving is exclusively generated on the caregiver's part. Partners in the caregiving relationship surely influence each other's behavior and moral impetus.

We see a similar process in Alice's case. She is reminiscing about the period of time following her husband's death from cancer. "I missed him, yes," she says, quickly adding, "but he had suffered for two years, and I never left his side. And he was not a complainer. So while he was ill, he was a sweetheart, real nice. So I did everything I could for him. And I didn't want him to linger on, suffering, the way he was suffering. So you think to yourself, 'You're going to start weeping and wailing. You're only

doing it for yourself. You're not thinking of what he was going through.'"
As with Sadie, caring for her husband brought rewards as well as difficulties for her: "He was a sweetheart, real nice." For the sake of her husband's well-being during his painful illness, Alice withheld expressing her
own emotional suffering. Was this a sign of generosity or of self-abnegation? Are the two separable? Are they joined more readily in women?

Sylvia might help us address those questions. I meet her one day at
Julie's soon after I begin field research there. Her husband has suffered
from Alzheimer's for the last three years, she tells me, and "he's a very sick
man." Caregiving demands unending physical work and emotional
resources from her, day and night. As a result, she perpetually feels
fatigued and demoralized. As she says, apart from taking care of her husband, "I have no life." I tell her it must be very hard for her. "Harder than
hard," she replies, suggesting that the situation is, indeed, terrible. Both
her doctor and her daughter—who offers her emotional support—have
pressed her to put her husband in a nursing home. But she feels extraordinarily conflicted about this possibility.

Almost a year later, when I am interviewing Sylvia at her home over a
deli lunch, she elaborates on her conflict. By now her husband goes to an
elder care center several mornings a week. But she feels the caregiving
demands are taxing her health. So, on the one hand, "My health is going
down, OK? I need a vacation. I feel I need a change, a vacation." Her
physician had more than a vacation in mind when he asked her, "What's
going to [happen] if you need a little surgery?" On the other hand, the
idea of putting her husband in a nursing home feels untenable to her at
the moment. "I am keeping him [at home] as long as I can, OK? My conscience bother me, you understand?... Listen. We been married fifty-
three years in September, September 25 coming be fifty-three years, OK?
We struggle together. We were hiding together [during the Second
World War in Europe]. We were working together.... Everything
together.... I would feel guilty." "Because you've gone through so much
with your husband, you feel you have an obligation to him," I venture. I
seem to have named her experience, for she says animatedly, "Absolutely.
Absolutely. That's it! That's it! Yeah."

I return the following week, when we pick up on this conversation. I
wonder whether Sylvia resents having continually to give of herself in a
situation that is so difficult, so nonreciprocal. "Sometimes I'm mad at my
husband, OK? Sometimes, because there was times I didn't like the way
he ate, OK? It was, you know, like husband and wife.... And I shouldn't.
I know I shouldn't. But I'm mad sometimes, and then I feel bad. Why
should I do that? I know I shouldn't. I know I shouldn't, OK? What you
call this?" "You're feeling," I suggest, "split in your feelings. Part of you

feels angry, and then you feel guilty about being angry." Evidently I've hit the nail on the head, for she responds, monosyllabically, "Yeah. Yeah. Yeah. Yeah. Yeah. Yeah."

Sylvia's self-abnegation in the face of her husband's illness is informed by a profound sense of responsibility born of a difficult shared life. It is not grounded in abstract moral principles, but in the reality of, together, having survived the war and its ravages and the demands of raising a family in the context of an immigrant experience. I don't know her wartime reality first-hand, and I would not presume to do so. I am moved by her narrative and by her fierce loyalty to her husband, whom she once admired as a "very accomplished man [who] used to read many newspapers as well as books," who was "educated at a *yeshiva* [school of higher Judaic learning]." But I want to know why Sylvia and so many other women interpret their incapacity to continue full-time caregiving as a moral failure. Their central experience seems to be that of guilt.

This realization hits me hard when I begin to get acquainted with older women. Mary put her mother in a nursing home when her mother broke her shoulder. "I had no choice," she tells me and several others as Julie does her hair. "I was alone and I needed to work." Mary went to the nursing home every day, spending all of Saturday and Sunday there. She would routinely bathe her mother herself because "I wanted to." She would occasionally bathe other residents of the nursing home as well, or at least wash their hair. Mary's pain about her need to put her mother in the home is visible and poignant. She tears up repeatedly. I say to her that she seems to have done above and beyond what anyone could have expected. She begins to cry, saying, "I still can't talk about this." She has not come to terms with these events, despite the fact that her mother has been dead for several years by now. Like other women, Mary received little assistance in caring for her mother. Mary's sister saw their mother on visit days; otherwise, "I was on my own."

Two months later, on a Friday morning, I strike up a conversation with Marion, who is sitting at Victoria's station, getting her hair colored. We talk about a variety of topics before she tells me that her husband died a bit over a year ago. After I express my condolences, she tells me she cared for him at home for six and a half years after he had a stroke. It finally got too hard for her, so she put him in a nursing home, something he very much did not want. At this point her eyes begin to well up. I surmise from what she has said that she feels guilty. The buzzer rings just now and she moves, with me in tow, to one of the hair-washing chairs. I notice that now she is crying in earnest. I drop down to my knees and, touching her hand, I tell her, "You did the best you could." She squeezes my hand, smiles ruefully through her tears, and whispers, "I hope so."

These are not isolated examples of women's pain. Many women communicate a similar experience, as does Teri when she tells me she put her mother in a nursing home only after her doctor told her she was "burning the candle at both ends." It was, in her words, "the hardest thing I've ever done." Once the loved one is under institutional care, the woman's caregiving does not cease, as we saw in Mary's case. Leah captures this tendency well. During her last years, her mother lived in a nursing home, but "I was there every day. Rain or shine, I went to the nursing home." During that time, Leah also worked full-time and cared for a child and a sick husband at home. Teri visited her mother every other day, taking turns with her sister. She took her mother's laundry to wash at home.

Why, then, do these women experience a sense of moral failure? Perhaps, in part, because in this society caregiving of the ailing or the elderly is seen as an individual responsibility—largely women's—and not that of the social body. A person's inability to care directly for parent or spouse is thus interpreted as a *personal* betrayal of the loved one. In addition, the expectation that women care for others is so deeply embedded in people's consciousness that the inability to do so is interpreted, not only as a lack of will, but as a transgression of a basic ethical imperative—that which calls women to sacrifice themselves for others. One example will suffice. Clara is speaking to me about a friend whose mother is a hundred years old.

> [She] is just fine, just fine. Her quality of life is not what it should be, only because she has this one daughter who is a nice enough person, *a little bit on the selfish side*, and has put her mother in a retirement home, although she's physically able, in every capacity. But [this daughter] felt that she just didn't want that service, giving to her mother, at this point in her life. So, the quality of life there ... must be very shabby. She's living among strangers. She's pushing the days away. (emphasis added)

Perhaps Clara knows more about this daughter's situation, or of her choice in the matter. From where I stand, Clara's judgment is harsh but accurately reflective of extant social expectations of women. Clara believes that selfishness explains the daughter's behavior. Would a similar judgment be made of a son? I suspect not. I see an articulation of the "family's claim" on the *woman's* time and resources here, something we have encountered repeatedly in the course of this chapter. It suggests that if the woman—for whatever reasons—chooses her own needs over someone else's, she is de facto viewed as self-interested and therefore irresponsible. The women I have cited who experience guilt may very well have internalized this social judgment. They undoubtedly ask themselves whether they could have done it any better—had *they* been better.

When we review the history of caregiving in the lives of Julie's customers, we see that women have taken very seriously their responsibilities to their children, husbands, parents, and other relatives, in addition to their housework. Some women, like Beth and Shelley, felt so strongly about children's need for their mother's care that they insisted on staying home while their children were growing up rather than getting paid jobs, though they could have used the income. Other women, like Evelyn, report great enjoyment in the tasks of childrearing and housekeeping. For many women, though, caring work carried substantial costs, as well. Reva and Teri's love for their jobs was thwarted by their husbands' demand that they devote themselves exclusively to home and family. Anna reports a happy marriage interrupted by fights about her desire to work for pay. Sylvia, who worked full-time in a business with her husband, had to do double-duty: She alone, and not her husband, had to work for home and family, as well, a pattern widespread in American families. Besides the unfairness in this distribution of labor, Sylvia felt deprived of friends—she simply had no time for socializing; this deprivation hurt her deeply. Sara single-handedly took care of her parents during their long illnesses. While she never resented this responsibility, she wistfully expresses the wish that someone could have shared this work. Recall that she had to quit her job during this time, a situation that did not seem to affect her adversely financially, but one that does so to many other women. Hence, caregiving as the exclusive province of women can often hurt women.

Some women—like Blanche—give of themselves wholeheartedly to the demands of an ailing parent or spouse, sometimes with a spirit of self-abnegation they themselves choose. The socialization of all women as caregivers, however, results in a coercive expectation that all women must do likewise, whether or not they want to or are able to do so. Sylvia is a case in point; her own health is being compromised at present as she cares, day in and day out, for a husband suffering from Alzheimer's. The consequence is that many study participants have been harmed by these expectations, experiencing guilt and a sense of moral failure when they are unable to care "well enough." The expectation that women as caregivers sacrifice their own needs for the sake of others perpetuates an unjust set of social relationships. I have already argued that the work of care has to be done, but the question of justice emerges here: Who is to do it? On whose terms? A just social order distributes benefits and burdens in a fair manner. Distribution based on gender alone is not fair, for there is nothing intrinsic in women that equips them to deal with the demanding work of caring for others. It burdens women with this task while privileging men with some choice in the matter. Since this work is difficult, undervalued, never-ending, and physically and emotionally depleting, it needs to be shared more equitably.

The question of equity may be closely linked to the issues of familial care and responsibility raised by Clara's narrative about the daughter who put her one hundred-year-old mother in a retirement home. That account raises the specter of the nursing home as a sometimes necessary but inadequate place of care. When I talk with participants about their concerns regarding their future, the nursing home is consistently mentioned with revulsion and fear. William F. May suggests that the nursing home "occupies the same place in the psyche of the elderly today that the poorhouse and the orphanage held in the imagination of Victorian children."[21] Martha, who worked full-time and was a widow then (she has since remarried), placed her mother in such an institution when she could no longer be cared for at home.

> I saw her change from a self-sufficient person to a vegetable. It was a horrible thing to watch, and I still think, Could I have done anything different? ... So I've seen what can happen to people. ... Well, I know what [the nursing home staff] do. They had [the patients] drugged most of the day. ... Five o'clock they give them their sedative, and they're ready to sleep. They're saving money on staff and they reduce their staff when they're in bed.[22]

Not surprisingly, Martha asserts that, based on this experience, she and her husband "decided that we never wanted that to happen to either of us." She is angered by the lack of respect for the person implied in this method of social control. Other women discuss the unpleasantness of the physical environment of nursing homes—even the better ones—especially the pungent smells of urine and disinfectants rather ubiquitous in these places. Implicitly or explicitly, however, the major problem associated with nursing homes is that the care is not furnished by family in a context that is really home. As Clara puts it, "She's living among strangers. She's pushing the days away." I suspect that "strangers" here mean both the caregivers and the other nursing home residents, and that simply being placed "among strangers" might be seen as an act of injustice by Clara and others in her situation.

From an objective perspective, one might argue that important and difficult aspects of caregiving may be done better by a "stranger." A nurse or an aide has been trained to do tasks like lifting, bathing, and cleaning the care-receiver's body of urine, feces, and sweat. Is the problem for Clara the strangers, I ask myself, or is it the institutional setting? I believe it is both.

A few participants—like Clara—have made provisions for "help" to be hired to take care of them at home should they become incapacitated. This suggests that to these individuals a nonfamily member is acceptable, providing the caregiving is done in one's own home. Home is seen by many people as a place of safety and comfort, especially during times of dependency. Did not Dorothy, in *The Wizard of Oz*, remind us—at least those of us who live in safe homes— that "there in no place like home"? The association of home with safety and the nursing home with fear has resonances with the traditional dichotomy, generated in the nineteenth century but still operative in people's thinking, between the private and the public spheres, discussed earlier. In that view, the private sphere is a haven from the vicissitudes of public life.

But there's more to it than that. At home the hired caregiver, working for wages, theoretically is expected to subscribe to the rules set by the care-receiver or by a stand-in, generally a family member. These rules would likely include treating the care-receiver with respect and dignity; honoring the person's wishes and stated needs, providing there is no mental impairment; in short, safeguarding the care-receiver's agency. While weak of body and therefore partially or completely dependent on the caregiver, the care-receiver might expect to remain a person with an intact will under these circumstances. This situation also opens up the possibility of a personal relationship between caregiver and care-receiver. Such a relationship lacks the broadly reciprocal context of relationships between parents and children or between spouses that we have seen. The caregiver is likely motivated by financial remuneration and perhaps by pride in a job well done, but not by filial or spousal obligation or long-term emotional closeness. Nonetheless, a personal relationship might still develop that transcends the impersonality of institutional caregiving as imagined or described by study participants.

In the nursing home environment, by contrast, the older person may envision a much greater loss of agency because the care received is no longer under her own control. What one eats and when one eats it, when one goes outdoors and when one stays in, when one wakes up and when one retires to sleep are decisions often taken away from the care-receiver. Staff members usually follow formal and at times seemingly arbitrary rules rather than respond to the particular needs of the care-receiver at any moment in time. Maybe this is what Clara meant when she said, "She's pushing the days away." And maybe this is what people fear when they contemplate their futures: to cease being agents of their own fate. There is not much one can do about physical deterioration, but the hope of all the women I interviewed is to remain mentally and morally intact, to remain, in so many words, captains of their own ships.

Caregiving for the Caregiver

We have seen again and again that women have spent much of their adult lives taking care of others: husbands, children, parents. Two questions now present themselves: What happens when these expert caregivers need care themselves? Who does this work? These women were raised with a strong ethic of familism that assumed a norm of reciprocity: Children would care for their parents in their old age, as parents took care of them in childhood. These women fulfilled *their* part of this implicit familial contract. But now there is hardly any certainty that the children will continue this tradition when the parents are no longer able to care for themselves.

Given current demographic patterns, it is possible, but unlikely, that many of the husbands of those now married will be in a position of caring for their wives. In the United States today, white women outlive men, on the average, by seven years, and most women in this study married men several years their senior. Recall, as well, that half of the women involved in intensive interviews are already widows. Consequently, the likelihood is that most, if not all, the women will be widows at some point in the future.

There seems to be widespread recognition of this likelihood among them. When asked about their concerns regarding the future, even currently married women name their children rather than their spouses as potential caregivers. I say this with caution, however, because not all envision their children in this role, and those who do seldom mean caregiving of the type they themselves extended to their own parents. Perhaps I should start with women's current relationships with their children in assessing the kind of care the women are currently receiving, this being a time prior to physical dependency.

Many of the women who are mothers seem to have positive and satisfying relationships with their children. In a minority of cases, such as Harriet's and Merle's, all the children live out of town. For most women, however, at least some of their children are nearby and in ongoing contact with them. Clara, for instance, has a very close relationship with her daughter. "We are best friends," she tells me, "and we share friends." We have seen that Shelley is also close to her two sons. Of her younger son, who lives in a neighboring state, she says, "He and I are as close as any parent can be with a child. . . . He's been a joy from the day he was born." Clara's daughter provides her with companionship and friendship. Shelley's sons give their mother the attentiveness and support she needs, frequently through telephone conversations. Beth delights in the closeness of her family and her relationships with her children. This is revealed especially during photo-elicitation, when the first thing she identifies in family photos is the physical touch between family members as an expression of love: "I'm looking at my hand again, and my husband, and my daughter's arms around me. . . . You see, my daughters, the hands on their brothers. . . . Look at my son's hands, look at the hands. Look it. You see that, with the hands?" She frequently sees her two daughters, who live nearby with their own families, and keeps in close touch with her two sons, who live out of state.

More common in my conversations with women, however, is a sense that their children are too busy for them, though this sentiment is often masked. Reva tells me that one cannot expect children's lives to revolve around the parents'. "The children love us, but they have their own lives," she says, adding that some women expect their children to call every day and get angry if they don't. "Children don't call because they're busy." In turn, she tries to keep busy with her own activities. Marny has two children in the area. She does not see them as much as she would like because "they have their own lives," a characterization that is repeatedly invoked as I talk to women about these matters.

I sense Evelyn's depression over the loss of her husband almost five years ago. I ask her if she has something to live for. She immediately responds, "No," adding that her daughter and family have their own lives, that her son has his own life. Her son lives with Evelyn now. After her husband died, she urged her son, who is single, to move into the family home. She likes hearing him move around in his office, located at home, but they do not spend much time together, only occasionally sharing a meal. He is considerate with her: "For instance, if he's going to get something to eat, he'll say, 'Would you like some? I'll make you some.' You know, things like that. But he's not demonstrative. He doesn't come out and put his arms around you, and, you know, say you're a good mother, or, you know what I mean. I don't know how to explain." What she probably means is that he is not providing her with the kind of emotional caring she needs, with the desire for physical touch she craves. Evelyn's daughter lives in a nearby suburb. She sees her only infrequently, as the daughter has a demanding career and children to attend to. This pains her. "I don't think she approves too much of the fact that I'm so depressed. And she's a psychiatric social worker and her husband's a psychiatrist. They've never once given me a word of encouragement. It's as though they've disowned me or something. Because of my nature, I suppose. I'm a terrible worrier, and a lot of things I get upset [about] very easily."

Dori—who was paralyzed in an automobile accident years back—is alone at home much of the time while her husband is working: "Ninety-nine and 44 one hundredths percent of the time. It makes me feel bad.

Some days I'm loaded with phone calls. . . . My children are not ones to call. They're busy with their own lives. . . . They don't bother to call unless they want something. They want something, they know who to call." Her daughter, who is twenty-nine, is completing college and lives in the same building as her brother and sister-in-law. Recalling her own youthful days, Dori says,

> People didn't move out unless they were married. And if you moved out before you were married you were a t–r–a–m–p. You couldn't even say that word. It was so totally different. Nowadays the kids can't wait to get out of college and get out of the house. Like it would be so much easier for my daughter to live closer [that is, in Dori's home] to [the university] and would be so much easier for her. "Mother!" That tone of voice. Like, "How did you ever manage to live this long?" . . . You'd think that home was so terrible that they couldn't live at home.

Dori regrets not seeing her children more often, "especially the two that [live in the area]. . . . I invite them all the time for dinner but they're always busy."

Evelyn clearly would like more attention from her daughter, as would Dori from her children. In this telling, these women interpret their children's lack of time for them in personal terms and appear to feel hurt as a result. In the absence of interviews with these children, I cannot represent their perspectives, which might tell a different story. Based on my experience and that of my contemporaries, that story might include the multiple role pressures experienced by the younger generation, making their lives extraordinarily complex and burdened, leaving less time for their parents than they might themselves desire.

Teri's account is different from Evelyn or Dori's. When people suggest that her daughter ought to spend more time with her, she feels angry. "My daughter has her own life!" she exclaims. "She works. She can't be holding my hand all the time!" The fact is that Teri sees her daughter virtually every week. She is also confident that should any crisis arise, it is her daughter who "will be there first."

The social and familial world has changed dramatically for many of the women in this study. For economic reasons, many of them lived for a time with their parents after marriage. Afterward, the younger couple settled somewhere nearby, where contact between families was frequent. In several cases parents lived in the same building as the now-married daughter. These women's children got to know their grandparents well. And, as we have seen, these women generally took on direct and long-term caregiving responsibilities for their ailing parents or otherwise secured help for them.

Several factors have radically changed intergenerational relationships between older parents and middle-aged adults since study participants cared for their parents. The frequently invoked statement that children "have their own lives" is suggestive. It assumes that the children's lives are separable from the parents'. Indeed, virtually all of these women's daughters are now employed, and hence much less available to address the needs of their mothers and fathers in old age. Social mobility and economic necessity have made for a drastic shift, as well, since many children are not physically present to oversee their aging parents' situations. As we have seen, study participants cared for their ailing parents for various reasons, impelled by obligatory and/or discretionary motivations. These women see care for aging parents as a moral obligation, linked to both Jewish tradition and American cultural practice. Beth Hess and Joan Waring note that in recent decades at least one dimension of filial responsibility has changed: There has been a shift from family to public responsibility of matters related to health and welfare, via Social Security and Medicare and the Older Americans Act. Whereas in the past elderly parents could make claims against their children for financial assistance or medical attention, today these claims are made against the state.[23]

Some women demur before conceding that, indeed, they would like to see more of their children and grandchildren. Blanche, for example, tells me that her daughter, who lives in the suburbs, is a very busy professional. She sees her grandchildren every few weeks. "At age seventy-five, I have my own life," she says defensively, only to add after a while in a more subdued manner that she'd like to see them more, "but now they have their own interests." To acknowledge unmet need is to acknowledge emotional dependency. The commitment to autonomy as a moral value is deeply internalized in these women, reflective, as it is, of a central American ideal. Consequently, admission of dependency, even upon one's children, generates a sense of vulnerability and shame. More specifically, dependency upon one's children may be construed as a role reversal: The parent has become a child in this sense, the child the parent. This perception often leads to the loss of self-worth.[24]

Concerns about autonomy and dependence become evident when I talk to participants about the future. "If I can't take care of myself," Leah says decisively, "I'd just as soon die. I'd hate to have to go to one of those smelly old people's homes, nursing homes. . . . If I got to the point where I couldn't take care of myself and I had to depend on somebody to feed me and dress me, I think I'd be ready to die then." Recently widowed, Leah has not discussed this eventuality with her stepson, to whom she is very close. Teri says she thinks a lot about the future, sometimes worrying about it. If it comes to the point where she can't take care of herself,

"I think I can rely on my daughter, but I really don't want to do this. That's why I want to be independent as long as I possibly can. . . . God willing, everything will come out OK. But I think of that often. 'Cause I don't want to be a burden on anybody."

Clara tells me she does not think about the possibility of being unable to take care of herself. "It would be a terrible blow to my pride because I have always been very self-sufficient and very independent. And I dislike putting people to task, to take care of me. . . . I know that I will not have to go to a nursing home and be among strangers, lose all my dignity." She would rely on her family to make necessary arrangements. "You saw my daughter," she reminds me. "Very loving, loyal, wonderful person. But I would not put the task on her. . . . I could afford to have the help that I would need [at home]."

Harriet's situation offers a contrast. She concedes that she no longer has the strength to manage her home. She sometimes thinks about the future "because I wonder how much longer I can keep the house going. . . . So, I say, 'My house and I are falling apart.'" Some people, including one of her sons, have suggested to Harriet that she sell the house, but she worries she might not be able to afford an apartment rental. "I say, 'As long as I can manage, I'll stay here.'" She has not discussed her future with her children.

Martha does not have children. Widowed twice in her youth, she has been married for the past six years. She does not worry about their future because "I've been through the worst. I think the important thing that I think about is that I just hope we both stay well. What I would be concerned about is if we became incapacitated. That's the worst thing, I think, that can happen." Beth is on the same wave length. She does not think much about the future. "I just go along and hope everything'll be OK." She works with old, ailing people; hence she adds, "I see it all the time. I just hope that mentally we'll be all right. That's all I'm hoping, dear God. 'Cause I see the Alzheimer's—poor people—and the forgetful people. It's very hard for a family to see that, it's just, sickness is hard, too, but mentally, as I say, dear God, we should have our mental capacities. . . . So I don't think about [it]. I just hope everything will be well."

Marny tries not to think about the future, either, as it frightens her. She worries about her husband's health and the possibility of being left behind. She also worries about "the cliché of not wanting to be a burden for my children." Though she has not discussed this with them, she is confident that, given their closeness, they "will take care of things."

Recently, Sadie moved to a residential facility. She has her own small apartment but eats meals in a communal dining hall. She is desperately unhappy with this arrangement, claiming that it was made without consulting her. Some time before, she says, her son had asked her about going into a nursing home, telling her that she could never live with him and his family. Stunned by his comment, Sadie recalls that she asked, "Have I ever said I wanted to?" Even now Sadie seems deeply wounded by this exchange. A year later, when I interview her in her new home, I ask her if she ever thinks about the future, about who is going to take care of her, should she need that. "Well, I always said there won't be a damn soul to take care of me," she responds. Then, surprisingly, she chuckles, then laughs outloud. "You know, I used to walk in the [long] hall we had when I was home alone [before her husband died], and I'd sing 'The Farmer in the Dell.'" She sings for me now, repeatedly, laughing: "The cheese stands alone, the cheese stands alone . . ."

Of the women I get to know at Julie's, Sylvia may very well be in most need of care right now. Her husband suffers from Alzheimer's and she provides most of his care; hence, she is often house bound. I ask her if her children—a daughter and a son—can give her some help. She responds, "They have their own lives." Sylvia notes that her daughter gives her moral support. "Oh, yeah. She's giving me support but she's got her problems, too, you know. I cannot complain. She's all right. She's a good girl. She's very understanding." They talk on the phone frequently, but Sylvia initiates most of the calls. "Well, she never got time to talk to me. Not because [it] is me, but she doesn't have time." Her daughter does not visit her frequently because "she is working, going to school; she is taking a master's degree, OK? She does when she can, OK? I haven't got no complaints on her whatsoever." I say, "You're taking care of your husband now. Do you worry about who's going to take care of you?" She replies, "I worry about maybe I die before him. Who's gonna take care of him? OK? OK? Yeah. You never know." She recognizes that worrying will not help solve her concerns. So she hopes "for the best, and I still think about it, what's going to be. I cannot, I'm tied up. I don't know what to do."

Beatrice went through a similar period of helplessness, fueled by different circumstances. Now eighty-two, Beatrice's husband is ninety years old. They have no children. "When I lost [various members of] my family, I looked around and I said, 'You know, he's eight or nine years older than I am.' And I said, 'What's going to happen [to me] if something should happen to [him]?' And I got frightened, frightened to death. It just took hold of me. But I fought it. It's terrible. It's the worst thing you could have. I'd rather have anything but that. So, thank God, I'm over it now." Beatrice got out of this difficult period of panic and anxiety via medical intervention. She now relies on weekly phone calls to a younger woman, married to the son of dear friends, now deceased, who monitors their situation. Beatrice's niece, who lives out of state and is in close touch, has also assured her that she'll "take the one that remains."

In general, women who are mothers expect that their children will arrange for the care they need, when they need it. Some have discussed it with them, others have not, simply assuming it. These are women whose expectations of care are shaped by the values to which they themselves were socialized as children.[25] Shelley is a good representative of this position. Saying that she is not concerned about the future, she adds, "I feel my children will work it out. I have a great deal of faith." Her confidence is supported by a very good and open relationship with her sons, by frequent phone conversations with them, and by the fact that one of them has in fact told her, "Mom, don't worry. I'm around. Don't worry." This reassurance gives her confidence and freedom from worry. Beyond that, however, Shelley asserts that "It's an insult to your children to make them feel like you don't trust them to do the right thing." What "the right thing" might be Shelley does not spell out.

The trust that children will care for them is not mere wishful thinking on the part on these older women, if we take more general statistical trends into account. Research findings consistently suggest that a very high percentage of disabled older people are cared for by families. Tish Sommers and Laurie Shields, for example, place this figure at 80 to 90 percent, adding that in "about three-fourth of the cases, the caregiver is a woman."[26]

Lucy is in the minority when she takes a negative view of parental expectations of filial responsibility. She and her husband, parents of two daughters, have made careful arrangements regarding their future, including payment for their funerals. "Your children are not liable to you," she asserts in her self-confident manner. "They are not legally liable. And I don't believe they should be morally liable. . . . The Asian faiths believe that you should take care of the elderly, as you well know. This is their belief. I think they're nuts. I don't think that you bring children into the world to take care of you." Tentatively, I mirror her thinking, "So you don't have any expectations that your children should take care of you." "I'd kill them [if they tried]," Lucy retorts. "Absolutely kill 'em. It's very much spelled out, on what we want these kids to do."

What will happen to these women is currently unknown. What is clear is that, for most, assumptions regarding parent-child relations are still informed by their socialization in childhood. While empirical research about the Jewish family is on its early stages, and myth and nostalgia often mix readily with reality, historian Paula Hyman writes that "the family appears to have occupied a central role in Jewish life throughout history."[27] Given the high percentage of Jewish women who are employed today, the Jewish commitment to familism expressed through caregiving by previous generations of women may well be changing. The old pattern was far from perfect, as we have seen, as the responsibility for caregiving has generally fallen, exclusively, on the shoulders of women.

As middle-aged women increasingly occupy employed positions, it is unacceptable, from the point of view of justice and equity, to expect that they continue to take sole responsibility for all familial caregiving, with all the implications that carries for their present lives and future well-being. It is time to address collectively the fact that caring is essential in the raising of children, in the nurturing of marital and other relationships, and in the attending of the old and ailing. Someone has to do it; this is vital work for the continuance of our society. Its essential place on the agenda of any decent society must be acknowledged, and ways must be found to valorize it and to disengage it from its gendered associations. In short, considerations of justice must both encourage and regulate the practice of care. Encouragement is needed because, as I have argued, caring is essential to human beings; by virtue of existing, persons deserve care. Regulation is necessary because under present social arrangements, it all too often falls unquestioningly, and often singularly, on the less powerful members of society, incurring unreasonable, because undistributed, costs of all sorts—emotional, physical, and economic.

Loss

I feel humbled sometimes when I review field and interview notes generated in the course of this study. I am confronted again and again by women who have lived a long time, experienced many joys and sorrows, and who typically remain vibrant and optimistic in their outlooks on life. I am no "spring chicken," as Grandma Ella would characterize women of middle age. I too have had my share of happiness and pain. But here the source of my humility is two-fold: women's tremendous courage, strength, and vulnerability in confronting major and life-transforming losses, on the one hand, and their willingness to discuss these experiences with me, a virtual stranger, on the other. I suspect study participants are unaware of the impact of their stories on me. After all, they generally told me about themselves in the course of one or two sittings. They recounted stories they had undoubtedly told and retold many a time. The audiotaping of those interviews has turned out to be far more than a convenient device for future recollection. From my vantage point today, the transcripts of these women's stories have become the texts of their lives, texts that I read and reread so that I feel I know these women far more than perhaps I have a right to. After all, I believe in reciprocity in relationships, and these women don't have the same access to my life as I do to theirs.[28] Hence yet another unresolved—and perhaps unresolvable—feature of ethnographic work stares me in the face.

In chapters 2 and 3, I discussed women's losses related to bodily changes—facial lines, graying hair, weight gain, physical limitations, illness, and so forth. This chapter has addressed central features of these women's work in their families, so I now turn to a consideration of the loss of loved ones, the impact of these losses on the women's lives, and their responses to these losses.

Let Marny's story serve as a preview. She recounts a poignant moment that happened about twelve years ago, when she was fifty-two and her daughter, Valerie, had recently been married. Marny, her husband, her parents, and Valerie and her new spouse were spending the weekend at Marny's country home in a neighboring state. Marny's father was ailing.

> We had a wonderful weekend. Valerie was young and vibrant with her husband. She had a video camera. I remember her [taping] because she wanted to have it on record. My dad—they must have seen he was deteriorating; they saw an era coming [to an end]. And it was very precious and very wonderful, and we loved being together. And they [the young couple] drove off . . . into the wild blue yonder . . . down the road. And I remember breaking down, and I could not say what was the matter. I cried. I was inconsolable. My father, who really at that point in time was not in touch with anybody's emotions . . . wanted to help me, but apparently I was inconsolable. I think this had to do with her being so young, and I love my son-in-law, and I love her. And I was proud of that, but I suddenly felt very alone or frightened. . . . I couldn't stop crying. I cried for an hour and a half. I was like a lunatic.

I ask Marny if in the intervening years she's been able to gain some insight into what happened to her at that moment. She is uncertain, but she understands that her reaction relates to her position between the generations. She concludes, "I do remember a definite sense of loss, an enormous sense of loss." Marny may well have been struck, on the one hand, by her daughter's entry into her own new family and hence her exit, in a manner of speaking, from Marny's; and, on the other, by Marny's knowledge that her father's life was at an end. Marny's identity as a mother and as a daughter was therefore dually threatened.

Women in this culture are socialized to define themselves in the context of their relationships. Some theorists persuasively argue that women's identity is largely shaped around issues of connection to and interdependence with others, leading to both positive and negative consequences.[29] The strength of this orientation is that women become especially good at social interaction and especially sensitive to other people's needs and feelings; they develop compassion and an ethic of responsibility and care.[30] The downside of this type of psycho-social development is that women tend to be less adept at developing strong ego boundaries and a sense of autonomy; often they depend too much on external validation to attain self-worth. The result of such an identity is that separation is especially painful for women. This becomes all the more so when separations are final, as in the case of the death of loved ones.

I recall when Grandma Ella lay deathly ill in the intensive care unit during one of her last visits to the hospital. She removed her wristwatch, telling me in a soft, weakened voice that she wanted me to have it. Then she added, with a big sigh, "Sufro por mi familia"—I suffer on my family's behalf. What she meant is that she was ready to die, but she knew the pain her death would cause us. It was the separation that was of greatest moment for her, and it was this pain she wanted to spare us. And so it is for some of the women of this study who anticipate their own deaths. Clara puts it best when she says, "The greatest trauma of growing old . . . is the fact that we leave this world and all the people in it, all the loved ones. This, I think, is the most traumatic. Not so much the dying as the leaving. The leaving. The separation."

The experience of loss is not reserved for the elderly, of course. It is part and parcel of the human condition. Nonetheless, Hess and Waring suggest that "most status passages of middle and old age involve losses," even as opportunities for growth are also present.[31] In other words, loss is far more abundant in the second half of life. Study participants have had their share, losing parents, siblings, children, and spouses.

Two women—Sylvia and Beth—lost parents at a very young age. Sylvia was not yet twenty when her father died. This was a major blow to her, as they had been very close. Some years later, after her marriage in 1942, she and her husband escaped the Nazi occupation in Poland by crossing the border into Russia. That was the last time she saw her mother. "Yeah. I left her. I left my mother," Sylvia says pensively. Except for one brother and two cousins, her whole family perished. "That's all that's left of the family, OK?" She interprets her time in America as a new lease on life for her, for her husband, and for her children.

Beth was twenty-two when her mother, age forty-seven, died suddenly of a blood clot in the brain. Her death "hit us like a ton of bricks." Beth struggles to understand why her mother had to die. On the one hand, she blames the doctor, who was advised that her mother did not feel well but did not hospitalize her. On the other hand,

> I believe in *beshert*. You know, what's meant to be. . . . My dear father passed away twenty years later—almost to the day—than I lost my dear mom. So then, it was very hard, but we managed to hold our lives together. . . . My only regret is that I don't have them both here. To be in my life, with my husband and my children and grandchildren. It hurts [especially during] bar mitzvahs, weddings. But thank God we had happy times that we don't forget.

Memory plays a healing role for Beth, as it does for Paula, who tells me that memories help her get past terrible times. Teri sometimes sits down comfortably in her living room chair and listens to old records. She enjoys the flood of memories the music evokes. They bring her solace; they reconnect her in a vivid way with loved ones who have passed on.

Marny's father lived a long life before he died. But his death was a major loss to Marny, nonetheless. "I adored my father." Then her mother had a major stroke. "My mother is still there, but I lost her." Her mother is no longer mentally present; Marny has already begun the mourning process.

"I could tell you about losses in my life," says Reva. "I lost my mother, father, and brother in one year. I put up three stones. My father was dying of cancer and my brother went to see him at the hospital. My brother dropped dead in the hospital elevator." It was a rough time. "I lived on a lot of tranquilizers." Merle's sister died suddenly, five years before her mother. "It was a terrible blow," Merle concedes, recognizing the untimely nature of this loss.

I tell Sara I am interested in knowing how women come to terms with the losses in their lives. "I'll never get over that. It's very traumatic. My two sisters, especially, because they left me the sole member of our family, and they died four months apart. . . . I haven't come to terms. I just know that that's what happened, and that's what I have to learn to live with. But I can't call it coming to terms." She is right, of course. She has taught me what experts also say: "People 'do not work through' bereavement. Rather, in accommodating to the loss, they are changed irrevocably."[32]

Shortly after I meet Clara at Julie's International Salon, she tells me she lost her "little sister," age sixty-six, to cancer four years ago. Tears come to her eyes as she talks, the pain still fresh. A year later, when I speak with Clara in her home, she returns to this subject. "I was just sorry that I couldn't find comfort, I couldn't find an answer for it. . . . She was seventeen years younger than I. And it was sort of a pseudo-mother relationship. She was my baby sister. I was her sister, but I was also her mother figure. Always. Always. Always." "How *did* you find comfort?" I venture to ask. "Well, you know, you realize that you have no choice. You have no choice. It's very difficult. She was so good. But we had a wonderful year. It wasn't wonderful that she was sick. But we had hours and hours of being alone and talking." Like Sara, Clara has no facile formula for getting past grief, for coming to terms with loss. She finds a measure of comfort, however, in the closeness she and her sister shared during the last year. Ironically, it is this very deep emotional connection that has allowed Clara to live with its absence.

A few women have had the terrible misfortune of losing children. Their accounts are brief and told in passing. I decide to respect the boundaries they have set up in the telling. Shelley is speaking of her grown sons. As an aside, she says, "See, when we had our first baby she was born dead. . . . They did not know what caused [her] death. That's another story. That was such a tragic time. I couldn't look at a baby buggy." Fran is chatting with Evelyn and me at the beauty shop. She is speaking of recent deaths in her family—her third husband and her daughter-in-law. She clarifies that the latter was married to her son, who died of a heart attack ten years ago. Evelyn is taken aback. She reacts, probably without thinking, by saying, "You lost your son? I want to die before my son or daughter." Fran retorts matter-of-factly, "I have to go on." Carmela's youngest son died instantly when, a few years ago, he was hit by a drunken driver. She thinks about this every day, concluding that this, like other things, was "in the Lord's hands." Carmela is in the minority here, as few women invoke traditional religious meanings to make sense of death and loss.

My mother was widowed when she was only fifty-eight, so I have seen at close hand the pain she experienced when my father died suddenly of a heart attack. Through her, I am familiar with the widow's intense grieving, loneliness, and the determination necessary to start a new life. Thus my mother has prepared me somewhat to hear about other women's spousal losses. There are definite commonalities. Yet it is also true that people mourn differently, respond to loss variously, and redirect their energies in alternative ways.

For the widows among the women of this study, the death of their husbands remains the most difficult and unfathomable of losses. In attempting to explain the meaning of losing a spouse, Evelyn, for example, says, "No one can possibly understand what it is like until it occurs. Because it's almost unexplainable." Gari Lesnoff-Caravaglia captures this sentiment when she writes that widows find that "they enter a foreign world." The most distressing aspect of widowhood, she argues, is the total lack of preparation for this experience. . . . Becoming a widow is very similar to finding one's self unexpectedly in a foreign country. Suddenly she is required to make important and costly purchases with a currency that is completely new to her, speak a language she has never before heard, and to commit herself to significant and irreversible decisions which are transmitted through an interpreter with a poor command of English. If we can appreciate the fear and bewilderment that such a situation would evoke, then we can begin to imagine what it is like to become a widow in a society that is characterized by sexism and a denial of the reality of death.[33]

I am especially taken by the vivid metaphors used to convey the chaos resulting from spousal loss. Evelyn acknowledges that she took her husband's death very hard. She concedes that, at first, "I think I was a little bit out of my head altogether. . . . I was more or less in shock. It took me an awful long time to come to the realization that my husband was gone forever, you know?" Evelyn recognizes that she has had a harder time than most widows dealing with this loss. She attributes her ongoing depression and continuing preoccupation with her husband's death—now almost five years later—to the fact that her husband was "really my whole life. . . . I lived vicariously [through him]. . . . I don't think I'll ever get used to it. [Other women] seem to cope better. For me it feels like it gets worse." Evelyn regrets that she did not go to college or have a career; she assumes that had she done so, she would now be meaningfully occupied rather than living in a permanent vacuum.

Evelyn's imagery involves mental health categories—being out of one's head, shock, depression. Reva's are more physical—bodily, in fact:

You lose your mate, which is like sawing part of your arm off, and that's it. You had a beautiful marriage, and you were treated like a queen and he was your king. . . . [Your losses] are always in your heart. I know a rabbi who once gave a speech. And he was saying that the [wound] is there and as days go by you can put a scab on it; it gets soft and rips off and starts breathing again. So that's exactly what happens. Sometimes I'll sit and cry and think about things, and how they could have been different if my husband was living. But I don't have the power. But I get up in the morning and I do what I have to do.

Metaphors of brokenness are not uncommon. Alice alludes to "picking up the pieces" after her husband's death. Teri also uses this kind of imagery in her narratives. "My husband died very suddenly. I just felt like my whole world crumpled." At another telling, she says, "At that time, I thought, 'This is the end. My world is just crushed!'" Both times, however, she repairs that brokenness in this manner:

> Then after a while I realized how good God was to us. Not only to him, taking him very quickly, but me [too]. Here is this great big guy in a wheelchair. A vegetable. I would have to watch him deteriorate. I don't think I could have taken that. But you see, He took him fast and that was it. So . . . things are never so bad that they couldn't be worse. . . . So you never forget, but time heals. You know what's done is done. You can't change it. And you wonder sometimes, "Why?" But it's not for us to say.

Though not a churchgoer,[34] Teri relies on a theologically informed worldview to interpret the tragedy of her husband's death and to prompt her to reconstruct her life. Added to that is a large dose of pragmatism: "You just go along, you know, one day after the next and try to think of all the good things. Don't sit back and feel sorry for yourself because that's not going to change it. It's never going to change." In this regard she captures most widows' strategies for rebuilding their lives.

Harriet, for example, reveals a similar pragmatic attitude. "It's something you can't help," she says. "You have to learn to live with it and take each day at a time. . . . There's nothing I could say or do that could change it." Alice has tried to maintain a positive attitude after the death of her husband eleven years ago and the subsequent loss of many friends.

> You know, you have to, because nobody else is going to do it for you. You have to sit down and make up your mind, "What do you want?" You're going to sit around and moan and groan for the rest of your life or you're going to get out? Well, I took up golf after he died, and that was quite a feat, I thought. I mean, you've got to pick up the pieces. Nobody's going to sit around and listen to you moan and groan. Nobody wants to hear you, "Oh, I lost the most important thing in my life." And OK, you have. But they don't care. They want to be helpful, but they don't want to have to listen to this day in, day out. . . . You can't bring them back.

Alice raises an important dimension in the experience of widowhood here: the need to change roles. As Phyllis Silverman and Adele Cooperband put it,

> To become a widow involves a search for a new definition of self as a single person. Without the benefit of a marital relationship which once framed and focused daily life, the widowed person must learn to live with loneliness and yet to find a purpose. It is necessary to learn to be a widow as one learns

to be a wife, or mother. . . . Widowhood involves working at living without. . . . Often the newly bereaved is expected to know immediately how to behave in this role, to have acquired this knowledge in an almost magical way.[35]

For Alice the job of working at being a widow was a self-conscious one. She used introspection as a way of helping her find how she was to live her life after her husband's death, and then she proceeded to implement her intentions.

This process is less clear for other women. We have seen that Evelyn, years after her husband's death, has yet to find a new role for herself. Likewise, Leah, who recently lost her second husband, struggles to figure out who she is now: "With him, I was something. Without him, I feel like nothing." But as she recalls the time following the death of her first husband, she says, "You wonder how you go on like that, and somehow the good Lord gives you the strength to go on. You can't believe that but you do." I ask if religion has helped her cope with loss. "I think so. You know, a person has to believe in something. You have to believe there is a supreme being and that things are going to get better. It must have been the faith that I had—that things were going to get better." This religious perspective may once again orient Leah toward a new self-definition. As with Teri, Leah's articulation of religious views is unusual among study participants.

Anna concedes that her husband's death—following forty-three years of marriage—was a terrible blow for her.[36] For a long time it was not possible for her to even talk about her memories. They were too painful. She attributes coming out of that initial period to her daughter, Jenny, who is retarded. "It keeps you on the straight and narrow. You have to do things. . . . What are you going to do? You have to keep going. . . . I'm one of the lucky ones. I have her. Most of these women [other widows at the beauty shop] don't have anyone."

A problem common among widows, according to researchers, is the absence of role models to teach them how to be widows.[37] At Julie's, women frequently play that role for each other. They are good at listening and at telling their own stories of grief and survival. Harriet tells me, "Sometimes you feel better when you talk to somebody your own age. You feel a little better, but it really doesn't make that much difference." In other words, the relief is temporary.

Loneliness is a frequent theme among them. Reva, widowed for eight years, tells me, "You never get used to eating alone." Anna says rather quietly, "It gets hard on the holidays," her eyes momentarily clouding with tears. Sadie says she is not particularly lonesome during the day, but the nights are hard. When her husband died, she would go to sleep very late "to make the night shorter." More than once Teri says, "It's kind of lonesome living alone." Then she adds, "I don't like this living alone. I don't like it, no. But this is my lot and I got to put up with it. I'm not miserable, but it would be so much nicer to have somebody in the house with me. That's not the way it's gonna be. Who am I to say? Do the best you can. So therefore I just love to have people come [to visit]. I just love it." Friendships and family ties ease the loneliness, of course. The situation is hardest for the widow whose physical condition is becoming limiting, whose children live in other places, and/or whose friendship circle is gradually shrinking.

Harriet meets all three criteria. When she went into the tavern business, her work demands led to her losing contact with friends. "So, more or less, now I'm on my own." Sometimes she feels lonely. "And sometimes I say, what the heck, that's the way it has to be." When her children suggest she take a trip, she dismisses that idea readily: She does not have the physical strength to do so. Even the idea of going to the airport is exhausting to her now. Later on in our conversation, she provides me with a more poignant image of her experience. "I get lonesome, and I'm alone in the house, and I'm watching TV. And I get so lonesome that I start walking back and forth in the house. That happens." The feeling passes, however, and she comforts herself with the thought that "there's nothing you can do about these things."

From the perspective of some people, there is something one can do, and that is to find another mate. This suggestion is universally met with dismissal, if not ridicule, by the widows I get to know. Pam and Shaina are sitting together at Julie's, chatting animatedly, as it is their wont to do. Pam, a widow for about six years, is recounting a phone call she received from a man shortly after her husband's death. It became clear after a few minutes of conversation that the man wanted a date. She quickly found an excuse and hung up the phone. Shaina promptly retorts, "Widowers think they are a godsend to women!" Pam answers, "Widowers think widows are hard up."

The fact is that the widows I encounter are not especially interested in meeting men. "I had the best and I don't want any more," says Alice decisively. "I loved my husband, and I still do. I wouldn't get tangled up with any old man today for nothing," declares Sadie. Reva is not adverse to going out to dinner on occasion. She claims there's nothing wrong with going out with the opposite sex. "You discuss things, that's beautiful, nothing wrong. But as far as moving in . . ." Her voice trails off as she expressively shakes her head back and forth, signaling an unmistakable "No." "Men are dependent on women. All of a sudden there's this big house, and the man says, 'What do I do now? That's the difference, especially when they retire. And you have your business. You get up in the morning, and you have your shirts pressed, and you have breakfast on the table . . . and your shirts are in the drawer, and your bed is made. It's a different story."

Harriet never dated following her husband's death. "I was never interested. I just wasn't. People say, 'Go out with a young guy.' You know what my answer is? 'I raised three children. I'm not about to raise another one. And that's it.' Could you see me going out with a younger guy? Oy, vey. The thought scares me." Teri tells me she finds ludicrous people's suggestion that she find herself a man. "At my age, what am I going to find? A tottering man who wants me to cook for him? Then are we going to sit and watch TV till one of us falls asleep?" In short, Teri's response is no way!

These comments express these women's fierce loyalty and devotion to the memory of their husbands. They suggest their awareness that their lives of care and service to others were shaped within the context of loving and long-term relationships with their spouses. They reveal, as well, an unwillingness to perpetuate that kind of self-sacrifice in the absence of a dialectic of care. They affirm women's sense of self independent of male presence. Perhaps this may be one of the positive aspects of older age: the capacity of women—even those raised with the most traditional of feminine orientations—to affirm their own needs as they reject the potential demands of a new mate. At this stage of their lives, they opt against a new family's claim on themselves. They may very well be thinking, "I always used to do for others. Now I do for myself."

CHAPTER FIVE

Energetic Anger

An Invitation to Resistance

❦

Anger must be the energy that has not yet found its right channel.
—Florida Scott-Maxwell, *The Measure of My Days*

We live in a society uncongenial to old age, at a far distance from the time when men and women alike used white powder on their wigs, or on their natural hair, to garner some of the respect then extended to the elderly. Few people seek out the old as repositories of wisdom and experience any longer. In this regard, the writer Allegra Taylor is an exception, for she literally searched the world in quest of older women who could be models for her own aging.[1] We commonly romanticize traditional cultures for their presumed positive treatment of older people; their attitudes, on the whole, may suggest a more positive orientation to old age than our own, but in actuality they have often revealed ambivalence, reflective, perhaps, of the existential fears associated with old age, loss, and death, or with the necessary power struggles between the generations.

In this book we have seen that in our socio-cultural order, older women must cope, not only with ageism, but with its conjunction with sexism, as well. We have witnessed repeatedly in these pages that the systemic devaluation of old age and of women's intrinsic worth have serious consequences for the well-being of older women. Inhabiting an older body— *being* an older body—comes to rob older women of respect and public visibility. The cultural values and social relations that have shaped their moral identities often make such women feel like moral failures, weighted down by guilt, shame, or the experience of insufficiency: for having wrinkles, for not being thin enough, or for their inability to continue caregiving tasks.

It is time that we begin a process of reconstructing old age by rejecting those elements in our cultural values and social structures that detract from older people's well-being. David Maitland believes that as people age they come to form part of a counterculture, one that passes judgment on socio-cultural values.[2] From that vantage point, some countercultural groups are already in existence. While Julie's International Salon ratifies some of the ways in which society at large judges and mistreats older women, as an unintentional community it also acts as a community of resistance, as an "oppositional community," to use Ann Ferguson's term.[3] There is no self-conscious ideology of liberation operative at Julie's, few pronouncements about the coercive norms of beauty and youth, and certainly no political agenda to take into the streets. Rather, resistance to socio-cultural oppressions is embedded in the way that older women treat one another—with respect, affection, and attentiveness; in conversations and gestures that affirm and hence make visible older women's pride in and attention to their bodies, and that acknowledge the pain, suffering, and loss that accompany embodiment; in discussions of their work of caring as work that is valuable, necessary, and demanding. Women in this context affirm their own experiences, experiences that are glossed over as insignificant or occluded from vision in other quarters. So while Julie's does not constitute a politically transforming community, it offers a safe space for older women to be themselves and to be supported in their lived experience, in contradistinction to what more commonly happens in the public sphere.

It is at Julie's, after all, that Beatrice enthusiastically exclaims as she gently caresses Teri's neck, "Isn't she pretty? And sweet, too." Or that Blanche bemoans Carmela's departure for the winter: "I am so sorry." Or that Carmela and Sara engage in spirited competition about their respective maladies. Or that women like Sylvia and Paula empathically discuss their caregiving to partners with Alzheimer's, or others share the burdens and the joys of cooking for a large crowd for the Passover seder.

It would be possible at this point in this study to end the story told by the customers of Julie's International Salon. But as a feminist social ethicist with commitments to social change, I cannot let the story end here. Until now this book has largely involved the inductive derivation of theoretical insights from the narratives of study participants themselves. At this juncture this study changes tone, as I move from a largely descriptive and interpretive orientation to a largely normative one, one whose goal is to find some concrete solutions to problems raised in this book. In concluding, I explore some existing and some prospective ways that unjust cultural assumptions and social practices, exposed in earlier chapters, can be resisted. The discussion that follows is suggestive and by no means exhaustive. I invite others to join me in this work of resistance.

In *Gender and Later Life*, sociologists Sara Arber and Jay Ginn strike an optimistic note when they write, "By rejecting the patriarchal ideal of femininity, by challenging the sexual division of labour, by asserting themselves as competent, strong, and resourceful, women can begin to reclaim their right to age without stigma."[4] Although I believe that these goals are easier named than achieved, they provide us with a compass to search for ways of addressing some of the problematics we have encountered in this book, which revolve around older women's experience of femininity, aging, and caring. In short, in what follows I attempt to address the social marginalization of older women and their devaluation as moral subjects.

Religious Values and Ritual as Mechanisms of Resistance

As someone trained in religion and social ethics, and of a religiously "musical" temperament,[5] I immediately think of religious institutions as potential settings for questioning unjust social values, as natural locales for doing the work of resistance. Of course, not all religious organizations fit this profile. Some behave in a "priestly" manner, while others act in "prophetic" ways, depending on the stance they take toward the larger society in which they are situated. A so-called priestly position mirrors the values and structures of society; it represents a conservative perspective, one that supports the status quo. A "prophetic" position challenges unjust social values and relations, condemning them for their failure to meet the tradition's normative aspirations. When it comes to the position of older people in this society, Beverly Harrison argues, "Many congregations are structured to marginalize older persons at every turn." In doing so, of course, they reveal the unquestioned embrace of extant socio-cultural values that injure the elderly, or, short of that, that fail to contribute to their well-being. Harrison calls for a prophetic stance when she argues that congregations must "take responsibility for not reproducing the alienated patterns of relating to older persons in the internal life of the church itself."[6]

David Maitland reveals a similar prophetic stance in his view of the church as a "Community of Support and Defiance": "Central to our vocation is the obligation to name and resist evil where and when we encounter it. Society's antipathy to whatever may be aging's proper agenda is, for me, such an evil. We need images that will encourage efforts to expose and to defy this evil."[7] While these authors write out of a Christian context, undoubtedly the same could be said about many Jewish and other religious congregations, as well.

Jewish and Christian traditions subscribe to the imperative to care for "the widow, the orphan, and the stranger"—the marginalized of the biblical world. This prophetic vision is not limited to those categories in our own time: All marginalized people must be attended to and included in our communities. Given the logic of their own traditions, Jews and Christians have an obligation to address the situation of older people today both within their own congregations and outside. Considering that 69 percent of Americans affiliate with a religious organization,[8] congregations have the capacity and opportunity to raise many people's consciousness about the experience of aging. They can utilize the talents and wisdom of their older members to educate their congregants about the reality of aging, the injustice of ageism, and the desirability of honoring and integrating older persons into all types of activities. In various ways religious organizations can function as communities of resistance: by affirming the givenness of aging, the reality that "it is for *whole* lives that we are made in God's image"[9] (emphasis added); by recognizing that older people may pursue interests that are different, neither better nor worse, than those of so-called "adulthood"; by noting the wide diversity among elders and in the experience of aging; by using older persons as models, "as witness that the fullness of life is possible into death." "To share this subversive work," Harrison argues, "is the serious business of ministry in our time."[10]

Another way in which religions can contribute to the well-being of older persons is to mobilize their religious resources for ritual-making in the interest of making the elderly visible and contesting existing power imbalances. Religions have long developed rituals to mark important moments in people's lives. Known as "rites of passage," these ceremonies facilitate the movement of the individual from one social status to another. In Judaism, for example, the *brit mila* (circumcision) celebrates the entry of the baby boy into the covenant with God; the wedding signals the passage of the bride and groom from single to married status; the bar mitzvah marks the religious maturity of the boy, and hence his entry into the community with full religious privileges and obligations. Considering Judaism's 4,000-year history, the move to introduce women-specific rituals parallel to those of men has been long in coming. For example, while bat mitzvah ceremonies of various types have been known for some time,[11] rituals fully equivalent to the bar mitzvah are of recent vintage. The past twenty years have been a fertile time in the development of Jewish women's rituals of all kinds. One such ceremony, known as the *brit bat*, in an effort to acknowledge publicly and in community the significance of a girl child's entry into the covenant.

Ritual does not only mark moments of significance in individuals' and communities' lives. It also serves to maintain power relations or to call them into question. So, for example, congregations that refuse to offer the bat mitzvah for girls or to support the brit bat for newborn girls are de facto affirming the importance of boys' rituals alone. They are in effect acknowledging the significance of ritual in people's lives—but only male people's lives matter in this instance. Institutions that try out new women's rituals make a *political* as well as a ceremonial statement.[12] They destabilize established power relations, calling for change in the direction of gender equality and inclusion. Other forms of inequality can be challenged, and need to be challenged, through the use of rituals. A case in point is ageism.

A variety of rituals that celebrate women's bodily experiences and transition points have been created in recent years, mostly by independent groups of women from a variety of established and newly emerging religious traditions. These include ceremonies that acknowledge the beginning and end of menstruation, childbirth, weaning, and entry into old age.[13] New rituals are emerging or have yet to be created that celebrate retirement, becoming a grandparent, leaving one's home, and entering a nursing home.[14] These kinds of rituals, done in communities, may be seen as acts of resistance against cultural values that militate against the importance of women's transitions, especially the transition into older age.

The "croning" ritual, which celebrates such a transition, might be of special significance in contesting our culture's dualistic preference for youth over old age, mind over body. For, as Penelope Washbourn observes, "The image of humanness that predominates [in] our industrialized society is based on the mind controlling the body. To be limited by our bodies, whether in sickness or death, or particularly by the female body processes, is considered weakness and threatens our 'normal' forms of mastery and self-control."[15] While Washbourn is addressing here the need for ritualizing the onset of menses as the entry into womanhood, I believe her observation applies equally to the need to respond to our society's judgment of the older woman's body. Celebratory rituals that applaud women's maturity and entry into old age—however defined—would serve as mechanisms of resistance against oppressive cultural premises. As Rosemary Ruether argues,

> The words for old women such as "crone," "hag," "witch," and "old bag" evoke images of women who are ugly, withered, decrepit, useless, repulsive, and evil. [A] "croning" liturgy transforms this negative connotation of ... old women into a positive one. It connects the word *crone* with *cronus* (time) and the wisdom of long life and experience. To become a "crone" is to become one of the "wise old women" who have gathered up the fruits of their long experience into profound understanding, and who serve as resources of wisdom for younger women.[16]

It was in this spirit, inspired by what I had learned from Julie's customers, that I planned a ceremony for my mother during her most recent visit to my home. I invited some of my good women friends, whose ages range from the early thirties to the late fifties. My daughter and the daughter of a friend joined us as we all sat down to a traditional "tea"— complete with finger sandwiches, trifle, and scones. I called all of us together, I told the group, because for a long time I had wanted to give my mother a special gift, and what seemed more precious than to bring her together with those women who are my special friends? But I also wanted to honor my mother, to show her off, if you will. An intelligent and intellectually restless woman, she never had the benefit of a college education. Since her retirement as a secretary nine years ago, she has turned her energies to reading the classics of Western thought as well as contemporary fiction, local and global. "How many mothers of our generation," I asked my friends, "call us on the phone to discuss Nietzsche, James Joyce, or the latest novel by Toni Morrison?" In short, I told the group, I called together a gathering for my mother because I wanted publicly to applaud her achievements in this stage of her life and to celebrate her as a model for the aging of younger women.

Following my remarks, my friends had the opportunity to introduce themselves, to describe their connection to me, and to reflect briefly on the nature of our shared event. People felt moved by the public, ritualized acknowledgment of intergenerational relationship expressed by our gathering. Several women talked about the physical distance that separates them from their mothers, especially significant now that their mothers (or more likely their fathers) are no longer able to travel. Some saw this event as an inspiration, as a model: They expressed the resolve to mark in some meaningful and public manner their next meeting with their mothers. One woman spoke of the beauty of this moment in light of the fact that she no longer has a mother, though she thinks about her every day of her life. Another hoped that eventually she and her daughter, now a young adult, could achieve the kind of relationship my mother and I evidently had achieved to make the present moment possible.

Such ceremonies provide alternative sources of success and status to women, so that appearance ceases to be the single measure by which women, especially older women, are evaluated. I would like to see these types of rituals entering the lives of established institutions, religious and otherwise. While currently they are making an important impact on the individuals and intentional communities that gather to celebrate them, placing them in the center of ongoing social life would serve larger and more ongoing communities of people.

Rejecting the Cultural Ideals of Youth and Femininity

"When a woman gets old," Sylvia tells me categorically, "she hates herself." Sylvia is the only person at Julie's International Salon to make such an extreme pronouncement on this matter. However, we have seen that aging presents many problems of self-esteem and worth for the participants of this study. Their aging female bodies often become the medium through which their moral integrity is challenged. I would wager that in this regard they represent many other women in American society today.

Of course, one needs to say at the outset that women's self-esteem depends, from an early age, on the approval of others. This is particularly the case when we focus on women in their embodied experience. In this study we have seen that whether or not a woman thought of herself as pretty or attractive in her youth was contingent on whether someone else— parent, friend, boyfriend, or husband—thought so, as well. I have argued that women's beauty in this society is assessed, by men and women alike, from the perspective of the male gaze. In like manner, the older person is evaluated by the gaze of youth; the older woman, via a double gaze—male and young. Jewish older women are sometimes subjected to a triple gaze: male, young, and the dominant culture's gaze.[17] In all three instances the actual woman is objectified, and she frequently objectifies herself.

As subordinate members of society, women have not had the power, historically, to represent themselves in public. Images of women, whether in literature or painting, traditionally were drawn by men, often as projections of male longings and fantasies, positive and negative. The actual woman herself was often lost in the process. More recently, visual images of women, in the cinema, television, or advertising, likewise fail to render women-defined representations. Such images do not simply reveal male perspectives; they also communicate the preferences or reflections of the ethnicity and class of those who create them. The attractive woman today is typically depicted as young; thin but with shapely breasts and legs; white or "exotic" looking; glamorous in dress, hair, and makeup; in a word, what contemporary public standards define as sexy.

The problem for women in this instance, of course, is that the vast majority do not and cannot fit the cultural ideal as popularly drawn. While some of the women I interviewed take this in stride, most fret about the loss of youth, slenderness, wrinkle-free faces, and natural hair color. Some work hard, via beauty shop care, dieting, and exercise to preserve an image as close to the ideal as they can, or short of that, one that resembles their own looks of times past. And since they are unable to do so or are unsuccessful in their efforts, many suffer pangs of guilt and insufficiency.

Theologian Ada María Isasi-Díaz, writing about the situation of His-
panic feminists in the U.S., asks, "How more invisible than invisible can
you be? ... Invisible invisibility has to do with people not even knowing
that they do not know you.... [Only] in the act of naming ourselves we are
born. Our lives are a constant struggle to be called by name.... others so
define you that they refuse to recognize the way you define yourself."[18] In
recent decades American women of all types have made tremendous
strides in naming and establishing themselves, not without struggle, as
competent, capable contributors to society in a myriad of ways. There has
not been the same effort invested in naming the self when it comes to
issues of bodily representation, however. It seems to me that women continue, by and large, to be defined by cultural expectations, typically internalized, that have been generated by others.

Considering the influence that the media, in general, and the advertising industry, in particular, have in post-industrial capitalism, it is virtually
impossible to imagine a scenario whereby advertisers, say, voluntarily
would come to represent women's bodies in realistic fashion. To show
women as they really are—in their multiple shapes, ages, weights, fashions—and to do so in an accepting, celebratory way, is to stop trying to
sell products designed to change them. As a rule, advertisers, working for
the corporate world, will do no such thing unless they are pressured to do
so.[19] So what, if any, options are open to women who would resist cultural
norms and social expectations if they only knew how? How might it be
possible for older women to feel good about their facial lines, their weight,
their stage of life? And how might our society learn to honor, respect, and
actually *see* them?

We see some glimmers of a response today as we witness women's
recent anger around litigation involving silicon-based breast enlarge-
ments. Many women in this study have refused to even consider cosmetic
surgery because of its potential harmful effects on their bodies. Sadie, for
example, insists that surgery is out of the question: "It wouldn't be healthy
for the body or my face." Concerned about their bodily well-being, Sadie
and others opt to "look their age" rather than to regain their more youthful, feminine looks via the surgeon's knife. This refusal may be seen as a
feminist response at two levels. At a personal level, it refuses the potential
loss for women of embodied personal integrity. At a collective level, it has
the potential to serve as a collective strategy by speaking to the power of
women as consumers to influence market conditions.[20] In my women's
studies classes I have perceived a similar feminist attitude of resistance
toward efforts to remake the female body to meet cultural norms. However, statistics suggest that cosmetic surgical options are increasing, not
decreasing, as their cost is lowered and their technology is perfected; there

is evidence that younger and younger women—and men—are beginning to opt for a surgical route to meet cultural standards of youth and beauty. Nonetheless, I believe that at the same time we are spying pockets of resistance in various quarters. There are growing numbers of people who are beginning to see that, as Jana Sawicki puts it, "Freedom does not basically lie in discovering or being able to determine who we are, but in rebelling against those ways in which we are already defined, categorized, and classified."[21]

Let us consider the mission of a group of older women meeting in San Francisco, featured in the video, *West Coast Crones:*

> We refuse the lie
> that it is shameful
> to be an old woman.
>
> We meet to
> build community and
> find new ways to combat
> ageism, sexism, and racism.
>
> We are inventing
> our own aging and
> sharing our experiences
> for our mutual enrichment.[22]

This group functions as an intentional community of resistance for its members, wherein dominant cultural expectations are examined, debunked, and, if necessary, actively resisted. These women are in the business of naming themselves as they rebuff the labels that the dominant culture places upon them. As Isasi-Díaz puts it, "in the act of naming ourselves we are born." When these women claim to be "inventing our own aging," they are in fact resisting external definitions and creating new meanings and visions for old age.

Meridel Le Sueur provides another instance of self-naming when she introduces her poem, "Rites of Ancient Ripening": "The title of this comes of the fact that I'm doing away with the word 'age.' Aging? You've heard of that? Aging or age or death? Aging? You never hear of anything in nature aging, or a sunflower saying, 'Well, I'm growing old,' and leaning over and vomiting. You know, it *ripens*, it drops its seed and the cycle goes on. So I'm ripening. For 'Age' you can say 'ripening.'"[23] In renaming the experience of aging, Le Sueur infuses it with new, positive, and evocative meaning. She is birthing new possibilities for herself and for others as she rejects inherited cultural meanings freighted with negativity. Baba Copper conveys a similar idea when she writes, "We need to reinvent the image of powerful, rebellious old women."[24] This is probably what Maggie Kuhn had in mind when she called her advocacy group for the aged the Gray Panthers. Jenny Joseph's whimsical poem, "Warning," expresses another image of rebellion. The first stanza reads,

> When I am an old woman I shall wear purple
> With a red hat which doesn't go, and doesn't suit me.
> And I shall spend my pension on brandy and summer gloves
> And satin sandals, and say we've not money for butter.
> I shall sit down on the pavement when I am tired
> And gobble up samples in shops and press alarm bells
> And run my stick along the public railings
> And make up for the sobriety of my youth.
> I shall go out in my slippers in the rain
> And pick the flowers in other people's gardens
> And learn to spit.[25]

Gerontologist Ruth Harriet Jacobs' answer to older women's situation is to recommend outrageousness. "RAGE is the middle of the word outrageous," she writes. "Rage occurs when we are frustrated, ignored, hurt, trivialized, denied needed resources, insulted, treated as second class individuals, and in other ways injured." She argues that "we can move beyond rage by being OUT RAGE OUS older women, refusing to accept the stereotypes or slights.... At 66, I have learned that if you are outrageous enough, good things happen. You stop being invisible and become validated." Jacobs' book, *Be An OUTRAGEOUS Older Woman*, provides modeling for circumventing and transgressing cultural expectations. Among her recommendations is for women to have "age pride, speak our ages proudly, and, if we sense discrimination, help others deal with it." One way she educates people about ageism is by proudly wearing a variety of buttons, which include: "RASP" (Remarkable Aging Smart Person); Youth Is a Gift of Nature: Aging Is a Work of Art; The Best Age Is the Age You Are; I *Am* Acting My Age; Age Isn't Important Unless You're Cheese; How Dare You Presume I'd Rather Be Young; Better Over the Hill than Under It; I've Stopped Lying about My Age.[26]

These examples point to ways in which older women can begin to name themselves, discover their own subjectivity, and hence contest some of the negative ways by which they are perceived, pictured, and named. But as Isasi-Díaz and Jacobs see it, and as I have suggested throughout this book, another problem is that of invisibility. Older women are seen from the vantage point of others, not their own; as a consequence, they are sometimes not seen at all. Efforts must therefore be made to make older women visible in the richness of their diversity.

The recent Canadian film, *Strangers in Good Company*, attempts to meet this goal.[27] It dramatizes several days in the lives of a group of older women who are stranded in the remote countryside when their bus breaks down. The women, a varied lot who are strangers to one another at the beginning of their journey, are revealed to one another, and to the viewer, as unique, distinctive personalities. These "characters" are authentic—the women are not professional actors. In employing this device, the film does a good job, not only of dispelling stereotypes, but of revealing the diversity of older women as well as their spirit and their beauty—inner and outer. It provides a good tool for naming older women's experience from their own perspective.

Another way to contest dominant representations of women is through the production of literature that reveals their subjectivity. Works of fiction have typically conveyed stereotypic representations of the old. In recent years a number of anthologies of photographs and writings—essays, fiction, poetry, dialogues, interviews—by and about older women have been published. They contest tired images as they present fresh portraits in their lively diversity.[28]

The discourses and mechanisms used by the dominant culture to name and subjugate Others can be contested in other ways, as well. One nonverbal dynamic involves the power of the gaze. As I have argued, the one who looks at another has the power to judge, and often to control. bell hooks reminds us that slaves were "denied their right to gaze" at whites, a prohibition clearly reflecting racialized power relations. hooks learned early on the power of the "oppositional gaze": "By courageously looking [back at whites], we defiantly declared, 'Not only will I stare. I want my look to change reality.' Even in the worse circumstances of domination, the ability to manipulate one's gaze in the face of structures of domination that would contain it, opens up the possibility of agency."[29] An oppositional gaze might be used by older women to begin to see, and then to deconstruct, the ways in which women—young and old—are represented in films, television, and ads. It might provide one vehicle for learning how to represent themselves from the perspective of their own experience and, consequently, to change the balance of power currently in favor of the male, young gaze.

In chapter 3, I discussed Alice and Clara's public self-presentations. Recall that when asked if she had ever experienced ageism, Alice said, "No, because I can put on an air that'll freeze them.... Pretend you have class." For her part, Clara argued that given their long life experience, older people ought to take control of the conversation at a social event rather than remaining silent and ignored. "I should be able to contain ... to maneuver the table." A new reading of Alice and Clara's strategies suggests to me that what they are arguing for is an oppositional stance, one that empowers the self by anticipating ageist bias and by contesting it in a preemptive way.

Another mechanism of resistance to cultural domination is the appropriation of the epithet, the derogatory remark, the denigrating name as one's own, but reconceptualized in one's own terms. I am reminded here of Melanie Kaye/Kantrowitz's search for a reappropriated Jewish identity—that of a Jewish lesbian. After recounting the experience of Jewish victimization through the centuries, she ventures into an exploration of Jewish women's resistance and valor in the years of the Second World War. She writes, "Most stories of the holocaust, like most other stories, have been told by and about men. I don't reject them for this, they are Jewish and mine. But as a woman, I need to know about the women, and that many Jews fought back, as they could, Jewish women among them." She makes annotated lists of such valiant women. "Those were Jewish women. I come from women who fought like that." Using this newly acquired knowledge to redefine traditionally denigrating labels, she concludes, "I want a button that says *Pushy Jew. Loud Pushy Jew. Loud Pushy Jew Dyke.*"[30]

What buttons might an older Jewish woman wear to contest received, denigrating meanings of her oldness? Of her Jewishness? Might she say, with Shaina, "I'm just an old bag" but mean something other than its surface meaning? When a woman gets called a "dog" because she refuses to live up to the image of beauty or glamour expected of her, might she wear a button that says, "I am a dog," contesting thereby the power of the social label, resisting the sting that is felt when one is told one does not fit in, one has missed the mark, one is unvirtuous? I expect only the very brave would risk, unaided, such transgression of social norms. It is virtually impossible for women—or anyone else—to find ways of transcending social definitions of femininity while standing alone against the array of cultural and economic forces stacked against them. Human beings are social beings, and complex problems call for collective solutions. A woman alone will not succeed in combating social norms and still remain within the social pale. But as a member of a group or a movement that supports her efforts, she has a much greater chance of surviving the inevitable rejection that will follow when she crosses boundaries and breaks rules. Hence the need for women to organize. Twenty women in a single locale wearing an "I am a dog" button would make a statement of resistance that would contest perceived personal idiosyncrasy; their message could not be readily ignored or dismissed on that account.

Kathryn Pauly Morgan offers a more radical performative form of revolt aimed at destabilizing the norms of femininity. It involves "revalorizing the domain of the 'ugly' and all that is associated with it.... Feminists can use [the fascination with the ugly] and explore it in ways that might be integrated with a revalorization of being old, thus simultaneously attacking the ageist dimension of the reigning ideology." Women "might constitute themselves as culturally liberated subjects," Morgan suggests, "through public participation in Ms. Ugly Canada/America/Universe/ Cosmos pageants *and use the technology of cosmetic surgery to do so.*"[31]

I support Morgan's proposal, save for her last recommendation, for to surgically convert the female body into an object of ugliness is as fetishizing as to make it into an object of beauty. But I find the idea of Ugly pageants compelling in its transgressive and destabilizing goals: It would effect an educational purpose and might open up some public dialogue about our cultural preoccupation with surface looks and the coercive norms of beauty and youth. But I would not want to see an Ugly pageant as an end in itself, as a way to replace one set of rigid standards by another by simply inverting the structures of oppression. Rather—and I expect this is Morgan's intent—its major purpose would be to lift up to ridicule any coercive set of cultural expectations, such as those we currently experience under the tyranny of the "beauty myth."[32]

Visibility Through Contact

Age segregation is undoubtedly partly responsible for older people's invisibility in this society. When I was a child in Chile, I remember birthday parties and social events that always included grandparents as well as parents and children. Likewise, study participants fondly recall many happy times when they lived in extended family arrangements, or when they raised their children in close proximity to their own parents and other relatives. Given social mobility, many children in the U.S.—my own daughter included—are raised with only occasional contact with grandparents and virtually no close relationship with other older persons. We also define our friendship circles almost exclusively along age-cohort lines. These patterns result in the separation of older persons from the lives of younger people, and, in turn, in their social invisibility. They become marginalized; they become Others.

A just society is inclusive of all its members, however. Efforts must therefore be made, by young and old alike, to find ways to integrate the interests, contributions, and concerns of older persons into the public agenda. Our predisposition to see older people as problems, to define them on younger people's terms, to devalue who they are must be actively contested.

A recent study conducted by the American Association of Retired Persons (AARP) demonstrates that negative images of aging begin early in an American child's life. Older children (ages 9 to 11) displayed more negative attitudes than younger children (ages 6 to 8), while boys' attitudes tended to be more negative than girls'. When using projective drawings, researchers found that "children who drew personalized older persons they knew, such as a grandfather, were more likely to portray the older person in positive ways. Children with generalized drawings of older persons they did not know were more likely to portray older adults in negative stereotypes."[33] In its national survey of teenagers, the AARP reports that teens "maintain several stereotypical beliefs about aging and being 'old'" and recommends that teens "should be encouraged to interact more regularly with older adults." Those teens who have frequent and regular interactions with older people "overwhelmingly report that the time spent is enjoyable."[34]

One way to combat the misrepresentation of older people in the minds of others, and in the public media, then, is to combat the kind of age segregation that leads to stereotyping. The AARP has developed a variety of programs designed to educate children regarding older people by bringing these diverse populations together. One such program involves older adults as volunteers in schools. These intergenerational partnerships benefit both students and older persons alike. Older adults may participate daily or weekly by tutoring, mentoring, and helping students and teachers in a variety of activities. They may offer occasional talks on careers, hobbies, travel, and other interests. In addition to contributing to the academic achievement of students, volunteers can offer emotional support, teach about aging, and provide needed grandparental figures to many children. In turn, they contribute in these ways to their communities, form friendships, and find in school contexts sources of personal growth, recognition, and achievement.[35]

Reva has volunteered for ten years in such an intergenerational program at a public elementary school in her neighborhood. Twice a week for several hours, she assists a teacher of young children in a variety of activities: educational tasks like marking papers, reading with children, cutting stencils; nurturing jobs like taking children to the bathroom, washing their hands, serving them lunch. Reva feels tremendous satisfaction, stimulation, and affirmation in this work. "The children are so bright, so bright.... It's wonderful for me, and they are most gracious; there are always gifts.... I love it! I love it!"

Generations United is a coalition of over one hundred national organizations—including the AARP, The Child Welfare League of America, The Children's Defense Fund, and the National Council on the Aging—

working on intergenerational issues and programs. In one of its recent publications, Generations United reports on intergenerational community service projects that position young and old people working together as community resources, "working as equal team members to help others. In the process, young and old learn about one another and strengthen their intergenerational ties as they perform service."[36]

Another way to make older people visible to the young in a balanced manner is to include materials about aging and the aged in school curricula. This applies to all school levels, including higher education. In university women's studies programs, for example, there is painfully little that is taught about, or written by, older women—an extension of the sociocultural ageism that removes older women from public view and social significance.

Expanding Older Women's Social Roles

In chapter 4 we saw that the caregiving work performed by women—young and old—on behalf of their families is unpaid and socially undervalued. A life spent doing this kind of work, as opposed to paid employment, has negative consequences for a woman's financial status in old age. The lack of value extended to caregiving contributes to the social invisibility and moral insignificance of older women and bodes ill for the satisfaction of their own needs for care in their very old age. Valorizing the work of caregiving, and removing it from its gendered associations, remains an important goal for a just society. It is a job of such large proportions, however, that its consideration lies beyond the scope of this book.[37] That being said, however, I agree with Kristine Baber and Katherine Allen that "as long as women and men do not have equal access to work opportunities and other means of accumulating social power, there will be asymmetry in caregiving responsibilities."[38]

Ruth Harriet Jacobs argues that older women's value is bound to increase with increased opportunities for expanded social roles. She imagines new roles by identifying society's unmet needs and older women's existing skills. Some of these roles would represent expansions of current ones. Some might be paid jobs, some could be volunteer positions. But it would take more than the willingness of individual women to change their roles, which in some cases would require training and other forms of social support. It would be a matter of public policy and hence of public will.[39] Considering that increasing numbers of women, including those who have been employed, will live two decades and more after turning sixty-five, opportunities for socially useful work seem financially prudent as well as socially responsible. Shelley, though over eighty, still works as an accountant about twelve hours per week. "I love it," she says enthusiastically. "It keeps my mind alert." Marion retired some time ago and misses her work. "It's the people. It gets lonesome not working." Recalling the job she had when she was a young woman, Sadie exclaims, "I loved it! I wish I could go to work today." Maybe people like Sadie and Marion could do so if the opportunity were available.

Older women, Jacobs suggests, could participate in educational institutions as teacher's aides or dorm advisers. The dorm director job would also provide housing for those older women who cannot afford to keep up their houses or rent suitable apartments. Older women interested in nurturing roles could help families in a variety of ways: by staffing homelike after-school centers, taking children to appointments or shopping for clothes, serving as telephone contacts for latchkey children, and as confidants to troubled families. In the health care field, older women could be trained to be liaisons between patients and health-care professionals, and to visit people in nursing homes. They could be advisers to those who construct and manage nursing homes, since "women who have managed homes know how to make places comfortable and attractive."[40]

Raised under an ethic of responsibility for others, older women might serve as models for more caring community relationships. Community service roles might include being confidants for insecure adolescents, young parents, or lonely people. Jacobs suggests that older caregivers could be given free training and interest-free loans or subsidies to upgrade day care establishments so they can be licensed. In the world of business, older women could create employment agencies specializing in older workers. They could be used as consultants by businesses interested in the elder market.

With some training, older women could play educational roles in a variety of settings, for example, giving talks on parenting problems and elder care. And they could be used in beneficial ways by the media. Jacobs concludes, "How long will it take for television to acknowledge that old women are wise, their faces showing the lines of experience? America will come of age when we see sixty- and seventy-year-old anchorwomen, just as we now have venerable male broadcasters.... Because television, films, radio, and print media influence public perceptions, they should be pioneers in utilizing the talents of older women and portraying them accurately and favorably. In the process, the overall image of older women would be enhanced."[41]

The model of older women's active participation in and contribution to society that Jacobs recommends is an appealing one. It reveals older women actively engaged with society in a mutually responsible manner. In like manner, in *The Fountain of Age*, Betty Friedan identifies and applauds quantities of people living adventuresome and interesting lives, involved in vital and exciting activities in their old age.[42] In this way Friedan persuasively contests the widespread yet inaccurate view that old age is a time of disease and decline of all kinds.

It may be necessary, however, to hold up another model for old age, alongside this one, to combat ageism and the invisibility of the old. Jacobs and Friedan advocate a form of "productive aging" that implicitly supports the dominant cultural view that a life well lived is a life of activity and busyness, and consequently, that a good old age is one in continuity with what has preceded it. As Harry Moody puts it, "Productive aging constitutes a reformulation of what later life should be in terms of the dominant values of the Modern Age: growth, energy, activity, accumulation, and efficacy in shaping the world around us." The ideal of productivity "will eventually ensnare us and defeat us," however, when we can no longer be "productive." Moody argues that "we need a wider vision of what late-life productivity may mean, a vision that includes values such as altruism, citizenship, stewardship, creativity, and the search for faith." Moody believes that productive aging should remain only as an option, not something that is imposed on people who may want a more conventional retirement and who have "no desire to be 'productive' in any of the various meanings of the term."[43]

Sylvia worked very hard her entire adult life, for the last thirty years of her work life in a demanding business with her husband. She "hated every day of it " and consequently she now feels relieved to be retired. So does Beatrice, who has devoted time as a volunteer in philanthropic organizations since her retirement. But she also likes to spend time with her husband and friends, and she now enjoys reading novels—those with a Jewish theme. "The older I get, the more I want to be Jewish. The older I get, [the more] I learn the *brachas* (ritual blessings)." She taught herself these blessings rather recently because "I want to belong to something." Though her husband does not wish to join a synagogue, Beatrice does, as she begins to explore her inner life and her need for ritual in her old age. Her needs in these matters become poignantly expressed as I am leaving her home after our long interview. Pointing to her chest, she explains, "I've been lonely. I've been lonely all my life. It hurts here; it aches here."

David Maitland calls for a rejection of the values of productivity by elders who wish to deepen their spirituality as they reflect on those inner questions left neglected during much of their adulthood. Such reflection necessarily leads to a questioning of external social values, and Maitland sees the possibility of older people becoming social critics: "The aging have a distinctive qualification for taking up the vocation of social criticism.... [They] can criticize with an awareness of both the achievements and the awesome failures of the period of history through which they have lived."[44] Given its emphasis on activity, our society does not currently honor the task of reflection that is necessary to bring integrity and coherence to a long life and to furnish meaning to old age and the inevitability of death. The work of resistance will entail turning our attention to the inner lives of older people and learning from their experiences, observations, and reflections. As Harrison sees it, the work of reclaiming "aging as a miracle of life, [as] a beautiful process that is part and parcel of abundant life, will take a united effort at subversion of the dominant political economy and its culture."[45]

Parting Words

The work of resistance that I have been discussing is not only theoretical for me. As far as I'm concerned, the status of older women is not of mere academic interest. With some luck, I and everyone else who is still young will become old some day. So despite some important similarities, ageism differs from other forms of systemic injustice, like racism or classism, because everyone will be subjected to its injuries unless significant change comes to pass. It is in our self-interest, and not only for the sake of others' well-being, to combat it. My commitment to resistance stems from another source, however: the knowledge and richness I have gained through my personal acquaintance with older women at Julie's International Salon. For me older women are no longer images on the screen or memories of my grandmothers. They are flesh-and-blood women I met at the salon, some of whom welcomed me into their homes and shared their lives with me in however incomplete a way, given the limitations of ethnographic work.

The last question I ask study participants during intensive interviews goes something like this: "What advice would you give younger women about life, given what you have learned?" Everyone has something substantive to say, something that reveals her own experience, her "take" on the tasks of life. Amidst longer narratives, some of which we have already examined in this book, women offer pithy statements that encapsulate their views:

Anna:	"Be yourself, but be a good person."
Lucy:	"Care about the truth. Whoever it is that you are, be who you are."
Sylvia:	"Care about the family, but also care about yourself."
Beth:	"Be a good person. Be kind. Help people. Do the very best you can so you can walk with your head held high."
Merle:	"Learn how to listen to what someone has to say."
Harriet:	"Don't try to outshine your next door neighbor."

Marny:	"Have a lot of interests."
Edie:	"Stick to who you are. Don't let men remake you."
Alice:	"Don't just get yourself in one little corner, of house and child, and forget that there's a world outside."
Sara:	"There are certain things in life that you must accept. You must accept, and you must have a philosophical attitude about it."
Martha:	"Look at what's really important, not at the shallow side of life."
Clara:	"Cement your loving relationships."
Shelley:	"Definitely be involved in something."
Beatrice:	"Be kind.... All we can do is be good to other people. I think that's why we're here."
Teri:	"Roll with the punches."
Reva:	"Be happy, be content with your life."

These teachings do not emerge from clever theorizing or philosophical speculation. They arise from the lived experience, both happy and sorrowful, of ordinary women, who in the seventh, eighth, or ninth decade of their lives agreed to talk to me so that their voices could be heard and the silence about their experience could be shattered. Allegra Taylor traveled around the world in search of older women's wisdom.[46] I had to drive only a few blocks to my neighborhood beauty shop.

Notes

Introduction

1. May Sarton, *As We Are Now* (New York: W. W. Norton and Company, 1973), 23.
2. Daniel Callahan, *Setting Limits: Medical Goals in an Aging Society* (New York: Simon & Schuster, 1987), 21; Jessie Allen, "The Front Lines," in *Women on the Front Lines: Meeting the Challenge of an Aging America*, ed. Jessie Allen and Alan Pifer (Washington, DC: Urban Institute Press, 1993), 1–2.
3. Thomas R. Cole, "Oedipus and the Meaning of Aging: Personal Reflections and Historical Perspectives," in *Aging and Ethics: Philosophical Problems in Gerontology*, ed. Nancy S. Jecker (Clifton, NJ: Humana Press, 1991), 95, 96.
4. See Barbara Macdonald with Cynthia Rich, *Look Me in the Eye: Old Women, Aging and Ageism*, expanded ed. (Minneapolis: Spinsters Press, 1991). Baba Copper believes that despite the field of gerontology and political organizations that promote the interests of the elderly, "we know next to nothing about what it is to be an old woman in this society." *Over the Hill: Reflections on Ageism Between Women* (Freedom, CA: Crossing Press, 1988), 85. There are some signs that feminists are beginning to turn their attention to women's older age, perhaps as a consequence of their own aging. See, for example, Letty Cottin Pogrebin's recent book, *Getting Over Getting Older: An Intimate Memoir* (Boston: Little, Brown and Company, 1996).
5. Barbara Macdonald, "Outside the Sisterhood: Ageism in Women's Studies," in *Women and Aging: An Anthology by Women*, ed. Jo Alexander, et al. (Corvallis, OR: Calix Books, 1986), 20.
6. Simone de Beauvoir, *The Coming of Age*, trans. Patrick O'Brian (New York: G. P. Putnam's Sons, 1972), 7.
7. Copper, 14.
8. Riv-Ellen Prell, "Rage and Representation: Jewish Gender Stereotypes in American Culture," in *Uncertain Terms: Negotiating Gender in American Culture*, ed. Faye Ginsburg and Anna Lowenhaupt Tsing (Boston: Beacon Press, 1990), 248–64; Gladys Rothbell, "The Jewish Mother: Social Construction of a Popular Image," in *The Jewish Family: Myths and Reality*, ed. Steven M. Cohen and Paula E. Hyman (New York: Holmes & Meier, 1986), 118–28.
9. Polly Young-Eisendrath, "The Female Person and How We Talk About Her," in *Feminist Thought and the Structure of Knowledge*, ed. Mary McCanney Gergen (New York: New York University Press, 1988), 169.
10. Caroline Evans and Minna Thornton, "Fashion, Representation, Femininity," *Feminist Review* 38 (Summer 1991): 48.

11. For gerontological studies of older women, see, for example, Sarah H. Matthews, *The Social World of Old Women: Management of Self-Identity*, Sage Library of Social Research, vol. 78 (Beverly Hills, CA: Sage Publications, 1979); Sara Arber and Jay Ginn, *Gender and Later Life: A Sociological Analysis of Resources and Constraints* (London: Sage Publications, 1991); Jessie Allen and Alan Pifer, eds., *Women on the Front Lines: Meeting the Challenge of an Aging America* (Washington, DC: Urban Institute Press, 1993).

    On feminine beauty, see, for example, Susan Brownmiller, *Femininity* (New York: Fawcett Columbine, 1984); Naomi Wolf, *The Beauty Myth: How Images of Beauty Are Used Against Women* (New York: William Morrow and Company, 1991); Susan Bordo, *Unbearable Weight: Feminism, Western Culture, and the Body* (Berkeley: University of California Press, 1993).

    Regarding the absence of books on older Jewish women, an exception is Sydelle Kramer and Jenny Masur, eds., *Jewish Grandmothers* (Boston: Beacon Press, 1976), which consists of brief memoirs by ten older Jewish women but lacks an analytic or interpretive dimension. Barbara Myerhoff devotes a chapter to a consideration of women in her classic study of elderly, European-born Jews in a California community center for older adults. *Number Our Days* (New York: E. P. Dutton, 1978).

    For a piece on beauty salons, see photographer Phyllis Ewen's "The Beauty Ritual," in *Images of Information: Still Photography in the Social Sciences*, ed. Jon Wagner (Beverly Hills, CA: Sage Publications, 1979), 43–57.

12. The dominant culture's gaze has been historically constructed; from the middle of the nineteenth to the middle of the twentieth centuries, that gaze was male, white, Anglo-Saxon, and Protestant. While some of the boundaries may have been eroded over the last half century, it seems to me that the dominant culture's gaze is still Christian.

13. Some feminist ethnographers working out of a social scientific perspective define their research and writing as action- or advocacy-based work, also moving beyond the strictly descriptive level of analysis. See, for example, Mary Margaret Fonow and Judith A. Cook, eds., *Beyond Methodology: Feminist Scholarship as Lived Research* (Bloomington: Indiana University Press, 1991) and Deborah A. Gordon, "Border Work: Feminist Ethnography and the Dissemination of Literacy," in *Women Writing Culture*, ed. Ruth Behar and Deborah A. Gordon (Berkeley: University of California Press, 1995), 372–89.

14. I find Jack Douglas' approach congenial to my own: "Rather than attempting to analyze moral experience in the abstract or independently of social context, we must . . . focus on the everyday uses of morality, both through linguistic statements and by other forms of communication, found in social interaction." "Deviance and Respectability: The Social Construction of Moral Meanings," in *Deviance and Respectability: The Social Construction of Moral Meanings*, ed. Jack D. Douglas (New York: Basic Books, 1970), 11.

15. Frida Kerner Furman, *Beyond Yiddishkeit: The Struggle for Jewish Identity in a Reform Synagogue* (Albany: State University of New York Press, 1987; Lanham, MD: University Press of America, 1994).

16. H. Richard Niebuhr, *The Responsible Self: An Essay in Christian Moral Philosophy* (New York: Harper and Row, 1963), 13.

17. Julie calculates that the salon serves about 200 customers per week. My intensive-interview sample thus roughly represents ten percent of the total.

18. For a detailed discussion of photo-elicitation as a research tool, see John Collier, Jr., and Malcolm Collier, *Visual Anthropology: Photography as a Research Method*, rev. and expanded ed. (Albuquerque: University of New Mexico Press, 1986).

19. In ethnographic work, data is collected on the basis of what participants tell the ethnographer and on observed behavior. I did not ask participants of this study to discuss their

sexual orientation, as this question might have been perceived as possibly offensive to women of their generation. None volunteered having a lesbian identity. My visits to participants' homes consistently revealed a heterosexual lifestyle, insofar as those women who do not at present live with a husband talked at length about the significance and centrality of the marital relationship in their lives. (The single divorced woman among participants in intensive interviews discussed her dates with men.)

20. See Sylvia Barack Fishman, *A Breath of Life: Feminism in the American Jewish Community* (New York: Free Press, 1993) and Riv-Ellen Prell, *Fighting to Become Americans: Jewish Women and Men in Conflict in the Twentieth Century* (Boston: Beacon Press, forthcoming).

21. It does not always follow, however, that insider status automatically circumvents problems of access. Despite my similarities to salon customers, in at least one instance I had to become integrated into the shop culture before I ceased to be perceived as an outsider. When a woman saw me at the shop for the first time, she light-heartedly announced to everyone that there was a "stranger" among them and they had better watch what they said. See Linda Williamson Nelson, "'Hands in the Chit'lins': Notes on Native Anthropological Research among African American Women," in *Unrelated Kin: Race and Gender in Women's Personal Narratives*, ed. Gwendolyn Etter-Lewis and Michele Foster (New York: Routledge, 1996), 183–99.

22. See Samuel C. Heilman, "Jewish Sociologist: Native-as-Stranger," *The American Sociologist* 15 (1980), 100–108.

23. Women's "experience" has been a central category in feminist studies of all types, including religion and ethics. More recently, it has become a problematic category for some scholars. See, for example, Sheila Greeve Devaney, "The Limits of the Appeal to Women's Experience," in *Shaping New Vision: Gender and Values in American Culture*, ed. Clarissa W. Atkinson, Constance H. Buchanan, and Margaret R. Miles (Ann Arbor: UMI Reseach Press, 1987), 31–49; Joan W. Scott, "'Experience,'" in *Feminists Theorize the Political*, ed. Judith Butler and Joan W. Scott (New York: Routledge, 1992); Mary McClintock Fulkerson, *Changing the Subject: Women's Discourses and Feminist Theology* (Minneapolis: Fortress Press, 1994); and Sonia Kruks, "Phenomenology, Feminism and 'Women's Experience'" (Paper delivered at the Annual Meeting of the American Political Science Association, Chicago, 31 August to 3 September, 1995). I believe we need to be careful to avoid false universalizations when using the category of women's experience. However, I also believe that there are selves whose experience of reality, shaped by socio-cultural realities, merits knowing about.

24. See, for example, James Clifford and George E. Marcus, eds., *Writing Culture: The Poetics and Politics of Ethnography* (Berkeley: University of California Press, 1986) and George Marcus and Michael M. J. Fischer, *Anthropology as Cultural Critique: An Experimental Moment in the Human Sciences* (Chicago: University of Chicago Press, 1986).

25. Judith Stacey writes, "In the last instance, an ethnography is a written document structured primarily by a researcher's purposes, offering a researcher's interpretations, registered in a researcher's voice." "Can there be a Feminist Ethnography?" in *Women's Words: The Feminist Practice of Oral History*, ed. Sherna Berger Gluck and Daphne Patai (New York: Routledge, 1991), 114.

26. Evelyn R. Rosenthal, "Women and Varieties of Ageism," in *Women, Aging and Ageism*, ed. Evelyn R. Rosenthal (Binghamton, NY: Harrington Park Press, 1990; originally published as the *Journal of Women & Aging* 2, no. 2, 1990), 6.

27. Shulamit Reinharz with the assistance of Lynn Davidman, *Feminist Methods in Social Research* (New York: Oxford University Press, 1992), 48.

28. Beverley Skeggs, "Theorising, Ethics and Representation in Feminist Ethnography," in

Feminist Cultural Theory: Process and Production, ed. Beverley Skeggs (Manchester: Manchester University Press, 1995), 197.

29. On this last point, see Valerie Ann Malhotra, "Research as Critical Reflection: A Study of Self, Time and Communicative Competence," in *A Feminist Ethic for Social Science Research*, ed. Nebraska Sociological Feminist Collective (Lewiston, NY: Edwin Mellen Press, 1988), 85.

30. On methodological and ethical dilemmas in feminist ethnography, see Skeggs; Stacey; Reinharz, chap. 3; Nebraska Sociological Feminist Collective; Liz Stanley, ed., *Feminist Praxis: Research, Theory and Epistemology in Feminist Sociology* (London: Routledge, 1990); Ruth Behar, *Translated Woman: Crossing the Border with Esperanza's Story* (Boston: Beacon Press, 1993); and Ruth Behar and Deborah A. Gordon, eds., *Women Writing Culture* (Berkeley: University of California Press, 1995).

Chapter One: Women's Territory

1. Ray Oldenburg, *The Great Good Place* (New York: Paragon House, 1989), 37.

2. Robert Harling, *Steel Magnolias* (Garden City, NY: Fireside Theater, 1986), 36.

3. Jeannie, Julie's sister, was also on staff during the period of participant observation, but she left with the birth of her second child.

4. Martin Buber, *Paths in Utopia*, trans. R. F. C. Hull (New York: Macmillan, 1950), 133, 135.

5. For example, Andrew Greeley writes, "It is the common store-house of stories that constitutes the community." *Religion as Poetry* (New Brunswick, NJ: Transaction Publishers, 1995), 43.

6. See Aristotle, *Nichomachean Ethics*, trans. David Ross (Oxford: Oxford University Press, 1925).

7. Mary E. Hunt, *Fierce Tenderness: A Feminist Theology of Friendship* (New York: Crossroad, 1992), 95, 98.

8. Janice G. Raymond, *A Passion for Friends: Toward a Philosophy of Female Affection* (Boston: Beacon Press, 1986), chap. 2.

9. See, for example, Nancy F. Cott, *The Bonds of Womanhood: "Woman's Sphere" in New England, 1780–1835* (New Haven: Yale University Press, 1977), chap. 5; Carroll Smith-Rosenberg, "The Female World of Love and Ritual: Relations Between Women in Nineteenth-Century America," in *A Heritage of Her Own: Toward a New Social History of American Women*, ed. Nancy F. Cott and Elizabeth H. Pleck (New York: Simon & Schuster, 1979), 311–42; Lillian Faderman, *Surpassing the Love of Men: Romantic Friendship and Love Between Women from the Renaissance to the Present* (New York: William Morrow and Company, 1981).

10. Jean Baker Miller, *Toward a New Psychology of Women* (Boston: Beacon Press, 1976), 83.

11. The acquisition of feminine or masculine personality traits is generally explained by two principal models. One is the process of socialization into gender roles. The other is the psychoanalytic theory of psycho-social development known as object-relations, popularized by Nancy Chodorow. See Chodorow's *The Reproduction of Mothering: Psychoanalysis and the Sociology of Gender* (Berkeley: University of California Press, 1978).

12. For recent analyses of women's friendships, see Hunt; Lillian Rubin, *Just Friends: The Role of Friendship in Our Lives* (New York: Harper and Row, 1985); Luise Eichenbaum and Susie Orbach, *Between Women: Love, Envy and Competition in Women's Friendships* (New York: Viking Penguin, 1988); and Pat O'Connor, *Friendships Between Women: A Critical Review* (New York: Guilford Press, 1992).

13. Paul H. Wright. "Gender Differences in Adults' Same- and Cross-Gender Friendships,"

in *Older Adult Friendship: Structure and Process*, ed. Rebecca G. Adams and Rosemary Bliesner (Newbury Park, CA: Sage Publications, 1986), 215.

14. Dorothy Jerrome, "The Significance of Friendship for Women in Later Life," *Ageing and Society* 1, no. 2 (July 1981), 177.

15. Hedva J. Lewittes, "Just Being Friendly Means a Lot—Women, Friendship, and Aging," in *Women in the Later Years: Health, Social, and Cultural Perspectives*, ed. Lois Grau in collaboration with Ida Susser (New York: Haworth Press, 1989), 141.

16. Susan E. Crohan and Toni C. Antonucci, "Friends as a Source of Social Support in Old Age," in *Older Adult Friendship: Structure and Process*, ed. R. G. Adams and R. Blieszner (Newbury Park, CA: Sage Publications, 1989), 133.

17. Joan C. Tronto persuasively argues that the association of caring work with the private sphere hides its social nature and leads to its devaluation. *Moral Boundaries: A Political Argument for an Ethic of Care* (New York: Routledge, 1993), 120.

18. W. J. Sauer and R. T. Coward, eds., *Social Support Networks and the Care of the Elderly: Theory, Research, and Practice* (New York: Springer Publishing Company, 1985).

19. Care and caring are often used interchangeably; I follow this practice. Some authors identify these terms as dispositions, while "caregiving" is assigned a behavioral component. My own view is that while care often involves an attitude, it must also involve action to be ethically significant.

20. Carol Gilligan, *In a Different Voice: Psychological Theory and Women's Development* (Cambridge: Harvard University Press, 1982).

21. Two proponents of these positions are, respectively, Nel Noddings and Joan Tronto. See Noddings' *Caring: A Feminine Approach to Ethics and Moral Education* (Berkeley: University of California Press, 1984) and Tronto's *Moral Boundaries*. See, also, the Symposium on Care and Justice in *Hypatia* 10, no. 2 (Spring 1995). I will return to these issues in chap. 4.

22. Gilligan, 63. "Caregiving" is often used in a fairly restrictive sense to connote the care of dependent others—children, the sick, and the elderly. See, for example, Emily K. Abel and Margaret K. Nelson, eds., *Circles of Care: Work and Identity in Women's Lives* (Albany: State University of New York Press, 1990). I think this usage is unnecessarily restrictive since friends often engage in these activities in what might be an interdependent fashion.

23. Barbara Hilkert Andolsen, "Justice, Gender, and the Frail Elderly: Reexamining the Ethic of Care," *Journal of Feminist Studies in Religion* 9, no. 1–2 (Spring–Fall 1993), 134.

24. I use this term to suggest expressions of women's experience shaped by socio-cultural, historical arrangements, not biological dimensions of femaleness.

25. Deborah Tannen, *You Just Don't Understand: Women and Men in Conversation* (New York: William Morrow and Company, 1990).

26. Rachel Josefowitz Siegel, "We Are Not Your Mothers: Report on Two Groups for Women Over Sixty," in *Women, Aging, and Ageism*, ed. Evelyn R. Rosenthal (New York: Harrington Park Press, 1990), 85.

27. Paula J. Caplan, *Between Women: Lowering the Barriers* (Toronto: Personal Library, 1981), 127.

28. Tannen, 114, 115.

29. Sally Yerkovich, "Gossiping as a Way of Speaking," *Journal of Communication* 27, no. 1 (1977), 192, 196.

30. May Sarton, *As We Are Now* (New York: W. W. Norton and Company, 1973), 66.

31. Beverly Wildung Harrison, "The Power of Anger in the Work of Love: Christian Ethics for Women and Other Strangers," in *Making the Connections: Essays in Feminist Social Ethics*, ed. Carol S. Robb (Boston: Beacon Press, 1985), 14.

32. Tronto, 119.

33. Arlie Russel Hochschild, *The Unexpected Community* (Englewood Cliffs, NJ: Prentice-Hall, 1973), 78.

34. Jacob Levine, "Humour as a Form of Therapy: Introduction to Symposium, " in *It's a Funny Thing, Humour*, ed. A. J. Chapman and H. C. Foot (Oxford: Pergamon Press, 1977), 127–37.

35. Mary Crawford, "Humor in Conversational Context: Beyond Biases in the Study of Gender and Humor," in *Representations: Social Constructions of Gender*, ed. R. K. Unger, sponsored by the Society for the Psychological Study of Social Issues (Amityville, NY: Baywood Publishing Company, 1989), 163.

36. Lee Edward Klosinski, *The Meals in Mark* (Ann Arbor: University Microfims International, 1988), 48.

37. See Marjorie L. DeVault, *Feeding the Family: The Social Organization of Caring as Gendered Work* (Chicago: University of Chicago Press, 1991).

38. Jerrome, 192.

39. See Hunt for her discussion on sacramentalizing friendship, 117ff.

40. Arlie Russel Hochschild, *The Managed Heart: Commercialization of Human Feeling* (Berkeley: University of California Press, 1983), 6. See, also, Mary Romero, *Maid in the U.S.A.* (New York: Routledge, 1992).

41. R. L. Kahn and T. C. Antonucci, "Convoys over the the Life Course: Attachment, Roles, and Social Support," in *Life-Span Development and Behavior*, vol. 3, ed. P. B. Bates and O. Brim (New York: Academic Press, 1980), 253–86.

42. Crohan and Antonucci.

Chapter Two: The Witch in the Mirror

1. Barbara A. Schreier, *Becoming American Women: Clothing and the Jewish Immigrant Experience, 1880–1920* (Chicago: Chicago Historical Society, 1994), 59, 64.

2. My assumption is that a woman's sex—her femaleness—is biologically based, whereas her gender—her femininity—is socially constructed.

3. Jean-Jacques Rousseau, *Emile or On Education*, introduction, translation and notes by Alan Bloom (New York: Basic Books, 1979), 365; Mary Wollstonecraft, *A Vindication of the Rights of Woman*, in *The Feminist Papers*, ed. Alice Rossi (Boston: Northeastern University Press, 1988), 57.

4. In his study of commercial advertisements, Erving Goffman notes a fundamental difference beween the way boys and girls are represented: "Boys, as it were, have to push their way into manhood, and problematic effort is involved. Girls merely have to unfold." *Gender Advertisements* (New York: Harper and Row, 1976), 38. Dorothy E. Smith writes, "Doctrines of femininity interpret women as producing themselves for men as extensions of men's consciousness and as objects of men's desire." *Texts, Facts, and Femininity: Exploring the Relations of Ruling* (London: Routledge, 1990), 191.

    The imperative to shape one's body to some standard of "attractiveness" is not exclusive to heterosexual practice. It also obtains in some dominant expressions of lesbian cultural practice, where the desire, of course, is to attract women.

5. Polly Young-Eisendrath argues: "Within our patriarchal society, the personal power of women is conveyed by her appearance. This power of appearance is the only socially condoned power openly afforded to all female persons in patriarchy." "The Female Person and How We Talk about Her," in *Feminist Thought and the Structure of Knowledge*, ed. Mary McCanney Gergen (New York: New York University Press, 1988), 169.

6. Lois W. Banner, *American Beauty* (Chicago: University of Chicago Press, 1983).

7. Kathy Peiss, "Making Faces: The Cosmetics Industry and the Cultural Construction of Gender, 1890–1930," in *Unequal Sisters: A Multi-Cultural Reader in U.S. Women's History*, 2d ed., ed. Vicki L. Ruiz and Ellen Carol DuBois (New York: Routledge, 1994), 372.

8. Peiss, 384, 391.

9. Susie Orbach, *Hunger Strike: The Anorectic's Struggle as a Metaphor for Our Age* (New York: W. W. Norton and Company, 1986), 72.

10. Stuart Ewen and Elizabeth Ewen, *Channels of Desire: Mass Images and the Shaping of American Consciousness* (Minneapolis: University of Minnesota Press, 1992), 70.

11. Naomi Wolf, *The Beauty Myth: How Images of Beauty Are Used Against Women* (New York: Anchor Books/Doubleday, 1991), 17. The diet and cosmetic industries do well when compared with 1992 federal social expenditures for education ($20 billion) and housing ($18 billion). U. S. Bureau of the Census, *Statistical Abstract of the United States: 1995*, 11th ed. (Washington, DC, 1995), table 583, p. 374.

12. Danae Clark writes that "lesbians have a long tradition of resisting dominant cultural definitions of female beauty and fashion as a way of separating themselves from heterosexual culture politically and as a way of signalling their lesbianism to other women in their subcultural group." She also recognizes that in recent years, many younger lesbians, especially, are rejecting the "anti-style" of the past and "finding a great deal of pleasure in playing with possibilities of fashion and beauty." "Commodity Lesbianism," in *The Lesbian and Gay Studies Reader*, ed. Henry Abelove, Michèle Aina Barale, and David M. Halperin (New York: Routledge, 1993), 188, 189. See, also, Arlene Stein, "All Dressed Up, but No Place to Go? Style Wars and the New Lesbianism," in *The Persistent Desire: A Femme-Butch Reader*, ed. Joan Nestle (Boston: Alyson Publications, 1992), 431–39.

   For alternatives to dominant beauty standards among African American women, see, for example, Noliwe M. Rooks' insightful study, *Hair Raising: Beauty, Culture, and African American Women* (New Brunswick, NJ: Rutgers University Press, 1996). See, also, Sheila Parker et al., "Body Image and Weight Concerns among African American and White Adolescent Females: Differences that Make a Difference," *Human Organization* 54, no. 2 (Summer 1995) and Midge Wilson and Kathy Russell, *Divided Sisters: Bridging the Gap Between Black Women and White Women* (New York: Anchor Books/Doubleday, 1996).

13. Wendy Cooper, *Hair: Sex Society Symbolism* (New York: Stein and Day/Publishers, 1971), 91.

14. Richard Corson, *Fashions in Hair: The First Five Thousand Years* (New York: Hillary House Publishers, 1971).

15. Cooper, 153, 164. Cooper (164) argues, however, that in the seventeenth century, a long line of "artist-hairdressers" arose in France, some of whom operated a hair salon "for ladies' hair."

16. Banner, 211.

17. Susan Brownmiller, *Femininity* (New York: Fawcett Columbine, 1984), 75.

18. Wolf, 157.

19. Wendy Chapkis, *Beauty Secrets: Women and the Politics of Appearance* (Boston: South End Press, 1986), 140.

20. Laura Mulvey, "Visual Pleasure and Narrative Cinema," *Screen* 16, no. 13 (August 1975), 17.

21. *New Shorter Oxford English Dictionary*, thumb index ed. (1993), s.v. "frump" and "dowdy."

22. Margaret R. Miles, *Carnal Knowing: Female Nakedness and Religious Meaning in the Christian West* (New York: Vintage Books, 1989), 147.

23. Tertullian, *De Cultu Fem.* 1, 1, cited by Rosemary Radford Ruether, "Misogynism and Virginal Feminism in the Fathers of the Church," in *Religion and Sexism: Images of Woman in*

the Jewish and Christian Traditions, ed. Rosemary Radford Ruether (New York: Simon and Schuster, 1974), 157.

24. Miles, 161.

25. See Nel Noddings, *Women and Evil* (Berkeley: University of California Press, 1989), chap. 2. I focus here on Christian culture's perspectives on women's bodies because all people living in American society partake of this worldview today, and, I assume, so do my study's participants. In addition, however, there is also a legacy of negative Jewish attitudes toward women's physicality from rabbinic rather than biblical sources. The provenance of such ideas is different from those of Christianity, and the negative views are sometimes balanced by positive attitudes. Nonetheless, such Jewish views may still be passed on in Jewish families, even in those that are no longer observant. See Judith Plaskow, *Standing Again at Sinai: Judaism from a Feminist Perspective* (San Francisco: Harper and Row, 1990). It goes without saying that negative perceptions of women's bodies did not stop in antiquity but have been added to these foundational views, especially in the current century.

26. Kathryn Pauly Morgan, "Women and the Knife: Cosmetic Surgery and the Colonization of Women's Bodies," *Hypatia* 6, no. 3 (Fall 1991), 37.

27. Pat Anderson, "The Cosmetic Industry: The Externalization of Women's Identity," paper prepared for the course "Psychology of Women" (Chicago: DePaul University, 1995).

28. Sandra Lee Bartky, "Narcissism, Femininity and Alienation," *Social Theory and Practice* 8, no. 2 (Summer 1982), 135, 136.

29. John Berger, *Ways of Seeing* (London: British Broadcasting Corporation and Penguin Books, 1972) 46, 47, 63.

30. Orbach, 36.

31. Susan Bordo, *Unbearable Weight: Feminism, Western Culture, and the Body* (Berkeley: University of California Press, 1993), 30.

32. Michel Foucault, *The History of Sexuality*, vol. 1: *An Introduction*, trans. Robert Hurley (New York: Vintage Books, 1990).

33. Fenja Gunn, *The Artificial Face: A History of Cosmetics* (Newton Abbot, Devon: David and Charles, 1973), 157.

34. Rosalind Coward, *Female Desires: How They Are Sought, Bought, and Packaged* (New York: Grove Press, 1985), 14.

35. I borrow this phrase from the subtitle of Mary Louise Bringle's book, *The God of Thinness: Gluttony and Other Weighty Matters* (Nashville: Abingdon Press, 1992).

36. African American women display a greater acceptance of larger body size and greater body weight than do white women. However, concurrent with the growth of the black middle class, there has been a rise in eating disorders among young African American women, perhaps suggesting a shift in attitudes. See Wilson and Russell, 97–102.

37. Orbach, 47, 61.

38. See Bordo.

39. Iris Marion Young, *Throwing Like a Girl and Other Essays in Feminist Philosophy and Social Theory* (Bloomington: Indiana University Press, 1990), 141–59.

40. Brownmiller, 33.

41. Bordo, 24–25.

42. On this last point, see Wolf, 200.

43. See Joanne Finkelstein, *The Fashioned Self* (Philadelphia: Temple University Press, 1991).

44. See Keith Walden, "The Road to Fat City: An Interpretation of the Development of Weight Consciousness in Western Society," *Historical Reflections/Reflexions Historiques* 12, no. 3 (1985), 331–73.

45. Bringle, 94.

46. Wolf, 184–85.
47. See Bordo.
48. Finkelstein, 68, 119.
49. Finkelstein, 182–83.
50. A Greek friend tells me that Greeks living in the United States make parallel claims about Greek looks. Another friend informs me that a common phrase among Irish Americans is, "You have the map of Ireland on your face." This may suggest that members of ethnic groups "read" the body for familiar clues.
51. Here Marny recognizes that Jewish identity is contextually constructed, a view that mirrors social psychological theory and research. See Simon N. Herman, *Jewish Identity: A Social Psychological Perspective* (Beverly Hills, CA: Sage Publications, 1977).
52. Sander Gilman, *The Jew's Body* (New York: Routledge, 1991), 191, 193.
53. Iris Marion Young, *Justice and the Politics of Difference* (Princeton: Princeton University Press, 1990), 123.
54. Charlotte Baum, Paula Hyman, and Sonya Michel, *The Jewish Woman in America* (New York: Plume Books, New American Library, 1976), 224–25.
55. Toni Morrison, *The Bluest Eye* (New York: Alfred A. Knopf, 1993).
56. An interesting image for a Jew to use in reference to her own experience. It clearly demonstrates the high degree to which many Jews have become acculturated into the larger Christian society in America.
57. See Schreier for a discussion of Jewish immigrant women's pressures toward Americanization.

Chapter Three: "What's My Alternative?"

1. Wendy Chapkis provides an insightful view of Jane Fonda, and, by extension, of the current American preoccupation with physical fitness: "If bulimia was Jane Fonda's secret vice, fitness is her public virtue. And yet the objective of both is remarkably similar—live but don't change." *Beauty Secrets: Women and the Politics of Appearance* (Boston: South End Press, 1986), 10.
2. For a more detailed cataloguing of the invisibility of older people—especially older women—in the print media, see Betty Friedan, *The Fountain of Age* (New York: Simon & Schuster, 1993), 35–38.
3. *The Chicago Tribune*, 4 Dec. 1991, sec. 5.
4. Jennie Keith, "Age in Social and Cultural Context: Anthropological Perspectives," in *Handbook of Aging and the Social Sciences*, 3d ed., ed. Robert H. Binstock and Linda K. George (San Diego: Academic Press, 1990), 91–111. A recent national study for the American Association of Retired Persons reports, "Respondents gave a wide variety of reasons for their perceptions of the age at which men and women become 'old.' This suggests that there is little consensus about benchmarks that indicate aging in the minds of Americans." American Association of Retired Persons, *Images of Aging in America: Final Report*, prepared by Kathy Speas and Beth Obenshain (Chapel Hill, NC: FGI Integrated Marketing, 1995), 21.
5. How our conception of old age is to be defined by a post-modern, information-based economy remains to be seen. For the connection between industrialism, capitalism, and views of old age, see Chris Phillipson, *Capitalism and the Construction of Old Age* (London: MacMillan, 1982) and Beverly Wildung Harrison, "The Older Person's Worth in the Eyes of Society," in *Making the Connections: Essays in Feminist Social Ethics*, ed. Carol S. Robb (Boston: Beacon Press, 1985), 152–66.
6. Malcolm H. Morrison, "Work and Retirement in an Older Society," in *Our Aging Society:*

Paradox and Promise, ed. Alan Pifer and Lydia Bronte (New York: W. W. Norton and Company, 1986), 341–65.

7. Barbara Myerhoff with Deena Metzger, Jay Ruby, and Virginia Tufte, "Aging and the Aged in Other Cultures: An Anthropological Perspective," in *Remembered Lives: The Work of Ritual, Storytelling, and Growing Older*, ed. Mark Kaminsky (Ann Arbor: University of Michigan Press, 1992), 113.

8. On Jewish views of old age, see Dayle A. Friedman, "The Crown of Glory: Aging in the Jewish Tradition," in *Celebration and Renewal: Rites of Passage in Judaism*, ed. Rela M. Geffen (Philadelphia: Jewish Publication Society, 1993), 202–25. For Christian perspectives, see Thomas R. Cole, *The Journey of Life: A Cultural History of Aging in America* (New York: Cambridge University Press, 1992).

9. Harry R. Moody, "The Meaning of Old Age," in *Aging and Ethics: Philosophical Problems in Gerontology*, ed. Nancy S. Jecker (Clifton, NJ: Humana Press, 1991), 64.

10. Keith, 94.

11. Stephen Sapp, *Full of Years: Aging and the Elderly in the Bible and Today* (Nashville: Abingdon Press, 1987), 36.

12. Florence Kluckhohn in Myerhoff, 114.

13. Myerhoff, 114.

14. William F. May, "The Virtues and Vices of the Elderly," in *What Does It Mean to Grow Old? Reflections from the Humanities*, ed. Thomas R. Cole and Sally A. Gadow (Durham, NC: Duke University Press, 1986), 47.

15. Terri L. Premo, *Winter Friends: Women Growing Older in the New Republic, 1785–1835* (Urbana: University of Illinois Press, 1990), 120–122. See, also, Cole, pt. I, *passim*. Given the tremendous rise in longevity in our own century, old age in previous centuries connoted a much younger chronological age. Instead of referring to people in their seventies and eighties, as in our own time, people in their fortiess and fifties were considered old.

16. May, 47.

17. Sally Gadow, "Recovering the Body in Aging," in *Aging and Ethics: Philosophical Problems in Gerontology*, ed. Nancy S. Jecker (Clifton, NJ: Humana Press, 1991), 115.

18. For an extended discussion of this theme, see Sapp and Cole.

19. People of all ages who are physically disabled in some way or suffer chronic illness understand first-hand some of the limitations experienced by the elderly. See Arthur Kleinman, *The Illness Narratives: Suffering, Healing & the Human Condition* (New York: Basic Books, 1988).

20. Penelope Washbourn, *Becoming Woman: The Quest for Wholeness in Female Experience* (New York: Harper and Row, 1977), 152.

21. On this point, see Cole.

22. Economic developments of the 1990s, particularly corporate downsizing, appear to be placing pressure upon middle-aged men to look younger in order to keep their jobs. See Amy M. Spindler, "It's a Face-Lifted, Tummy-Tucked Jungle Out There," *New York Times*, Sunday, 9 June 1996, sec. 3.

23. Elaine Hatfield and Susan Sprecher, *Mirror, Mirror . . . The Importance of Looks in Everyday Life* (Albany, NY: State University of New York Press, 1986), 44: 292. The connection made between youth and beauty—and its converse—is not limited to the American context. Simone de Beauvoir attributes to Lévi-Strauss the observation that the Nambikwara Indians "have a single word that means 'young and beautiful' and another that means 'old and ugly.'" *The Coming of Age*, trans. Patrick O'Brian (New York: G. P. Putnam's Sons, 1972), 5.

24. Sara Arber and Jay Ginn, *Gender in Later Life: A Sociological Analysis of Resources and Constraints* (London: Sage Publications, 1991), 45.

25. See Paul Thompson, Catherine Itzin, and Michele Abendstern, *I Don't Feel Old: The Experience of Later Life* (Oxford: Oxford University Press, 1990) for another study showing older people's tendency not to feel as old as they are chronologically.

26. See Emily Martin, *The Woman in the Body: A Cultural Analysis of Reproduction* (Boston: Beacon Press, 1987) for a discussion of women's tendency to alienate the body from the self.

27. Arber and Ginn, 45.

28. Erving Goffman, *Stigma: Notes on the Management of Spoiled Identity* (Englewood Cliffs, NJ: Prentice-Hall, 1963).

29. According to Sheila Parker et al., "Among African Americans less emphasis is placed in being young as a criteria [*sic*] for being beautiful. . . . Beauty is not associated with a short window of opportunity as it is in dominant White culture." "Body Image and Weight Concerns among African American and White Adolescent Females: Differences that Make a Diference," *Human Organization* 54, no. 2 (Summer 1995), 110.

30. Gadow, 116.

31. Ibid.

32. Martin Buber, *I and Thou*, trans. Walter Kaufman (New York: Charles Scribner's Sons, 1970).

33. Morton A. Lieberman and Sheldon S. Tobin, *The Experience of Old Age: Stress, Coping, and Survival* (New York: Basic Books, 1983), chap. 10.

34. See, for example, F. Leonard with T. Sommers and V. Dean, *Not Even Dogcatcher: Employment Discrimination and Older Women*, Gray Paper No. 8 (Washington, DC: Older Women's League, 1982). While today older men are also at risk of losing their jobs to younger people, it is not necessarily due to their graying hair; in fact, in many quarters gray hair is often thought to make men look distinguished.

35. Gari Lesnoff-Caravaglia, "Introduction," in *The World of the Older Woman: Conflicts and Resolutions*, ed. Gari Lesnoff-Caravaglia, Frontiers in Aging Series, vol. 3 (New York: Human Sciences Press, 1984), 9.

36. Susan Sontag, "The Double Standard of Aging," in *No Longer Young: The Older Woman in America*, Proceedings of the 26th Annual Conference on Aging (Ann Arbor, MI: Institute of Gerontology, University of Michigan and Wayne State University, 1975), 34.

37. Arber and Ginn, 47.

38. As a drama critic, George Bernard Shaw expressed preference for Eleanora Duse, the Italian actress, who wore no cosmetics, over Sara Bernhart, "mistress of makeup": "Her wrinkles are her credentials of humanity." As we have seen, appreciation for the untampered-with female face, especially when lined, is rare in late twentieth-century America. Cited in Studs Turkel, *Coming of Age: The Story of Our Century by Those Who've Lived It* (New York: New Press, 1995), xx.

39. See, for example, Arber and Ginn; Friedan; Jo Harrison, "Women and Ageing: Experience and Implications," *Ageing and Society* 3, no. 2 (July 1983): 209–35; Barbara Macdonald with Cynthia Rich, *Look Me in the Eye: Old Women, Aging and Ageism* (San Francisco: Spinsters, Ink, 1983); Leah Cohen, *Small Expectations: Society's Betrayal of Older Women* (Toronto: McClelland and Stewart, 1984); Baba Copper, *Over the Hill: Reflections on Ageism Between Women* (Freedom, CA: Crossing Press, 1988); *Women's Studies Quarterly* 17, no. 1 and 2 (Spring/Summer 1989); and Evelyn R. Rosenthal, ed., *Women, Aging, and Ageism* (Binghamton, NY: Harrington Park Press, 1990). Thomas Cole (*Journey*, 233) cautions against some anti-ageist positions that emerged in the 1970s, which suggested that apart from chronological age, there are no real differences between the young and the old: "The fashionable stereotype of old age showed no more tolerance or respect for the intractable vicis-

situdes of aging than the old negative stereotype. While health and self-control had been previously understood as virtues reserved for the young and middle-aged, they were increasingly demanded of the old as well."

40. Baba Copper, "Voices: On Becoming Old Women," In *Women and Aging: An Anthology by Women*, ed. Jo Alexander et al. (Corvallis, OR: Calix Books, 1986), 54.

41. Copper, *Over the Hill*, 20.

42. Alasdair MacIntyre, *After Virtue: A Study in Moral Theory*, 2d ed. (Notre Dame, IN: University of Indiana Press, 1984), 204.

43. According to Lesnoff-Caravaglia, "To be noticed, an older woman has to be an exceptional individual." "Double Stigmata: Female and Old," in *The World of the Older Woman: Conflicts and Resolutions*, ed. Gari Lesnoff-Caravaglia, Frontiers in Aging Series, vol. 3 (New York: Human Sciences Press, 1984), 12. Alternatively, Myerhoff (114) writes, "Ironically, it is often the individual's refusal to demonstrate or accept old age, the very demonstration that *flaunts* his status, which wins him respect and attention."

44. Copper, *Over the Hill*, 40.

Chapter Four: "The Cheese Stands Alone"

1. See Susan A. Glenn, *Daughters of the Shtetl: Life and Labor in the Immigrant Generation* (Ithaca and London: Cornell University Press, 1990), chap. 1.

2. Susan Moller Okin, *Justice, Gender, and the Family* (New York: Basic Books, 1989), 141, 158.

3. Barbara Hilkert Andolsen, "Justice, Gender, and the Frail Elderly: Reexamining the Ethic of Care," *Journal of Feminist Studies in Religion* 9, no. 1–2 (Spring–Fall 1993), 134.

4. Ruddick does not literally mean mother here, but rather, parent. She uses mother as a way of acknowledging the empirical reality that historically it is women who have done the work of parenting. Sara Ruddick, *Maternal Thinking: Toward a Politics of Peace* (New York: Ballantine Books, 1989), 17–21.

5. Marjorie L. Devault, *Feeding the Family: The Social Organization of Caring and Gendered Work* (Chicago: University of Chicago Press, 1991).

6. Carol Gilligan, *In a Different Voice: Psychological Theory and Women's Development* (Cambridge, MA: Harvard University Press, 1982).

7. Marilyn Waring, *If Women Counted: A New Feminist Economics* (San Francisco: Harper and Row, 1988), 227.

8. Kristine M. Baber and Katherine R. Allen, *Women & Families: Feminist Reconstructions* (New York: Guilford Press, 1992), 206.

9. Jane Addams, *Twenty Years at Hull-House* (Chicago: University of Illinois Press, 1990), 71.

10. Gunhild O. Hagestad writes, "Television, newpapers, and popular magazines portray the old as a frail, dependent group that represents a drain on national and family resources. . . . Similarly, recent research and policy debates have tended to emphasize the neediness and dependency of the old, depicting them as a drain on scarce resources. Yet there is a striking lack of perception of the old as *constituting a resource*, a lack that ignores economic as well as psychological realities." "The Aging Society as a Context for Family Life," in *Aging and Ethics: Philosophical Problems in Gerontology*, ed. Nancy S. Jecker (Clifton, NJ: Humana Press, 1991), 135.

11. Joan C. Tronto, *Moral Boundaries: A Political Argument for an Ethic of Care* (New York: Routledge, 1993), 106.

12. Tronto, 107.

13. Alexis J. Walker et al., "Motives for Parental Caregiving and Relationship Quality," *Family Relations* 39 (1990), 51–56.

14. A few women, like Sara and Sadie, tell me they did the lion's share of their parents' care-taking, with sisters playing a minimal role. In the absence of interviews with these sisters, I am unable to assess the reasons for this unequal division of labor. Employment or other family demands may account for it. For various reasons, some women's identities may also be more thoroughly related to caregiving activities.

15. Susan E. Foster and Jack A. Brizius, "Caring Too Much? American Women and the Nation's Caregiving Crisis," in *Women on the Front Lines: Meeting the Challenge of an Aging America*, ed. Jessie Allen and Alan Pifer (Washington, DC: Urban Institute Press, 1993), 55.

16. Anna Quindlen, *One True Thing* (New York: Random House, 1994), 25.

17. Paula Dressel and Ann Clark, "A Critical Look at Family Care," *Journal of Marriage and the Family* 52 (August 1990), 778.

18. Jessie Allen, "Caring Work and Gender Equality in an Aging Society," in *Women on the Front Lines*, ed. Allen and Pifer, 229.

19. Andolsen, 132–34. See, also, Tronto (112–14) for a view of care as "gendered, raced, and classed."

20. This term was suggested to me by Elizabeth Kelly, personal communication.

21. William F. May, "The Virtues and Vices of the Elderly," in *What Does It Mean To Grow Old? Reflections from the Humanities*, ed. Thomas R. Cole and Sally A. Gadow (Durham, NC: Duke University Press, 1986), 46.

22. The last observation is supported by Jaber F. Gubrium's classic empirical study of a nursing home, *Living and Dying at Murray Manor* (New York: St. Martin's Press, 1975).

23. Beth B. Hess and Joan M. Waring, "Parent and Child in Later Life: Rethinking the Relationship," in *Child Influences on Marital and Family Interaction: A Life-Span Perspective*, ed. Richard M. Lerner and Graham B. Spanier (New York: Academic Press, 1978), 242.

24. Hess and Waring, 251–52.

25. Hess and Waring, 242.

26. Tish Sommers and Laurie Shields, *Women Take Care: The Consequences of Caregiving in Today's Society* (Gainesville, FL: Triad Publishing Company, 1987), 21.

27. Paula E. Hyman, "Introduction: Perspectives on the Evolving Jewish Family," in *The Jewish Family: Myths and Reality*, ed. Steven M. Cohen and Paula E. Hyman (New York: Holmes and Meier Publishers, 1986), 7.

28. I am reminded of Reva's generosity in responding to my request that she participate in intensive interviewing. I was touched when she readily agreed, saying, "I will help you. I don't mind."

29. See, for example, Nancy Chodorow, *The Reproduction of Mothering: Psychoanalysis and the Sociology of Gender* (Berkeley: University of California Press, 1978); Lillian B. Rubin, *Intimate Strangers: Men and Women Together* (New York: Harper and Row, 1983).

30. Gilligan, p.

31. Hess and Waring, 252.

32. Phyllis S. Silverman and Adele Cooperband, "Widow-to-Widow: The Elderly Widow and Mutual Help," in *The World of the Older Woman: Conflicts and Resolutions*, ed. Gari Lesnoff-Caravaglia, Frontiers of Aging Series, vol. 3 (New York: Human Sciences Press, 1984), 144.

33. Gari Lesnoff-Caravaglia, "Widowhood: The Last Stage of Wifedom," in *The World of the Older Woman*, ed. Gari Lesnoff-Caravaglia, 137, 142.

34. Teri is one of two Christians I interviewed in depth. Alice is the other.

35. Silverman and Cooperband, 145.

36. Notice yet another bodily metaphor of brokenness here—a blow—one that we encounter several times in this section on loss.

37. Silverman and Cooperband, 155.

Chapter Five: Energetic Anger

1. Allegra Taylor, *Older Than Time: A Grandmother's Search for Wisdom* (London: Aquarian/Thorsons, 1993).

2. David J. Maitland argues that the elderly constitute a counterculture by virtue of their detachment from dominant cultural attitudes. I like his notion of a counterculture but believe it functions more accurately as a political goal (or vocation, to use his language) to be achieved rather than as an accurate description of most older people's existing views. *Aging as Counterculture: A Vocation for the Later Years* (New York: Pilgrim Press, 1991).

3. Ann Ferguson, "Feminist Communities and Moral Revolution," in *Feminism and Community*, ed. Penny A. Weiss and Marilyn Friedman (Philadelphia: Temple University Press, 1995), 372.

4. Sara Arber and Jay Ginn, *Gender and Later Life: A Sociological Analysis of Resources and Constraints* (London: Sage Publications, 1991), 49.

5. The notion of a religiously "musical" temperament is a take-off on Max Weber's famous characterization of himself as "religiously unmusical." H. H. Gerth and C. Wright Mills, eds., *From Max Weber: Essays in Sociology* (New York: Oxford University Press, 1946), 25.

6. Beverly Wildung Harrison, "The Older Person's Worth in the Eyes of Society," in *Making the Connections: Essays in Feminist Social Ethics*, ed. Carol S. Robb (Boston: Beacon Press, 1985), 164.

7. Maitland, 171.

8. U. S. Bureau of the Census, *Statistical Abstracts of the United States: 1995*, 115th ed. (Washington, DC, 1995), table 83, p. 68.

9. Maitland, 96.

10. Harrison, 166.

11. See Jenna Weissman Joselit, *The Wonders of America: Reinventing Jewish Culture, 1880–1950* (New York: Hill and Wang, 1994), 127ff., for an account of these developments.

12. E. M. Broner, "Honor and Ceremony in Women's Rituals," in *The Politics of Women's Spirituality: Essays on the Rise of Spiritual Power Within the Feminist Movement*, ed. Charlene Spretnak (Garden City, NY: Anchor Books, 1982), 236.

13. For an exploration of diverse feminist liturgical and ritual experiments, see Marjorie Procter-Smith and Janet R. Walton, eds., *Women at Worship: Interpretations of North American Diversity* (Louiville, KY: Westminster/John Knox Press, 1993).

14. Dayle A. Friedman, "The Crown of Glory: Aging in the Jewish Tradition," in *Celebration & Renewal: Rites of Passage in Judaism* (Philadelphia: Jewish Publication Society, 1993), 221. This last set of rituals may be used, of course, for women or men alike.

15. Penelope Washbourn, "Becoming Woman: Menstruation as Spiritual Challenge," in *Womanspirit Rising: A Feminist Reader in Religion*, ed. Carol P. Christ and Judith Plaskow (San Francisco: Harper and Row, 1992), 254.

16. Rosemary Radford Ruether, *Women-Church: Theology and Practice of Feminist Liturgical Communities* (San Francisco: Harper and Row, 1986), 206. For an example of a Christian croning ritual, see Ruether, 207–9; for a Jewish counterpart, see Marcia Cohn Spiegel, "Becoming a Crone," *Lilith* 21 (Fall 1988), 18–19. See, also, Edna M. Ward, ed., *Celebrating Ourselves: A Crone Ritual Book* (Portland, ME: Astarte Shell Press, 1992).

17. While Jewish women may be seen from the perspective of the gentile, Christian, or non-ethnic gaze, women of color are subjected, as well, to the white gaze.

18. Ada María Isasi-Díaz, "Toward an Understanding of *Feminismo Hispano* in the U. S. A.," in *Women's Consciousness, Women's Conscience: A Reader in Feminist Ethics*, ed. Barbara Hilkert Andolsen, Christine E. Gudorf, and Mary D. Pellauer (Minneapolis: Winston Press, 1985), 51.

19. Business ethicists would do well to investigate the moral obligations of business regarding the representation of women—young and old—in advertising and to press businesses to meet such obligations.

20. Kathryn Pauly Morgan, "Women and the Knife: Cosmetic Surgery and the Colonization of Women's Bodies," *Hypatia* 6, no. 3 (Fall 1991), 42.

21. Jana Sawicki, *Disciplining Foucault: Feminism, Power, and the Body* (New York: Routledge, 1991), 27.

22. Madeline Muir (producer and director), *West Coast Crones*, exec. prod. Kathy Wolfe (Box 64, New Almaden, CA 95042: Wolfe Video, 1991).

23. Meridel Le Sueur, "Remarks From 1983 Poetry Reading," in *Women and Aging: An Anthology by Women*, ed. Jo Alexander et al. (Corvalis, OR: Calyx Books, 1986), 9.

24. Baba Copper, *Over the Hill: Reflections on Ageism Between Women* (Freedom, CA: Crossing Press, 1988), 59.

25. Jenny Joseph, "Warning," in *When I Am an Old Woman I Shall Wear Purple*, ed. Sandra Haldeman Martz (Watsonville, CA: Papier-Mache Press, 1991), 1.

26. Ruth Harriet Jacobs, *Be An Outrageous Older Woman—a RASP* (Manchester, CT: Knowledge, Ideas, and Trends, 1991), 1, 165, 168.

27. National Film Board of Canada, *Strangers in Good Company*, prod. David Wilson, dir. Cynthia Scott (New York: First Run-Icarus Film, 1990).

28. For anthologies about the aged, in general, see, for example, Thomas R. Cole and Mary G. Winkler, eds., *The Oxford Book of Aging* (Oxford: Oxford University Press, 1994) and Margaret Cruikshank, ed., *Fierce with Reality: An Anthology of Literature on Aging* (St. Cloud, MN: North Star Press of St. Cloud, 1995). For collections by and about older women, see, for example, Jo Alexander et al., eds., *Women and Aging: An Anthology by Women* (Corvallis, OR: Calyx Books, 1986); Janet Ford and Ruth Sinclair, *Sixty Years On: Women Talk About Old Age* (London: Women's Press, 1987); Sandra Haldeman Martz, ed., *When I Am an Old Woman I Shall Wear Purple* (Watsonville, CA: Papier-Mache Press, 1991); Peggy Downes et al., eds., *The New Older Woman: A Dialogue for the Coming Century* (Berkeley: Celestial Arts, 1996).

29. bell hooks, *Black Looks: Race and Representation* (Boston: South End Press, 1992), 115–16.

30. Melanie Kaye/Kantrowitz, "Some Notes on Jewish Lesbian Identity," in *Nice Jewish Girls: A Lesbian Anthology*, ed. Evelyn Torton Beck (Trumansburg, NY: The Crossing Press, 1982), 40, 42.

31. Morgan, 45–46.

32. The term is Naomi Wolf's. *The Beauty Myth: How Images of Beauty Are Used Against Women* (New York: Anchor Books/Doubleday, 1991).

33. American Association of Retired Persons, *Images of Aging: Children's Attitudes: Summary Report* (January 1995), n. p.

34. American Association of Retired Persons, *Images of Aging in America: National Teen Survey: Summary Report* (January 1995), 16.

35. American Association of Retired Persons and National Association of Partners in Education, *Becoming a School Partner: A Guidebook for Organizing Intergenerational Partnerships in Schools* (American Association of Retired Persons, 1992), 7, 23.

36. "Publication Offers Tips on Young and Old Serving Together," *Generations United Newline* (Summer 1994), 3.

37. For a model of justice regarding family gender roles, see Susan Moller Okin, *Justice, Gender, and the Family* (New York: Basic Books, 1989), chap. 8.

38. Kristine M. Baber and Katherine R. Allen, *Women and Families: Feminist Reconstructions* (New York: Guilford Press, 1992), 174.

39. The following suggestions about new roles for older women are taken from Ruth Harriet Jacobs, "Expanding Social Roles for Older Women," in *Women on the Front Lines: Meeting the Challenge of an Aging America*, ed. Jessie Allen and Alan Pifer (Washington, DC: Urban Institute Press, 1993), 207–14.

40. Jacobs, 209.

41. Jacobs, 214.

42. Betty Friedan, *The Fountain of Age* (New York: Simon & Schuster, 1993).

43. Harry R. Moody, "Age, Productivity, and Transcendence," in *Achieving a Productive Aging Society*, ed. Scott A. Bass, Francis G. Caro, and Yung-Ping Chen (Westport, CT: Auburn House, 1993), 36, 38, 36.

44. Maitland, 144.

45. Harrison, 166.

46. Taylor.

✣ Works Cited ✣

Abel, Emily K., and Margaret K. Nelson, eds. *Circles of Care: Work and Identity in Women's Lives*. Albany, NY: State University of New York Press, 1990.

Addams, Jane. *Twenty Years at Hull-House*. Chicago: University of Illinois Press, 1990.

Alexander, Jo, Debi Berrow, Lisa Domitrovich, Margarita Donnelly, and Cheryl McLean, eds. *Women and Aging: An Anthology by Women*. Corvalis, OR: Calyx Books, 1986.

Allen, Jessie. "Caring Work and Gender Equality in an Aging Society." In *Women on the Front Lines: Meeting the Challenge of an Aging America*, edited by Jessie Allen and Alan Pifer, 221–39. Washington, DC: Urban Institute Press, 1993.

———. "The Front Lines." In *Women on the Front Lines: Meeting the Challenge of an Aging America*, edited by Jessie Allen and Alan Pifer, 1–10. Washington, DC: Urban Institute Press, 1993.

Allen, Jessie, and Alan Pifer, eds. *Women on the Front Lines: Meeting the Challenge of an Aging America*. Washington, DC: Urban Institute Press, 1993.

American Association of Retired Persons. *Images of Aging: Children's Attitudes: Summary Report* (January 1995).

———. *Images of Aging in America: Final Report*, prepared by Kathy Speas and Beth Obenshain. Chapel Hill, NC: FGI Integrated Marketing, 1995.

———. *Images of Aging in America: National Teen Survey: Summary Report* (January 1995).

American Association of Retired Persons and National Association of Partners in Education. *Becoming a School Partner: A Guidebook for Organizing Intergenerational Partnerships in Schools*. American Association of Retired Persons, 1992.

Anderson, Pat. "The Cosmetic Industry: The Externalization of Women's Identity." Paper prepared for the course "Psychology of Women." Chicago: Depaul University, 1995.

Andolsen, Barbara Hilkert. "Justice, Gender, and the Frail Elderly: Reexamining the Ethic of Care." *Journal of Feminist Studies in Religion* 9, no. 1–2 (Spring–Fall 1993), 127–45.

Arber, Sara, and Jay Ginn. *Gender and Later Life: A Sociological Analysis of Resources and Constraints.* London: Sage Publications, 1991.

Aristotle. *Nichomachean Ethics.* Translated by David Ross. Oxford: Oxford University Press, 1925.

Baber, Kristine M., and Katherine R. Allen. *Women & Families: Feminist Reconstructions.* New York: Guilford Press, 1992.

Banner, Lois W. *American Beauty.* Chicago: University of Chicago Press, 1983.

Bartky, Sandra Lee. "Narcissism, Femininity and Alienation." *Social Theory and Practice* 8, no. 2 (Summer 1982), 127–43.

Baum, Charlotte, Paula Hyman, and Sonya Michel. *The Jewish Woman in America.* New York: Plume Books, New American Library, 1976.

Behar, Ruth. *Translated Woman: Crossing the Border with Esperanza's Story.* Boston: Beacon Press, 1993.

Behar, Ruth, and Deborah A. Gordon, eds. *Women Writing Culture.* Berkeley: University of California Press, 1995.

Berger, John. *Ways of Seeing.* London: British Broadcasting Corporation and Penguin Books, 1972.

Bordo, Susan. *Unbearable Weight: Feminism, Western Culture, and the Body.* Berkeley: University of California Press, 1993.

Bringle, Mary Louise. *The God of Thinness: Gluttony and Other Weighty Matters.* Nashville: Abingdon Press, 1992.

Broner, E. M. "Honor and Ceremony in Women's Rituals." In *The Politics of Women's Spirituality: Essays on the Rise of Spiritual Power Within the Feminist Movement,* edited by Charlene Spretnak, 234-44. Garden City, NY: Anchor Books, 1982.

Brownmiller, Susan. *Femininity.* New York: Fawcett Columbine, 1984.

Buber, Martin. *I and Thou.* Translated by Walter Kaufman. New York: Charles Scribner's Sons, 1970.

———. *Paths in Utopia.* Translated by R. F. C. Hull. New York: Macmillan, 1950.

Callahan, Daniel. *Setting Limits: Medical Goals in an Aging Society.* New York: Simon & Schuster, 1987.

Caplan, Paula J. *Between Women: Lowering the Barriers.* Toronto: Personal Library, 1981.

Chapkis, Wendy. *Beauty Secrets: Women and the Politics of Appearance.* Boston: South End Press, 1986.

Chodorow, Nancy. *The Reproduction of Mothering: Psychoanalysis and the Sociology of Gender.* Berkeley: University of California Press, 1978.

Clark, Danae. "Commodity Lesbianism." In *The Lesbian and Gay Studies Reader,* edited by Henry Abelove, Michele Aina Barale, and David M. Halperin, 186–201. New York: Routledge, 1993.

Clifford, James, and George E. Marcus, eds. *Writing Culture: The Poetics and Politics of Ethnography.* Berkeley: University of California Press, 1986.

Cohen, Leah. *Small Expectations: Society's Betrayal of Older Women.* Toronto: McClelland and Stewart, 1984.

Cole, Thomas R. *The Journey of Life: A Cultural History of Aging in America.* New York: Cambridge University Press, 1992.

———. "Oedipus and the Meaning of Aging: Personal Reflections and Historical Perspectives." In *Aging and Ethics: Philosophical Problems in Gerontology*, edited by Nancy S. Jecker, 92–111. Clifton, NJ: Humana Press, 1991.

Cole, Thomas R., and Mary G. Winkler, eds. *The Oxford Book of Aging.* Oxford: Oxford University Press, 1994.

Collier, Jr., John, and Malcolm Collier. *Visual Anthropology: Photography as a Research Method.* Revised and expanded ed. Albuquerque: University of New Mexico Press, 1986.

Cooper, Wendy. *Hair: Sex Society Symbolism.* New York: Stein and Day Publishers, 1971.

Copper, Baba. *Over the Hill: Reflections on Ageism Between Women.* Freedom, CA: Crossing Press, 1988.

———. "Voices: On Becoming Old Women." In *Women and Aging: An Anthology by Women*, edited by Jo Alexander, Debi Berrow, Lisa Domitrovich, Margarita Donnelly, and Cheryl McLean, 47–57. Corvallis, OR: Calix Books, 1986.

Corson, Richard. *Fashions in Hair: The First Five Thousand Years.* New York: Hillary House Publishers, 1971.

Cott, Nancy F. *The Bonds of Womanhood: "Woman's Sphere" in New England, 1780–1835.* New Haven: Yale University Press, 1977.

Coward, Rosalind. *Female Desires: How They Are Sought, Bought, and Packaged.* New York: Grove Press, 1985.

Crawford, Mary. "Humor in Conversational Context: Beyond Biases in the Study of Gender and Humor." In *Representations: Social Constructions of Gender*, edited by R. K. Unger, 155–66. Sponsored by the Society for the Psychological Study of Social Issues. Amityville, NY: Baywood Publishing Company, 1989.

Crohan, Susan E., and Toni C. Antonucci. "Friends as a Source of Social Support in Old Age." In *Older Adult Friendship: Structure and Process*, edited by R. G. Adams and R. Blieszner, 129–46. Newbury Park, CA: Sage Publications, 1989.

Cruikshank, Margaret, ed. *Fierce with Reality: An Anthology of Literature on Aging.* St. Cloud, MN: North Star Press of St. Cloud, 1995.

de Beauvoir, Simone. *The Coming of Age.* Translated by Patrick O'Brian. New York: G. P. Putnam's Sons, 1972.

Devaney, Sheila Greeve. "The Limits of the Appeal to Women's Experience." In *Shaping New Vision: Gender and Values in American Culture*, edited by Clarissa W. Atkinson, Constance H. Buchanan, and Margaret R. Miles, 31–49. Ann Arbor: UMI Reseach Press, 1987.

DeVault, Marjorie L. *Feeding the Family: The Social Organization of Caring as Gendered*

Work. Chicago: University of Chicago Press, 1991.

Douglas, Jack. "Deviance and Respectability: The Social Construction of Moral Meanings." In *Deviance and Respectability: The Social Construction of Moral Meanings*, edited by Jack D. Douglas, 3–30. New York: Basic Books, 1970.

Downes, Peggy, Patricia Faul, Virginia Mudd, and Ilene Tuttle. *The New Older Woman: A Dialogue for the Coming Century*. Berkeley: Celestial Arts, 1996.

Dressel, Paula, and Ann Clark. "A Critical Look at Family Care." *Journal of Marriage and the Family* 52 (August 1990), 769–82.

Eichenbaum, Luise, and Susie Orbach. *Between Women: Love, Envy and Competition in Women's Friendships*. New York: Viking Penguin, 1988.

Evans, Caroline, and Minna Thornton. "Fashion, Representation, Femininity," *Feminist Review* 38 (Summer 1991), 48–66.

Evelyn R. Rosenthal, ed. *Women, Aging, and Ageism*. Binghamton, NY: Harrington Park Press, 1990.

Ewen, Phyllis. "The Beauty Ritual." In *Images of Information: Still Photography in the Social Sciences*, edited by Jon Wagner, 43–57. Beverly Hills, CA: Sage Publications, 1979.

Ewen, Stuart, and Elizabeth Ewen. *Channels of Desire: Mass Images and the Shaping of American Consciousness*. Minneapolis: University of Minnesota Press, 1992.

Faderman, Lillian. *Surpassing the Love of Men: Romantic Friendship and Love Between Women from the Renaissance to the Present*. New York: William Morrow and Company, 1981.

Ferguson, Ann. "Feminist Communities and Moral Revolution." In *Feminism and Community*, edited by Penny A. Weiss and Marilyn Friedman, 367–97. Philadelphia: Temple University Press, 1995.

Finkelstein, Joanne. *The Fashioned Self*. Philadelphia: Temple University Press, 1991.

Fishman, Sylvia Barack. *A Breath of Life: Feminism in the American Jewish Community*. New York: Free Press, 1993.

Fonow, Mary Margaret, and Judith A. Cook, eds. *Beyond Methodology: Feminist Scholarship as Lived Research*. Bloomington: Indiana University Press, 1991.

Ford, Janet, and Ruth Sinclair. *Sixty Years On: Women Talk About Old Age*. London: Women's Press, 1987.

Foster, Susan E., and Jack A. Brizius. "Caring Too Much? American Women and the Nation's Caregiving Crisis." In *Women on the Front Lines: Meeting the Challenge of an Aging America*, edited by Jessie Allen and Alan Pifer, 47–73. Washington, DC: Urban Institute Press, 1993.

Foucault, Michel. *The History of Sexuality*. Vol. 1: *An Introduction*. Translated by Robert Hurley. New York: Vintage Books, 1990.

Friedan, Betty. *The Fountain of Age*. New York: Simon & Schuster, 1993.

Friedman, Dayle A. "The Crown of Glory: Aging in the Jewish Tradition." In *Celebration and Renewal: Rites of Passage in Judaism*, edited by Rela M. Geffen, 202–25.

Philadelphia: Jewish Publication Society, 1993.

Fulkerson, Mary McClintock. *Changing the Subject: Women's Discourses and Feminist Theology.* Minneapolis: Fortress Press, 1994.

Furman, Frida Kerner. *Beyond Yiddishkeit: The Struggle for Jewish Identity in a Reform Synagogue.* Albany: State University of New York Press, 1987; Lanham, MD: University Press of America, 1994.

Gadow, Sally. "Recovering the Body in Aging." In *Aging and Ethics: Philosophical Problems in Gerontology,* edited by Nancy S. Jecker, 113-20. Clifton, NJ: Humana Press, 1991.

Gerth, H. H., and C. Wright Mills, eds. *From Max Weber: Essays in Sociology.* New York: Oxford University Press, 1946.

Gilligan, Carol. *In a Different Voice: Psychological Theory and Women's Development.* Cambridge, MA: Harvard University Press, 1982.

Gilman, Sander. *The Jew's Body.* New York: Routledge, 1991.

Glenn, Susan A. *Daughters of the Shtetl: Life and Labor in the Immigrant Generation.* Ithaca: Cornell University Press, 1990.

Goffman, Erving. *Gender Advertisements.* New York: Harper and Row, 1976.

———. *Stigma: Notes on the Management of Spoiled Identity.* Englewood Cliffs, NJ: Prentice-Hall, 1963.

Gordon, Deborah A. "Border Work: Feminist Ethnography and the Dissemination of Literacy." In *Women Writing Culture,* edited by Ruth Behar and Deborah A. Gordon, 372–89. Berkeley: University of California Press, 1995.

Greeley, Andrew. *Religion as Poetry.* New Brunswick, NJ: Transaction Publishers, 1995.

Gubrium, Jaber F. *Living and Dying at Murray Manor.* New York: Martin's Press, 1975.

Gunn, Fenja. *The Artificial Face: A History of Cosmetics.* Newton Abbot, Devon: David and Charles, 1973.

Hagestad, Gunhild O. "The Aging Society as a Context for Family Life." In *Aging and Ethics: Philosophical Problems in Gerontology,* edited by Nancy S. Jecker, 123–46. Clifton, NJ: Humana Press, 1991.

Harling, Robert. *Steel Magnolias.* Garden City, NY: Fireside Theater, 1986.

Harrison, Beverly Wildung. "The Older Person's Worth in the Eyes of Society." In *Making the Connections: Essays in Feminist Social Ethics,* edited by Carol S. Robb, 152–66. Boston: Beacon Press, 1985.

——— "The Power of Anger in the Work of Love: Christian Ethics for Women and Other Strangers." In *Making the Connections: Essays in Feminist Social Ethics,* edited by Carol S. Robb, 3–21. Boston: Beacon Press, 1985.

Harrison, Jo. "Women and Ageing: Experience and Implications." *Ageing and Society* 3, no. 2 (July 1983), 209–35.

Hatfield, Elaine, and Susan Sprecher. *Mirror, Mirror . . . The Importance of Looks in Everyday Life.* Albany, NY: State University of New York Press, 1986.

Heilman, Samuel C. "Jewish Sociologist: Native-as-Stranger." *The American Sociolo-*

gist 15 (1980), 100–108.

Herman, Simon N. *Jewish Identity: A Social Psychological Perspective*. Beverly Hills, CA: Sage Publications, 1977.

Hess, Beth B., and Joan M. Waring. "Parent and Child in Later Life: Rethinking the Relationship." In *Child Influences on Marital and Family Interaction: A Life-Span Perspective*, edited by Richard M. Lerner and Graham B. Spanier, 241–73. New York: Academic Press, 1978.

Hochschild, Arlie Russel. *The Managed Heart: Commercialization of Human Feeling*. Berkeley: University of California Press, 1983.

———. *The Unexpected Community*. Englewood Cliffs, NJ: Prentice-Hall, 1973.

hooks, bell. *Black Looks: Race and Representation*. Boston: South End Press, 1992.

Hunt, Mary E. *Fierce Tenderness: A Feminist Theology of Friendship*. New York: Crossroad, 1992.

Hyman, Paula E. "Introduction: Perspectives on the Evolving Jewish Family." In *The Jewish Family: Myths and Reality*, edited by Steven M. Cohen and Paula E. Hyman, 3–13. New York: Holmes and Meier Publishers, 1986.

Isasi-Díaz, Ada María. "Toward an Understanding of *Feminismo Hispano* in the U. S. A." In *Women's Consciousness, Women's Conscience: A Reader in Feminist Ethics*, edited by Barbara Hilkert Andolsen, Christine E. Gudorf, and Mary D. Pellauer, 51–61. Minneapolis: Winston Press, 1985.

Issue on Ageism. *Women's Studies Quarterly* 17, no. 1 and 2 (Spring/Summer 1989).

Jacobs, Ruth Harriet. *Be an Outrageous Older Woman—a RASP*. Manchester, CT: Knowledge, Ideas, and Trends, 1991.

———. "Expanding Social Roles for Older Women." In *Women on the Front Lines: Meeting the Challenge of an Aging America*, edited by Jessie Allen and Alan Pifer, 207–14. Washington, DC: Urban Institute Press, 1993.

Jerrome, Dorothy. "The Significance of Friendship for Women in Later Life." *Ageing and Society* 1, no. 2 (July 1981), 175–98.

Joselit, Jenna Weissman. *The Wonders of America: Reinventing Jewish Culture, 1880–1950*. New York: Hill and Wang, 1994.

Joseph, Jenny. "Warning." In *When I Am An Old Woman I Shall Wear Purple*, edited by Sandra Haldeman Martz. Watsonville, CA: Papier-Mache Press, 1987.

Kahn, R. L., and T. C. Antonucci. "Convoys over the the Life Course: Attachment, Roles, and Social Support." In *Life-Span Development and Behavior*, vol. 3, edited by P. B. Bates and O. Brim, 253–86. New York: Academic Press, 1980.

Kaye/Kantrowitz, Melanie. "Some Notes on Jewish Lesbian Identity." In *Nice Jewish Girls: A Lesbian Anthology*, edited by Evelyn Torton Beck, 28–44. Trumansburg, NY: Crossing Press, 1982.

Keith, Jennie. "Age in Social and Cultural Context: Anthropological Perspectives." In *Handbook of Aging and the Social Sciences*. 3d ed., edited by Robert H. Binstock and Linda K. George, 91–111. San Diego: Academic Press, 1990.

Kleinman, Arthur. *The Illness Narratives: Suffering, Healing & the Human Condition.* New York: Basic Books, 1988.

Klosinski, Lee Edward. *The Meals in Mark.* Ann Arbor: University Microfims International, 1988.

Kramer, Sydelle, and Jenny Masur, eds. *Jewish Grandmothers.* Boston: Beacon Press, 1976.

Kruks, Sonia. "Phenomenology, Feminism and 'Women's Experience.'" Paper delivered at the Annual Meeting of the American Political Science Association, Chicago, 31 August-3 September, 1995.

Leonard, F., with T. Sommers and V. Dean. *Not Even Dogcatcher: Employment Discrimination and Older Women.* Gray Paper No. 8. Washington, DC: Older Women's League, 1982.

Lesnoff-Caravaglia, Gari. "Double Stigmata: Female and Old." In *The World of the Older Woman: Conflicts and Resolutions,* edited by Gari Lesnoff-Caravaglia, 11–20. Frontiers in Aging Series, vol. 3. New York: Human Sciences Press, 1984.

———. "Introduction." In *The World of the Older Woman: Conflicts and Resolutions,* edited by Gari Lesnoff-Caravaglia. Frontiers in Aging Series, vol. 3. New York: Human Sciences Press, 1984.

———. "Widowhood: The Last Stage of Wifedom." In *The World of the Older Woman: Conflicts and Resolutions,* edited by Gari Lesnoff-Caravaglia, 137–43. Frontiers of Aging Series, vol. 3. New York: Human Sciences Press, 1984.

Le Sueur, Meridel. "Remarks From 1983 Poetry Reading." In *Women and Aging: An Anthology by Women,* edited by Jo Alexander, Debi Berrow, Lisa Domitrovich, Margarita Donnelly, and Cheryl McLean, 9–19. Corvalis, OR: Calyx Books, 1986.

Levine, Jacob. "Humour as a Form of Therapy: Introduction to Symposium." In *It's a Funny Thing, Humour,* edited by A. J. Chapman and H. C. Foot, 127–37. Oxford: Pergamon Press, 1977.

Lewittes, Hedva J. "Just Being Friendly Means a Lot—Women, Friendship, and Aging." In *Women in the Later Years: Health, Social, and Cultural Perspectives,* edited by Lois Grau in collaboration with Ida Susser, 139–59. New York: Haworth Press, 1989.

Lieberman, Morton A. and Sheldon S. Tobin. *The Experience of Old Age: Stress, Coping, and Survival.* New York: Basic Books, 1983.

Macdonald, Barbara. "Outside the Sisterhood: Ageism in Women's Studies." In *Women and Aging: An Anthology by Women,* edited by Jo Alexander, Debi Berrow, Lisa Domitrovich, Margarita Donnelly, and Cheryl McLean, 20–25. Corvallis, OR: Calix Books, 1986.

Macdonald, Barbara, with Cynthia Rich. *Look Me in the Eye: Old Women, Aging and*

Ageism. Expanded ed. Minneapolis: Spinsters Press, 1991.

MacIntyre, Alasdair. *After Virtue: A Study in Moral Theory*. 2d ed. Notre Dame, IN: University of Indiana Press, 1984.

Maitland, David J. *Aging as Counterculture: A Vocation for the Later Years*. New York: Pilgrim Press, 1991.

Malhotra, Valerie Ann. "Research as Critical Reflection: A Study of Self, Time and Communicative Competence." In *A Feminist Ethic for Social Science Research*, edited by the Nebraska Sociological Feminist Collective, 82–99. Lewiston, NY: Edwin Mellen Press, 1988.

Marcus, George, and Michael M. J. Fischer. *Anthropology as Cultural Critique: An Experimental Moment in the Human Sciences*. Chicago: University of Chicago Press, 1986.

Martin, Emily. *The Woman in the Body: A Cultural Analysis of Reproduction*. Boston: Beacon Press, 1987.

Martz, Sandra Haldeman, ed. *When I Am An Old Woman I Shall Wear Purple*. Watsonville, CA: Papier-Mache Press, 1991.

Matthews, Sarah H. *The Social World of Old Women: Management of Self-Identity*. Sage Library of Social Research, vol. 78. Beverly Hills, CA: Sage Publications, 1979.

May, William F. "The Virtues and Vices of the Elderly." In *What Does It Mean to Grow Old? Reflections from the Humanities*, edited by Thomas R. Cole and Sally A. Gadow, 43–61. Durham: NC: Duke University Press, 1986.

Miles, Margaret R. *Carnal Knowing: Female Nakedness and Religious Meaning in the Christian West*. New York: Vintage Books, 1989.

Miller, Jean Baker. *Toward a New Psychology of Women*. Boston: Beacon Press, 1976.

Moody, Harry R. "Age, Productivity, and Transcendence." In *Achieving a Productive Aging Society*, edited by Scott A. Bass, Francis G. Caro, and Yung-Ping Chen, 27–40. Westport, CT: Auburn House, 1993.

———. "The Meaning of Old Age." In *Aging and Ethics: Philosophical Problems in Gerontology*, edited by Nancy S. Jecker, 51–92. Clifton, NJ: Humana Press, 1991.

Morgan, Kathryn Pauly. "Women and the Knife: Cosmetic Surgery and the Colonization of Women's Bodies," *Hypatia* 6, no. 3 (Fall 1991), 25–53.

Morrison, Malcolm H. "Work and Retirement in an Older Society." In *Our Aging Society: Paradox and Promise*, edited by Alan Pifer and Lydia Bronte, 341–65. New York: W. W. Norton and Company, 1986.

Morrison, Toni. *The Bluest Eye*. New York: Alfred A. Knopf, 1993.

Muir, Madeline (producer and director). *West Coast Crones*. Kathy Wolfe, executive producer. Box 64, New Almaden, CA 95042: Wolfe Video, 1991.

Mulvey, Laura. "Visual Pleasure and Narrative Cinema." *Screen* 16, no. 13 (August 1975), 6–18.

Myerhoff, Barbara. *Number Our Days*. New York: E. P. Dutton, 1978.

Myerhoff, Barbara, with Deena Metzger, Jay Ruby, and Virginia Tufte. "Aging and the Aged in Other Cultures: An Anthropological Perspective." *Remembered Lives: The Work of Ritual, Storytelling, and Growing Older*, edited by Mark Kaminsky, 101–126. Ann Arbor: University of Michigan Press, 1992.

National Film Board of Canada. *Strangers in Good Company*. Produced by David Wilson, directed by Cynthia Scott. New York: First Run-Icarus Films, 1990.

Nelson, Linda Williamson. "'Hands in the Chit'lins': Notes on Native Anthropological Research among African American Women." In *Unrelated Kin: Race and Gender in Women's Personal Narratives*, edited by Gwendolyn Etter-Lewis and Michele Foster, 183–99. New York: Routledge, 1996.

Niebuhr, H. Richard. *The Responsible Self: An Essay in Christian Moral Philosophy*. New York: Harper and Row, 1963.

Noddings, Nel. *Caring: A Feminine Approach to Ethics and Moral Education.* Berkeley: University of California Press, 1984.

———. *Women and Evil*. Berkeley: University of California Press, 1989.

O'Connor, Pat. *Friendships Between Women: A Critical Review*. New York: Guilford Press, 1992.

Okin, Susan Moller. *Justice, Gender, and the Family*. New York: Basic Books, 1989.

Oldenburg, Ray. *The Great Good Place*. New York: Paragon House, 1989.

Orbach, Susie. *Hunger Strike: The Anorectic's Struggle as a Metaphor for Our Age*. New York: W. W. Norton and Company, 1986.

Parker, Sheila, Mimi Nichter, Mark Nichter, Nancy Vuckonic, Colette Sims, and Cheryl Ritenbaugh. "Body Image and Weight Concerns among African American and White Adolescent Females: Differences that Make a Difference." *Human Organization* 54, no. 2 (Summer 1995), 103–14.

Peiss, Kathy. "Making Faces: The Cosmetics Industry and the Cultural Construction of Gender, 1890–1930." In *Unequal Sisters: A Multi-Cultural Reader in U.S. Women's History*. 2d ed. Edited by Vicki L. Ruiz and Ellen Carol DuBois, 372–94. New York: Routledge, 1994.

Phillipson, Chris. *Capitalism and the Construction of Old Age*. London: MacMillan, 1982.

Plaskow, Judith. *Standing Again at Sinai: Judaism from a Feminist Perspective*. San Francisco: Harper and Row, 1990.

Pogrebin, Letty Cottin. *Getting Over Getting Older: An Intimate Memoir*. Boston: Little, Brown and Company, 1996.

Prell, Riv-Ellen. *Fighting to Become Americans: Jewish Women and Men in Conflict in the Twentieth Century*. Boston: Beacon Press, forthcoming.

———. "Rage and Representation: Jewish Gender Stereotypes in American Culture." In *Uncertain Terms: Negotiating Gender in American Culture*, edited by Faye Ginsburg and Anna Lowenhaupt Tsing, 248–64. Boston: Beacon Press, 1990.

Premo, Terri L. *Winter Friends: Women Growing Older in the New Republic, 1785–1835*.

Urbana: University of Illinois Press, 1990.

Procter-Smith, Marjorie, and Janet R. Walton, eds. *Women at Worship: Interpretations of North American Diversity*. Louiville, KY: Westminster/John Knox Press, 1993.

"Publication Offers Tips on Young and Old Serving Together." *Generations United Newline* (Summer 1994), 3.

Quindlen, Anna. *One True Thing*. New York: Random House, 1994.

Raymond, Janice G. *A Passion for Friends: Toward a Philosophy of Female Affection*. Boston: Beacon Press, 1986.

Reinharz, Shulamit, with the assistance of Lynn Davidman. *Feminist Methods in Social Research*. New York: Oxford University Press, 1992.

Romero, Mary. *Maid in the U.S.A*. New York: Routledge, 1992.

Rooks, Noliwe M. *Hair Raising: Beauty, Culture, and African American Women*. New Brunswick: Rutgers University Press, 1996.

Rosenthal, Evelyn R. "Women and Varieties of Ageism." In *Women, Aging and Ageism*, edited by Evelyn R. Rosenthal, 1–6. Binghamton, NY: Harrington Park Press, 1990; originally published as the *Journal of Women & Aging* 2, no. 2 (1990).

Rothbell, Gladys. "The Jewish Mother: Social Construction of a Popular Image." In *The Jewish Family: Myths and Reality*, edited by Steven M. Cohen and Paula E. Hyman, 118–28. New York: Holmes and Meier, 1986.

Rousseau, Jean-Jacques. *Emile or On Education*. Introduction, translation and notes by Alan Bloom. New York: Basic Books, 1979.

Rubin, Lillian B. *Intimate Strangers: Men and Women Together*. New York: Harper and Row, 1983.

———. *Just Friends: The Role of Friendship in Our Lives*. New York: Harper and Row, 1985.

Ruddick, Sara. *Maternal Thinking. Toward a Politics of Peace*. New York: Ballantine Books, 1989.

Ruether, Rosemary Radford. *Women-Church: Theology and Practice of Feminist Liturgical Communities*. San Francisco: Harper and Row, 1986.

Sapp, Stephen. *Full of Years: Aging and the Elderly in the Bible and Today*. Nashville: Abingdon Press, 1987.

Sarton, May. *As We Are Now*. New York: W. W. Norton and Company, 1973.

Sauer. W. J., and R. T. Coward, eds. *Social Support Networks and the Care of the Elderly: Theory, Research, and Practice*. New York: Springer Publishing Company, 1985.

Sawicki, Jana. *Disciplining Foucault: Feminism, Power, and the Body*. New York: Routledge, 1991.

Schreier, Barbara A. *Becoming American Women: Clothing and the Jewish Immigrant Experience, 1880–1920*. Chicago: Chicago Historical Society, 1994.

Scott, Joan W. "'Experience.'" In *Feminists Theorize the Political*, edited by Judith Butler and Joan W. Scott, 22–40. New York: Routledge, 1992.

Siegel, Rachel Josefowitz. "We Are Not Your Mothers: Report on Two Groups for

Women Over Sixty." In *Women, Aging, and Ageism*, edited by Evelyn R. Rosenthal, 81–89. New York: Harrington Park Press, 1990.

Silverman, Phyllis S., and Adele Cooperband. "Widow-to-Widow: The Elderly Widow and Mutual Help." In *The World of the Older Woman: Conflicts and Resolutions*, edited by Gari Lesnoff-Caravaglia, 144–61. Frontiers of Aging Series, vol. 3. New York: Human Sciences Press, 1984.

Skeggs, Beverley. "Theorising, Ethics and Representation in Feminist Ethnography." In *Feminist Cultural Theory: Process and Production*, edited by Beverley Skeggs, 190–206. Manchester: Manchester University Press, 1995.

Smith, Dorothy E. *Texts, Facts, and Femininity: Exploring the Relations of Ruling.* London: Routledge, 1990.

Smith-Rosenberg, Carroll. "The Female World of Love and Ritual: Relations Between Women in Nineteenth-Century America." In *A Heritage of Her Own: Toward a New Social History of American Women*, edited by Nancy F. Cott and Elizabeth H. Pleck, 311–42. New York: Simon & Schuster, 1979.

Sommers, Tish, and Laurie Shields. *Women Take Care: The Consequences of Caregiving in Today's Society.* Gainesville, FL: Triad Publishing Company, 1987.

Sontag, Susan. "The Double Standard of Aging." In *No Longer Young: The Older Woman in America*, 31–39. Proceedings of the 26th Annual Conference on Aging. Ann Arbor, MI: Institute of Gerontology, University of Michigan and Wayne State University, 1975.

Spiegel, Marcia Cohn. "Becoming a Crone." *Lilith* 21 (Fall 1988), 18–19.

Spindler, Amy M. "It's a Face-Lifted, Tummy-Tucked Jungle Out There." *New York Times*, Sunday, 9 June 1996, sec. 3.

Stacey, Judith. "Can there be a Feminist Ethnography?" In *Women's Words: The Feminist Practice of Oral History*, edited by Sherna Berger Gluck and Daphne Patai, 111–19. New York: Routledge, 1991.

Stanley, Liz, ed. *Feminist Praxis: Research, Theory and Epistemology in Feminist Sociology.* London: Routledge, 1990.

Stein, Arlene. "All Dressed Up, but No Place to Go? Style Wars and the New Lesbianism." In *The Persistent Desire: A Femme-Butch Reader*, edited by Joan Nestle, 431–39. Boston: Alyson Publications, 1992.

Symposium on Care and Justice. *Hypatia* 10, no. 2 (Spring 1995).

Tannen, Deborah. *You Just Don't Understand: Women and Men in Conversation.* New York: William Morrow and Company, 1990.

Taylor, Allegra. *Older Than Time: A Grandmother's Search for Wisdom.* London: Aquarian/Thorsons, 1993.

Terkel, Studs. *Coming of Age: The Story of Our Century by Those Who've Lived It.* New York: New Press, 1995.

Tertullian, *De Cultu Fem.* 1, 1. Cited by Rosemary Radford Ruether, "Misogynism and Virginal Feminism in the Fathers of the Church." In *Religion and Sexism:*

Images of Woman in the Jewish and Christian Traditions, edited by Rosemary Radford Ruether, 150–83. New York: Simon & Schuster, 1974.

Thompson, Paul, Catherine Itzin, and Michele Abendstern, *I Don't Feel Old: The Experience of Later Life*. Oxford: Oxford University Press, 1990.

Tronto, Joan C. *Moral Boundaries: A Political Argument for an Ethic of Care*. New York: Routledge, 1993.

U. S. Bureau of the Census. *Statistical Abstract of the United States: 1995*. 11th ed. Washington, DC, 1995.

Walden, Keith. "The Road to Fat City: An Interpretation of the Development of Weight Consciousness in Western Society." *Historical Reflections/Reflexions Historiques* 12, no. 3 (1985), 331–73.

Walker, Alexis J., Clara C. Pratt, and Hwa-Yong Shinn. "Motives for Parental Caregiving and Relationship Quality." *Family Relations* 39 (1990), 51–56.

Ward, Edna M., ed. *Celebrating Ourselves: A Crone Ritual Book*. Portland, ME: Astarte Shell Press, 1992.

Waring, Marilyn. *If Women Counted: A New Feminist Economics*. San Francisco: Harper and Row, 1988.

Washbourn, Penelope. "Becoming Woman: Menstruation as Spiritual Challenge." In *Womanspirit Rising: A Feminist Reader in Religion*, edited by Carol P. Christ and Judith Plaskow, 246–58. San Francisco: Harper San Francisco, 1992.

———. *Becoming Woman: The Quest for Wholeness in Female Experience*. New York: Harper and Row, 1977.

Wilson, Midge, and Kathy Russell. *Divided Sisters: Bridging the Gap Between Black Women and White Women*. New York: Anchor Books/Doubleday, 1996.

Wolf, Naomi. *The Beauty Myth: How Images of Beauty Are Used Against Women*. New York: William Morrow and Company, 1991.

Wollstonecraft, Mary. *A Vindication of the Rights of Woman*. In *The Feminist Papers*, edited by Alice Rossi. Boston: Northeastern University Press, 1988.

Wright, Paul H. "Gender Differences in Adults' Same- and Cross-Gender Friendships." In *Older Adult Friendship: Structure and Process*, edited by Rebecca G. Adams and Rosemary Bliesner, 197–221. Newbury Park, CA: Sage Publications, 1986.

Yerkovich, Sally. "Gossiping as a Way of Speaking." *Journal of Communication* 27, no. 1 (1977), 192–96.

Young, Iris Marion. *Justice and the Politics of Difference*. Princeton: Princeton University Press, 1990.

———. *Throwing Like a Girl and Other Essays in Feminist Philosophy and Social Theory*. Bloomington: Indiana University Press, 1990.

Young-Eisendrath, Polly. "The Female Person and How We Talk About Her." In *Feminist Thought and the Structure of Knowledge*, edited by Mary McCanney Gergen, 152–72. New York: New York University Press, 1988.

Index